# Translation Theories Explained

*Translation Theories Explained* is a series designed to respond to the profound plurality of contemporary translation studies. There are many problems to be solved, many possible approaches that can be drawn from neighbouring disciplines, and several strong language-bound traditions plagued by the paradoxical fact that some of the key theoretical texts have yet to be translated.

Recognizing this plurality as both a strength and a potential shortcoming, the series provides a format where different approaches can be compared, their virtues assessed, and mutual blind spots overcome. There will also be scope for introductions to specific areas of translation practice. Students and scholars may thus gain comprehensive awareness of the work being done beyond local or endemic frames.

Most volumes in the series place a general approach within its historical context, giving examples to illustrate the main ideas, summarizing the most significant debates and opening perspectives for future work. The authors have been selected not only because of their command of a particular approach but also in view of their openness to alternatives and their willingness to discuss criticisms. In every respect the emphasis is on explaining the essential points as clearly and as concisely as possible, using numerous examples and providing glossaries of the main technical terms.

The series should prove particularly useful to students dealing with translation theories for the first time, to teachers seeking to stimulate critical reflection, and to scholars looking for a succinct overview of the field's present and future.

Anthony Pym
Series Editor

# Translation in Systems

*Descriptive and System-oriented Approaches Explained*

Theo Hermans

Routledge
Taylor & Francis Group

LONDON AND NEW YORK

First published 1999 by St. Jerome Publishing

Published 2014 by Routledge
2 Park Square, Milton Park, Abingdon, Oxon OX14 4RN
711 Third Avenue, New York, NY 10017, USA

*Routledge is an imprint of the Taylor & Francis Group, an informa business*

Copyright © Theo Hermans 1999

ISBN 13: 978-1-900650-11-3 (pbk)
ISSN 1365-0513

*British Library Cataloguing in Publication Data*
A catalogue record for this book is available from the British Library.

# Contents

# Preface

The account presented in this book is narrower than the subtitle suggests, especially as regards the word 'descriptive'. Not all descriptive approaches to translation will be covered. A great deal of historical, contrastive and other research, much of it descriptive in nature, is being conducted all over the world. Many of these studies simply get on with the job, without explicit theoretical or methodological reflection, or without consciously aligning themselves with other descriptive work being done elsewhere. It would be futile to attempt to survey this vast and ever growing body of research.

My subject is more limited. It consists primarily of an approach to translation which was elaborated in the 1970s, gained prominence during the following decade, and is still going strong. It has become known under various names: Descriptive Translation Studies, the Polysystems approach, the Manipulation school, the Tel Aviv-Leuven axis, the Low Countries group, and even, incongruously, Translation Studies. In the last ten years or so it has become widely recognized that the emergence of this descriptive and systemic model marked one of the paradigmatic sea-changes in the study of translation.

There are other limitations. Since I can cope with only a handful of Western languages, much of the material that ought to have been considered remains beyond my reach. This applies particularly to publications in Hebrew, but no doubt there is relevant research also in many other languages inaccessible to me. Translation studies need translation, in more than one sense.

For better or worse, I have played a small part in the approach explained in the present book. This creates a problem of critical distance, and of personal pronouns. While I am happy to acknowledge sympathy for many of the views to be presented, I intend to keep a certain distance from them. In this I am helped by the realization that in recent years my own scepticism has only increased, not as regards the fundamental orientation and value of most descriptive and system-based work, but with respect to a range of specific points and issues. No doubt this scepticism pervades my presentation of them. It also makes it slightly easier for me to avoid speaking of the group of researchers identified with descriptive and systemic studies in terms of 'we'.

The aim of this book is threefold: to explain the descriptive and systemic approach to the study of translation; to engage critically with some of the key ideas; and to suggest possible directions for further theoretical and methodological reflection.

Theo Hermans

# Acknowledgements

Part of the research for this book was conducted during a sabbatical term generously supported by the Humanities Research Board of the British Academy.

The University of Durham's Publications Board kindly granted permission to quote at length from John McFarlane, 'Modes of Translation', *Durham University Journal*, June 1953.

The author and publisher are also grateful to Farrar, Straus and Giroux, LLC and Benedict B. C. Fitzgerald for permission to reprint the extract from Robert Fitzgerald's English translation of Homer's *Odyssey*, published by Doubleday, 1961; Faber and Faber Limited for permission to reprint the extract from Ezra Pound's *Seventy Cantos*, published by Faber and Faber, 1950; and International Thomson Publishing for permission to reprint the extract from Richmond Lattimore's English translation of Homer's *Odyssey*, published by Harper, 1967.

# Preamble: Mann's Fate

Thomas Mann knew exactly why translation mattered. Every language in the world is a minority language because no single language is spoken by the majority of the world's population. If you happen to be a writer working in one of these minority languages, especially if it is not one of the larger minority languages like English or Chinese but a smaller one like German, your books need to be translated if they are to find a readership beyond the confines of their original tongue. If your work is translated, especially if it is translated into several languages or into one of the world's larger languages, it can reach audiences many times the size of that of the original publication. But there is a corollary. For those potentially vast audiences who read your work in translation because they are unable to read it in the original, the translations determine the impression those readers will form of you as a writer. Through translation writers can escape the prison house of their language, but they are then dependent on translators for the perception of their work in the wider world. Books which are translated may carry the original writer's name on the cover, but the actual words between the covers are written by translators.

Realizing this, Thomas Mann showed a keen interest in the translation of his books into English. His first and highly successful novel, *Buddenbrooks*, had come out in German in 1900; by the time his most ambitious work till then, *The Magic Mountain*, appeared in 1924, the American publisher Alfred Knopf had acquired the exclusive right to distribute Mann's work in the United States. There is grim irony in the fact that in the course of the 1930s the Nazis would suppress Mann's books in his native Germany and even deprive him of his German citizenship. In 1938 he emigrated to the US. There, a German writer in exile with no prospect of having his books distributed in Germany, he was more dependent on translation than he could ever have imagined. It was Mann's fate to be translated.

How well was he served by his main translator into English, the American Helen Lowe-Porter, who would be responsible for English versions of *Buddenbrooks* (1924), *The Magic Mountain* (1927), the four volumes of *Joseph and His Brothers* (1934-44), *Doctor Faustus* (1948) and other titles? The question recently received a pretty decisive answer, even though the arbiter's conclusions caused a brief flurry of controversy. Let us look into the issue for a moment.

In a page-long article in *The Times Literary Supplement* of 13 October 1995 Timothy Buck wiped the floor with Helen Lowe-Porter's translations. He subsequently made his case at greater length in a virulent but well-documented essay in a scholarly journal (Buck 1996). The *TLS* article drew several responses. First Lawrence Venuti criticized Timothy Buck's criticism of the Lowe-Porter translations, then David Luke, himself a translator of Thomas Mann's *Death in Venice*, leapt to Buck's defence, Venuti responded again, so did Luke, and finally, in January 1996, the two surviving daughters of Helen Lowe-Porter added their contribution.

There are some interesting things to be learned from Timothy Buck's attack, and from the responses to it. Buck begins by stressing that Helen Lowe-Porter produced "the authorized translations of nearly all of Mann's *oeuvre*, so that in most cases it is on her mediation that anglophones unversed in German are dependent for access to Mann's work" (1995:17). He recognizes that the translations proved commercially successful. Over a hundred thousand copies of *Doctor Faustus* were printed for the Book of the Month Club edition alone. On the whole, they were received favourably to very favourably by the critics. Buck also concedes that Lowe-Porter's prose generally reads well and that she "would often come up with imaginative, idiomatic renderings" (1996:910). But that is as far as it goes. The overall verdict is devastating. The translations are "seriously flawed", "unsound, erratic", marred by "unnecessary, arbitrary deviations from the author's texts" and an "extraordinary number of major or even catastrophic errors", the work, in short, of "an ambitious, startlingly underqualified translator, who plainly did not know her own limitations" (1996:919). The judgement is backed up with abundant evidence. Buck details Lowe-Porter's inadequate grasp of German by listing numerous omissions and blatant mistranslations (of the kind: *breitbeinig*, meaning 'with his legs apart', rendered as 'with big bones'). He denounces the unwarranted liberties she takes when she refashions Mann's syntax and roughly chops up the carefully crafted German sentences, adds touches or entire phrases of her own, and puts an insidious slant on some passages, altering the reader's perception of who does what in particular scenes. While young Tadzio in *Death in Venice* is described as 'turning his profile towards the watching Aschenbach', in Lowe-Porter's version it is Aschenbach who is 'sitting so that he could see Tadzio in profile' (Buck 1995:17; 1996:914). The imprecision and licence of Lowe-Porter's translation, Buck observes, "patently calls in question the very use here of the term 'translation'" (1995:17).

Buck also delves into the background of the whole affair. He points out that it was the American publisher Alfred Knopf and not the author who had the right to choose the translator, and that Knopf expressly overruled Mann's preference for another candidate. He contrasts the very different views which Mann and Lowe-Porter held on the subject of translation. Mann himself, who, incidentally, doubted in 1925 that a woman would be up to the task of translating so intellectually demanding a novel as *The Magic Mountain*, once wrote in a letter to Lowe-Porter that in principle he favoured translations of his work that were "as literal and accurate as the foreign language will allow". Lowe-Porter took a much freer approach and declared in the Translator's Note to *Buddenbrooks* that she had set herself "the bold task of transferring the spirit first and the letter so far as might be" (Buck 1996:901-902). Nevertheless Mann publicly praised her efforts, expressing his reservations only in private or in guarded, ambivalent statements. Perhaps, Buck suggests, he knew the publisher would not replace her anyway, perhaps he was too busy with other things, or reluctant to endanger the flow of dollar royalties, or maybe his personal feelings of friendship for his translator outweighed his misgivings about her competence. Whatever the reasons, Buck concludes, we are landed with 'a pseudo-Mann', English versions undeserving to be called translations. Which only highlights the need for a fresh, reliable translation. Alas, the new translation of *The Magic Mountain* by John Woods published in 1995, though better than Lowe-Porter's, is still not good enough. The solution lies with the publishers. They should provide an 'English Mann' that does justice to the real Mann (Buck 1997).

The details of the brief polemic that followed Timothy Buck's *TLS* article do not need to detain us. In speaking up for Lowe-Porter, Lawrence Venuti focused on two points. Our contemporary standards of accuracy in translation, he argued, differ from those in the past; and translation always involves re-interpretation according to the values prevalent in the here and now of the translator. David Luke, siding with Timothy Buck against Venuti, replied with examples showing that the unacceptable frequency of basic howlers in both Lowe-Porter's and Woods' translations were not a matter of interpretation but simply of a defective command of German grammar and a failure to make proper use of the dictionary, demonstrating *en passant* Venuti's own less than firm hold on the German language. Venuti wisely kept his silence after this, but in a final contribution Lowe-Porter's daughters quoted at length from a 1943 letter by their mother in which she spoke about her endeavour to produce in her translations an overall effect comparable to that of the original, reminding the reviewer that he "has to look at the whole, not pick out sentences, if he means to judge the translation at all".

Who won the argument in the end? Not Lawrence Venuti, so much is certain. His point about interpretation blew up in his face, and the one about changing canons of accuracy remained a dead letter. The way Helen Lowe-Porter's daughters used their mother's own words to highlight her philosophy of translation (their term) was cunning and timely but overshot the mark, failing to address the central objection concerning grammar and the dictionary which Buck and Luke had raised. No, there can be little doubt that Buck and Luke emerged the clear winners. Luke's conclusion that "[t]he continuing circulation of debased versions of one of the great German writers of this century is a continuing scandal" therefore also stands. New and better renderings are required. The wish to see the debased versions replaced with adequate translations provided the motive for Timothy Buck's public attack in the first place. If as a result the publishers are shamed into appropriate action, culture will have been done a good turn and the world will be a better place. So the case is closed.

Or is it? If it were, this book would end here. Why go on if there are no more questions to be asked? But maybe there are further questions that are worth asking. After all, however deplorable they may be, Helen Lowe-Porter's translations exist. They were and are read. We cannot simply wish them away. Whether we lament or applaud their presence and their impact, they are facts of life, an undeniable part of history, like East Enders, or Margaret Thatcher's memoirs, or Van Meegeren's forged Vermeers. Even if we wish the Lowe-Porter translations had never been produced, the mere fact of their existence, and of their effect on generations of readers, should be reason enough to take a closer look at them, not just in order to damn them but to try to account for their appearance.

That means approaching them from a somewhat different angle. Critical evaluation, the apportioning of praise or censure, need not be the exclusive or even the primary aim. Perhaps explanation can be. If we take this other path, we could begin by taking stock, not of what we feel there should have been, but of what, for better or for worse, there *is*. Applied to the Lowe-Porter translations this might mean accepting them as they are, warts and all, and then trying to figure out why they look the way they do, what factors and conditions account for their production, why they were received as they were, what actual impact they had, why there are some – Timothy Buck among them – who think they should not be called translations at all.

Specific questions that could be asked about this case include the following:

- What about the publisher Alfred Knopf's right to pick a translator of his own choosing, against the author's wishes if necessary? How did such legal arrangements come into being? How do they affect the selection of translators in other cases? What were the relations between publishers, authors and translators at the time, or at other times?
- Assuming we can differentiate between plain grammatical errors and interpretive choices (can we?), what do we make of Helen Lowe-Porter's more deliberate omissions, additions and alterations? How much room for manoeuvre did she in fact have, and who determined this? Should we not, before passing judgement on the translator, compare her position and her performance with that of some of her contemporaries? Why is it that she apparently worked so slowly – are there personal, social, economic reasons for it? Is it at all relevant that despite Mann's misgivings about a woman translator's ability to cope with *The Magic Mountain* she saw herself, in her own words, as "a confirmed and express proponent of what in those long-ago days was called 'woman's rights'" (Thirlwall 1966:11)?
- Considering that the Lowe-Porter translations were generally well received by the critics and proved commercially successful, could it be that the translator was correctly anticipating reader expectations? Can

we perhaps account for the nature of the translations in these terms? How common or idiosyncratic were Helen Lowe-Porter's views on translation at the time? How does her output compare with that of other translators working for the same publisher, with other literary translators working from German, with other translators generally?

- Is it at all possible to gauge the effect of translations on actual readers, in this case for example by comparing German readers' impressions of Thomas Mann in German with the responses of Anglophone readers of Lowe-Porter's versions? Are there other ways of measuring the real impact of her translations? What if, as Lawrence Venuti suggests but fails to substantiate, there are differences between what was permissible in translations in the 1920s and '30s and what we want to see in a translation today? How can we find out about these things?

- Should we also try to assess the assessors? Timothy Buck tells us unambiguously what he associates with 'faithful translation': the translator should neither add to nor subtract from the content of the original, respect the author's intentions and refrain from offering 'wild interpretations' (1996:904, 911, 914). Could it be that his criticism of Helen Lowe-Porter's practice reveals little more than the clash between diverging conceptions of what translation is or should be? Is translation possible without adding or subtracting or interpreting, wildly or not, and who is to judge? What if we set this case against translations from other times and places in which the original content was added to or subtracted from, authorial intentions were violated and wild interpretations were rife – and the texts in question were still called 'translations'?

The list is obviously not exhaustive, but it gives an indication. In all these cases, the questions are geared not so much to gauging the quality of individual translations, upholding particular principles as to what constitutes a good translation, or guaranteeing the quality of new translations to be made. Rather, the aim is to delve into translation as a cultural and historical phenomenon, to explore its context and its conditioning factors, to search for grounds that can explain why there is what there is.

If we set out on a course of this kind, other, more general questions readily follow. Questions such as:

- If there are conflicting views on whether a given text is a translation or not, how do we resolve the matter? Can we distinguish between what is translation and what is not? On what basis? How do we know a translation when we see one?

- If we want to analyse a given translation and characterize its relation with the original text, how do we go about it? Are there set procedures, methodologies, rules of thumb that we can apply?

- Can we measure or otherwise assess the impact of translations? Are there models for doing this? How do we handle the values and connotations, the tell-tale signs of interpretive moves, the ideological slant entering translation, *any* translation, whether it is labelled 'good' or 'bad', praised or damned?
- What about ideas about translation – where do we find them, what determines their nature, how do they change and develop? How do we read, interpret and account for them – and where do we then place our own ideas, my own ideas about translation? What is their relevance for the practice of translation anyway? And to what extent do ideas about translation and translatability have cultural significance?
- What about the interrelations between these various questions? For example, can we study individual translations without taking into account ideas about what constituted (good) translation at the time? Can we study translations one by one, or should we look at larger wholes, other translations (which ones?), the broader context? How much context do we need? Are there ways of determining the historical significance of translation at a given time, for a given community?

It is with questions like these that the present book is concerned. Not all of them will be answered. As will become clear, some of the questions themselves are more complex and challenging than may appear at a first glance. Others rebound on the questioner. Of course, they may not be the correct questions to ask of translation – who can tell? But they are both productive and realistic, in that they take translation as it comes rather than as we might have wished it. They focus less on what translation should have been, could have been, or might have been, than on what it *is* – or better: how it appears to be, how it presents itself to us.

# 1. An Invisible College

## Names

The approach to translation and to studying translation set out in the following chapters goes under different names. This is not unusual. Many names of movements or currents of thought in the arts, the humanities or the sciences are not the invention of the people most directly concerned but given by outsiders. The Russian Formalist literary critics of the beginning of the twentieth century spoke of themselves as 'morphologists' and 'specifiers', but their opponents branded them as 'formalists'. The Cubist painters took their name from a remark made by a hostile reviewer that their canvases looked as if covered with little cubes. When the protagonists of a particular approach themselves make efforts to devise a name and propagate it, there is usually an agenda behind it. They want to stand out, to be recognized as different from some existing approach. The Expressionists wrote and painted in direct opposition to the older Impressionists. Postmodernism and Poststructuralism see themselves emphatically as coming after, and calling into question the assumptions of, Modernism and Structuralism. These names have an oppositional edge to them which allows us to glimpse a programme of action.

The labels attached to the approach which forms the subject of this book are partly donned and partly given by others. We need to sort them out first, without necessarily settling on a single designation.

The term most commonly used is 'descriptive', as in 'the descriptive approach' or 'descriptive translation studies'. It dates from the early 1970s and derives its polemical force from the deliberate opposition to 'prescriptive' translation studies. Seen in this light the term 'descriptive translation studies' signals the rejection of the idea that the study of translation should be geared primarily to formulating rules, norms or guidelines for the practice or evaluation of translation or to developing didactic instruments for translator training. On the positive side 'descriptive' points to an interest in translation as it actually occurs, now and in the past, as part of cultural history. It seeks insight into the phenomenon and the impact of translation without immediately wanting to plough that insight back into some practical application to benefit translators, critics or teachers. Because it focuses on the observable aspects of translation, it has also been called 'empirical'. And because it holds that the investigation of translation may as well start with the thing itself and its immediate environment, i.e. with translations and their contexts rather than with source texts, the term 'target-oriented' translation studies also applies, distinguishing this perspective from 'source-oriented' approaches.

But 'descriptive', 'empirical' and even 'target-oriented translation studies' are rather unspecific terms. Plenty of work on, say, medieval or

eighteenth-century translation, or on linguistic aspects of translation, is descriptive in the sense of being non-prescriptive, empirical in its concern with
existing translations, and target-oriented in that it engages with translations
rather than the originals which gave rise to them. In the present book the
terms refer in the first instance to the approach adopted by the group of researchers who will be introduced in the second part of this chapter; by extension
it applies to other work carried out along these lines.

It is a matter of historical accident that the American James Holmes, a
pioneer of descriptive translation studies, also proposed in 1972 the name
'translation studies' as the designation, in English, of the scholarly preoccupation, whether theoretical, empirical or applied, with any and all aspects
of translation. The term is now commonly used and refers to the entire field of
study. Confusingly, however, 'translation studies' has on occasion been taken
to mean the specifically descriptive line of approach (for example, in Koller
1990). Fortunately this usage is now rare. In the following pages 'translation
studies' means the whole discipline.

The approach known as 'descriptive translation studies' is sometimes
referred to as the 'polysystem approach', after one of its prominent concepts.
The term 'polysystem' was invented by the Israeli scholar Itamar Even-Zohar
and has also found application outside the world of translation, especially in
literary studies. We can also speak, more broadly, of a 'systemic' perspective
on translation, which would then include other system-theoretic concepts apart
from the polysystem concept. It is good to bear in mind, though, that one can
perfectly well operate along descriptive lines without taking on board any
systems or polysystems ideas.

Occasionally the term 'Low Countries group' is heard in connection with
the approach described here. This is because several of its proponents work in
or hail from Flanders and the Netherlands. The term is inappropriate because
obviously too narrow. It ignores not only the seminal role played by Gideon
Toury and Itamar Even-Zohar together with a number of other Israeli scholars,
but also the contributions made by researchers elsewhere in Europe and the
United States as well as in Turkey, Korea, Brazil, Hong Kong and other places.
Designations like 'Tel Aviv school' or 'Tel Aviv-Leuven school' are equally
inappropriate, for similar reasons. Descriptive translation studies cannot be
reduced to two or three individuals or centres. It is not a unified approach.

Finally, there is the term 'Manipulation group' or 'Manipulation school'.
It derives from the collection of essays called *The Manipulation of Literature*
(Hermans 1985a). The word 'manipulation' in the book's title was suggested
by André Lefevere. The term 'Manipulation group', coined by Armin Paul
Frank (1987:xiii), gained currency through Mary Snell-Hornby's account of
this approach (1988:22-26) as one of the two main schools of thought in translation studies in Europe in the 1980s. The designation picks up one of the
more provocative claims in the introduction to *The Manipulation of Litera-*

*ture*, to the effect that, from the target perspective, "all translation implies a degree of manipulation of the source text for a certain purpose" (Hermans 1985a:11).

All the above terms are in use and appear to have entered the first reference works on translation studies (the *Dictionary of Translation Studies*, Shuttleworth & Cowie 1997, the *Routledge Encyclopedia of Translation Studies*, Baker 1998, and the *Handbuch Translation*, Snell-Hornby, Hönig *et al.* 1998). In the following pages I shall employ the designations 'descriptive', 'empirical' and 'target-oriented' approach, 'polysystems' and 'systemic' approach and 'Manipulation school/group' more or less interchangeably, depending on the context. This does not mean that everyone discussed in this book would want to label their own work indiscriminately with any or all of these names; but I trust most can live with most of them.

## Invisible Colleges

The descriptive and systemic perspective on translation and on studying translation was prepared in the 1960s, developed in the 1970s, propagated in the 1980s, and consolidated, expanded and overhauled in the 1990s. It introduced itself to the wider world in 1985 as "a new paradigm" in translation studies (Hermans 1985a:7).

Now, 'paradigm' is a big word. Its deployment at the time was obviously a rhetorical move, designed to highlight the oppositional, novel and radical aspects of the new stance. It sounds somewhat self-conscious, and contains an element of defiance. It might also signal an attempt by its proponents to prove their intellectual credentials by showing an awareness of theoretical issues. The term itself derives from the philosophy of science.

The idea of paradigms was made popular by Thomas Kuhn's famous book *The Structure of Scientific Revolutions*, first published in 1962. Although Kuhn did not provide a definition of his key term, for our purposes a paradigm can be understood as "a model of scientific achievement that sets guidelines for research", and as "a means for conducting research on a particular problem, a problem-solving device" (Crane 1972:7, 29). In his book Kuhn rejected the common conception that knowledge in the sciences grows cumulatively, and instead proposed a different and more discontinuous pattern. The normal state occurs in periods of what he called 'normal science', during which the implications of a particular paradigm are explored. In time an increasing number of paradoxes, incompatibilities, contradictions and unresolved questions may lead to a crisis and to a 'paradigm shift', a revolution, when a radically new way of looking is proposed, hotly debated, and finally accepted by at least part of the scientific community as a promising way forward. From that moment onwards research is conducted on a new footing as the new paradigm is explored, which means another period of 'normal science' has begun.

Kuhn's book is concerned with momentous changes in the history of science. He discusses Copernicus, Newton, Darwin, Poincaré, Einstein and other giants. To call on his notion of paradigms in the context of translation studies, a discipline of huge ambition but as yet modest dimension and achievement, looks a bit overblown. On the other hand, Kuhn's book proved so successful that the term has been subject to inflationary use in all sorts of disciplines. In any case, in the postscript which he added to the second edition in 1969, Kuhn pointed out that a revolution "need not be a large change, nor need it seem revolutionary to those outside a single community" (Kuhn 1970:181). In the same postscript he stressed that a paradigm "governs, in the first instance, not a subject matter but rather a group of practitioners. Any study of paradigm-directed or of paradigm-shattering research must begin by locating the responsible group or groups" (1970:180). If he were to rewrite his book, he added, he would probably put more emphasis on these groups of practitioners than on the abstract notion of a paradigm.

This idea provides me with a convenient point of entry. The paradigm, or, as Kuhn's postscript also calls it, the 'disciplinary matrix' (1970:182) to be explained in the following chapters, has undoubtedly proved successful, inspirational, controversial, liberating and problematic, all at the same time. Before we launch into its central ideas, its applications and implications, it will be useful to take Kuhn's advice and look at the group of practitioners behind it. We have a perfectly appropriate frame for this in Diana Crane's notion of the 'invisible college', a network of researchers working within a given paradigm (Crane 1972).

With her 'invisible college' Crane offers a model of the growth and diffusion of knowledge in scientific and scholarly communities. The model, which builds on Kuhn's work, is applicable to both the sciences and the humanities. The emphasis however is very much on the social organization of research areas and on the role of communities and networks of researchers. The central claim is that scientific and scholarly practice is not a matter of disembodied ideas spontaneously combusting and gaining acceptance from eerily rational minds. There is a social as well as a cognitive aspect to the process. It involves practitioners working in an institutional environment, regular personal contacts and a sense of solidarity, and a material as well as an intellectual infrastructure.

Diana Crane discerns a pattern in the way new ideas and paradigms emerge and spread. She describes this as a contagion process. Seminal ideas are first tried out in a small circle, early enthusiasts then infect others, which leads to an exponential growth in the production of research until a plateau is reached with voluminous output but few new ideas, after which stagnation sets in, followed by decline – and, of course, new sets of different ideas. In other words, when a paradigm runs its natural course, it goes through a series of stages (Crane 1972:40, 67ff):

- first, interesting hypotheses, theories, discoveries and methodological principles attract a group of like-minded researchers who reach consensus on key issues;
- soon a small number of highly productive individuals develop a theoretical apparatus, set priorities for research, recruit collaborators and train students, and maintain contact with colleagues;
- next, we witness an exponential increase in publications and in new recruits, allowing the central ideas to be elaborated and tested;
- eventually the novelty wears off, the rate of innovation declines, the exploration of the key ideas loses impetus, theoretical and methodological anomalies open up, some members drop out;
- finally the leading researchers develop increasingly specialized interests, or divide into factions over controversial issues; this may result in adjustments and new directions for research, or in breakdown and the eventual emergence of a different paradigm.

In the crucial early stages the guiding ideas are formulated, and they continue to provide the main focus. Their authors are also the ones most frequently cited by fellow researchers. The model stresses the element of solidarity. An invisible college constitutes a personal and intellectual network, with regular informal contacts, joint ventures and publications, frequent cross-referencing in articles and books, and, for the central players, a long-term commitment to the field and to the basic ideas.

**Manipulation College?**

The growth and diffusion of the descriptive/systemic/manipulation paradigm in translation studies can be described with almost uncanny ease in terms of Diana Crane's invisible college.

Among the first exchanges that would lead to the crystallization of a coherent 'disciplinary matrix' was the meeting of minds, in the 1960s, between the Amsterdam-based American translator and theorist James Holmes and a Czechoslovak group including Jiří Levý, Anton Popovič and František Miko. They were interested in such things as structuralist literary theory, the role of translation as part of literary history, ways of describing differences between translations and originals from stylistic or generic points of view, and the distinctive features of translation in relation to other 'metatexts', i.e. texts which speak about existing texts. Levý died in 1969, aged 41, Popovič in 1984, and the Czechoslovak group eventually fell silent. By that time however contacts had been established with, on the one hand, Itamar Even-Zohar and his colleague Gideon Toury, two researchers at Tel Aviv University, both with strong theoretical interests, and, on the other, several Flemish academics including José Lambert at Leuven University, Raymond van den Broeck, who worked at a translator training institute in Antwerp, and André Lefevere, who had studied at Essex University, taught briefly in Hong Kong and then at Antwerp, and would later settle in Austin, Texas.

The decisive stage of theory formation occurred during a series of three relatively small-scale conferences, all held in English. The first took place in Leuven in 1976, the second in Tel Aviv in 1978, and the third in Antwerp in 1980. The proceedings of the first conference were published as *Literature and Translation* (Holmes, Lambert & Van den Broeck 1978), those of the second in a special issue of the journal *Poetics Today* (vol. 2, no. 4, 1981, edited by Even-Zohar and Toury), and those of the third in the Michigan-based semiotics journal *Dispositio* (vol. 7, nos. 19-21, 1982, edited by Lefevere). The names of the conference organizers and proceedings editors are those of the key figures in the descriptive and systemic paradigm. Others who attended and/or spoke at one or more of the conferences and continued to be associated with the group include Susan Bassnett (Warwick University), Katrin van Bragt (Leuven), Lieven D'hulst (Leuven and then Antwerp), Zohar Shavit (Tel Aviv), Maria Tymoczko (Massachusetts), Shelly Yahalom (Tel Aviv) and Theo Hermans (Warwick and then London). Among slightly later recruits are Dirk Delabastita (Leuven and subsequently Namur), Saliha Paker (Istanbul), Theresa Hyun (Seoul, Toronto) and others.

The early years saw the emergence of a personal network and the elaboration of a consensus on key ideas. Bearing the 'invisible college' model in mind, it is striking that despite their international dispersion members of the network share a number of obvious features. All have been involved in university-based research and possess a background in literary studies with an active interest in comparative literature and literary history. The growth of the paradigm also coincided with personal career patterns. Of the old guard, Even-Zohar, Lefevere, Van den Broeck and Lambert had gained their doctorates around 1970 with dissertations on either translation or comparative literature topics. Around the mid 1970s they could still be regarded as young Turks, eager to make their mark. All the others mentioned in the previous paragraph obtained their PhD degrees in the course of the 1970s or later, and most went on to tenure tracks and professorial chairs in the 1980s and '90s. Clearly, the diffusion of the paradigm owes much to this upward academic mobility and the opportunities created by it.

In the paradigm's early, formative stages most of the key texts, including Even-Zohar's *Papers in Historical Poetics* (1979) and Toury's *In Search of a Theory of Translation* (1980) as well as the three collections of conference papers, appeared in quite obscure publications. This made group solidarity doubly important, in the form of cross-referencing, joint editing or writing ventures and a collective profile. It also contributed to the atmosphere within the network, whose members preferred to see themselves as radical, innovative, combative and theoretically sophisticated. The example of the Russian

Formalist circles was never far away. Lambert and Lefevere were aware of the Russian Formalist writings which had reached the West in the 1960s; Even-Zohar would quote them in Russian. Individuals brought their own expertise and interests: Even-Zohar had his polysystem hypothesis, Toury his empirical emphasis, Lambert a large-scale research project on translation history, Lefevere a preoccupation with philosophy of science, and Holmes a synthetic view spanning the theory and practice of translation. The chemistry worked.

Expansion followed. Susan Bassnett's introductory *Translation Studies* (1980, revised 1991), which became popular, bore traces of the new approach; its index featured Holmes, Lefevere, Levý and Popovič, alongside more traditional names like Catford and Eugene Nida, as the modern translation scholars most frequently mentioned. In 1985 *The Manipulation of Literature* presented work by some of the paradigm's key players to a wider audience; despite its exorbitant price and homespun appearance (it must be among the last books in the world to have been prepared camera-ready on an electric golfball typewriter) the book proved an unexpected success. Controversy helped to give the main ideas an airing. While Mary Snell-Hornby's *Translation Studies* (1988) depicted the Manipulation school as a major presence, she was also sharply critical (but sounded a markedly more positive note in the revised 1995 edition). The rather more conservative Peter Newmark, writing in 1991, dismissed the Manipulation group for their lack of interest in the criticism and evaluation of translations, and lambasted them, not unreasonably, for their "turgid style, an obsession with dates [...] and a paucity of translation examples" (1991:107).

By the early 1990s the exponential increase in publications and recruits was manifest. Lambert and Toury had set up the journal *Target* in 1989. Although *Target* was (and is) not tied to a particular school of thought, the editorial in the first issue emphasized the journal's intention to focus on theoretical and descriptive studies and on the need to 'contextualize' translation (Lambert & Toury 1989:6). *Target* soon established itself as one of the leading scholarly journals in the field, featuring a higher than average volume of work bearing the empirical imprint. The amount of citation and cross-referencing to prominent exponents of the descriptive approach is striking.

In a different context, the presence of a translation studies lobby in the international comparative literature establishment, engineered by Lambert and Lefevere, had already begun to bear fruit by the mid 1980s, when workshops on translation had become a regular feature of the triennial congresses of the International Comparative Literature Association (ICLA). Again, while the workshops did not subscribe to a specific theoretical line, the fact that they were planned and organized by a committee chaired successively by Lambert, Lefevere, Hermans and Theresa Hyun guaranteed ample exposure for the Manipulation model, as some of the congress proceedings bear out (e.g.

Lambert & Lefevere 1993, Lambert & Hyun 1995). Also of a literary nature, but at a different level, was the interaction between the Manipulation group and the cluster of research projects on translation history in Germany which ran at Göttingen University from 1985 till 1997. The Göttingen programme was the largest concentrated research effort on the history of translation ever undertaken. Several of its individual projects entered into debate, both sympathetic and critical, with the descriptive paradigm (see Chapters 5 and 11).

Perhaps the most effective vehicle for the propagation of the paradigm has been the series of international summer courses on translation research training, masterminded by Lambert and held annually since 1989, first in Leuven and more recently Misano (Italy), under the name of CERA and then CETRA. To date some two hundred young or not so young researchers have gone through these courses. Once again, the CETRA programme does not set out to indoctrinate the innocent or convert the unbelieving, but the active presence of individuals close to the descriptive paradigm does its work. Invited 'CETRA professors' have included Toury, Bassnett and Lefevere (as well as others: Hans Vermeer, Albrecht Neubert, Mary Snell-Hornby, Daniel Gile, Anthony Pym, Yves Gambier and Lawrence Venuti), while the regular staff of 'supervisors' taking part every summer includes Delabastita, D'hulst and Hermans.

Two further things became noticeable by the early 1990s. One bears on Diana Crane's fourth stage: after the period of consolidation and exponential growth, the rate of innovation declines and the exploration of key ideas loses impetus. Nowhere is this more in evidence than in two volumes brought out by key figures in the paradigm, Even-Zohar's essays collected as 'Polysystem Studies' in a special one-man issue of *Poetics Today* (Even-Zohar 1990), and Toury's *Descriptive Translation Studies and Beyond* (1995). Both books revised, refined and redefined earlier positions (Even-Zohar 1978 and Toury 1980 respectively), but contained disappointingly little that was new in theoretical or methodological terms, and scarcely any engagement with competing views and ideas.

The other development points elsewhere, towards the reorientation and expansion of the paradigm in different directions. Among its most visible signs was the collection *Translation, History and Culture* edited by Bassnett and Lefevere in 1990. In their introduction they argued that the study of translation was moving on from a formalist phase to a consideration of the broader political and cultural contexts in which translation, like other modes of 'rewriting', creates images of other texts. Power and manipulation would be key issues in what they hailed as the 'cultural turn' in translation studies. The volume featured gender-based and postcolonial contributions and essays on the mass media as well as more traditional material. Lefevere and Bassnett went on separately and jointly to pursue the increased emphasis on institutional and ideological factors (e.g. Lefevere 1992, Bassnett & Lefevere 1998), while Lambert turned his attention to the mass media and the policies and politics behind them. Others have added similar accents.

The 'invisible college' model suggests that after stage four comes stage five: anomalies opening up, key researchers dropping out, progressive specialization, break-up into factions, terminal decline. It would be a classic error, though, to mistake the model for reality. Some stagnation there certainly is. As I suggested, some of Even-Zohar's and Toury's recent work has lost its edge. James Holmes died in 1986 at the age of 62, André Lefevere in 1996, aged 50. Anomalies and contradictions within the paradigm are being exposed; in fact the present book intends to add to this internal criticism and rethinking. In his *Becoming a Translator* Douglas Robinson recently observed that in the late 1980s and 1990s "new trends in culturally oriented translation theory", especially feminist and postcolonial approaches, "expanded upon and to some extent displaced descriptive translation studies" (1997a:233). He may be right. But as the quote implies by foregrounding both expansion and displacement, the picture is more complex than the simple application of the 'invisible college' model makes it out to be.

The empirical paradigm has in a sense become part of a broader, less clearly defined trend, which, to an extent, it also helped to foster by drawing attention to translation as a force and an instrument in cultural history. Some of the guiding concepts and insights of the descriptive paradigm are now common currency in translation studies. The call to contextualize translation has lost none of its relevance, even if the way in which contextualization is to be achieved seems less obvious. In this respect the paradigm's systemic and sociological dimensions in particular leave plenty of scope for innovative thought.

Still, Diana Crane's notion of an 'invisible college' has served us well. In providing a model of the growth and diffusion of a particular paradigm in translation studies, it has helped us to recognize that the success of scholarly ideas depends on context – on material as well as intellectual circumstances, and on a critical mass of committed individuals in the right places. The critical mass is important. It guarantees continuity over time as well as the influx of new faces and ideas to generate questioning, dissent, debate, revision and innovation. The quantitative aspect thus has a qualitative impact. Compare it with the ever-present issue of whether translation studies constitute a discipline or not. In itself the question is without interest. If I like putting up garden sheds, who cares whether my hobby is called building, or carpentry, or gardening? A rose by any other name. But it matters at other levels. The acknowledgement by one's peers in the scholarly community of the validity of this kind of pursuit can be a key factor when it comes to attracting students or chalking up points in research assessments. Recognition as a discipline makes for a stronger position in competing for funds and resources, which are necessary to fill posts, dispose of a book-buying budget, attend conferences, exchange information, attract researchers, in short to build both the material and intellectual infrastructure within which new ideas have better chances of germinating.

In the next chapter I want to show the importance of having in place a critical mass of enthusiasts by tracing some of the more isolated efforts made before the descriptive paradigm came together. As will become clear, several of the basic ideas were around early on, but it took an invisible college to shape and launch them as a programme.

# 2. Lines of Approach

We can appreciate the relevance of an invisible college as a network of committed individuals by looking at the stage preceding the emergence of the descriptive paradigm. Most of the ideas which coalesced with the Manipulation group had been expressed before, but they had not found echoes. John McFarlane's essay 'Modes of Translation', published in the *Durham University Journal* in 1953, was one of those forlorn calls, a voice in the wilderness. A decade later a more concerted effort began to take shape with the work of some Czech and Slovak scholars, notably Jiří Levý, František Miko and Anton Popovič . They thought along structuralist lines and aimed at a systematic exploration of translation. Their meeting with James Holmes would lead directly to the new 'disciplinary matrix'. Let us look at some of these early efforts, partly because they define some of the key concerns of the descriptive paradigm, and partly because they will demonstrate the extent to which new ideas build on existing ones. Throughout, the frame of reference is that of literary studies.

## 'Diagnostic rather than hortatory'

The phrase comes from McFarlane's 'Modes of Translation'. James Holmes recognized the essay's pioneering role when he had McFarlane invited as a guest of honour to the 1976 Leuven conference which marked the beginning of the Manipulation group. It is a remarkable piece for its time. I will retrace its argument and quote its conclusion at some length. The essay as a whole seeks to overturn many of the traditional assumptions the descriptive paradigm would also, and more forcefully, argue against.

There is nothing new in McFarlane's starting point. Translation, he observes, is generally disparaged today. We recognize its practical value, but especially where literature is concerned we are only too ready to brand an imperfect translation as a 'travesty' or worse. However, the reason for this, McFarlane claims, is not so much the appalling badness of most translations or the incompetence of translators, but the way we have come to think about translation and its feasibility. If we despise translation because it fails to live up to our expectations, this is because our expectations are unreasonable. We want translation to square the circle and express frustration when this cannot be done. We demand that it reconcile the irreconcilable and then gloat over its necessary failure.

McFarlane quotes Wilhelm von Humboldt writing in 1796 to A.W. Schlegel: "All translating seems to me an attempt to solve an impossible problem" ("Alles Übersetzen scheint mit schlechterdings ein Versuch zur Auflösung einer unmöglichen Aufgabe", 1953:78). This is because the task we commonly set translation is that of combining what McFarlane terms "Accuracy of rendering with Grace of expression" (1953:78-79). The remainder of the essay demonstrates the pointlessness and futility of criticism which insists on translation meeting these unattainable requirements. In the process McFarlane demolishes the requirements themselves. His main target is the notion of 'Accuracy'. Accuracy in translation involves the search for an equivalent content or sense, covering both substantial and stylistic meaning, which are thought to reside in the words of the original. Does Accuracy then result in literal, word-for-word translation? That would be a mistake, McFarlane argues. What words mean is determined by the context in which they occur. Since literal translation is obsessed with words or even their component parts and takes no account of context, any mode of translation based on literalism as a standard for Accuracy is fundamentally false.

If meaning is not a matter of isolated words, how complex is it? McFarlane distinguishes referential from emotive meaning. Referential meaning draws on the "powers of symbolic reference" (1953:84) of the language, but since languages are not exactly parallel in this respect, and symbolic reference is not very precise, no precise equivalence between precise symbols can ever be attained. Emotive meaning refers to the power of words to move. In lyrical poems emotive meaning may actually be more important than referential meaning. If in translating such texts we want to retain this primacy, we are surely justified in "employing a different referential symbolism in order to obtain equivalence in this all-important emotive meaning" (1953:85). Where does that leave Accuracy, though? In addition, language never functions on one level of meaning only, but always on several simultaneously. Even if translators were able to separate out all the different strands of meaning in a text, there would still be no way of re-combining their equivalents into one coherent unit in another language. Different languages are differently structured. Bearing in mind linguistic constraints of this order, McFarlane concludes that "[t]o deny merit to translation – to deny certain formulations even the right to call themselves translation – simply because there is not equivalence *in all respects at once* is a facile yet much practised perversion of criticism" (1953:87).

The final twist in the argument involves the question of who in fact determines the meaning of a text, especially in literature. Is there a fixed, identifiable meaning to be determined in the first place? McFarlane draws on I.A. Richards's *Principles of Literary Criticism* (1924), one of the seminal works of English and American New Criticism, to show that divergent readings of literary texts often co-exist. There are similar divergences between what a speaker may have intended and what a hearer actually makes of the speaker's words. If, then, different interpretations yield different meanings, we can never properly speak of *the* meaning of a text, hence, by implication, "we can never talk about *the* translation; there will inevitably be different translations deriving from different meanings, all of them perhaps equally valid but none of them an 'ideal' or a 'true' one" (1953:89). Even so, a translator who takes as a starting point the effect a poem had on him or her as a reader is likely to be reproached for injecting too much subjectivity into the translation. If the translator takes the alternative route and attempts to get under the poet's skin and repeat the genesis of the original utterance, it will be objected that this requires a totally bilingual poet – and here McFarlane quotes Rilke, who wrote French with virtually the same ease as he did German but found, to his own surprise, that he wrote differently in French compared with German.

The complexity and elusiveness of meaning, then, is such that we cannot derive an absolute standard of Accuracy for translation from it. Translation cannot produce total accuracy because there is no way of determining what total accuracy would consist of. It is therefore pointless to continue to think of translation in terms of demands for equivalence "in all respects at once". What we need instead, McFarlane contends, is a different approach to translation, an approach which accepts translation as it is rather than as we might wish it to be, and which wants to gain insight into its nature rather than to urge it to perform the impossible. Therefore the intent of his essay, McFarlane concludes, has been

> ... to underline the need for some new, provisional theory of translation – 'new' in the sense that it should be diagnostic rather than hortatory, that it should be concerned not with unreal ideals and fictional absolutes but actualities, and that it should not hesitate to use the instruments of modern semantic theory; and 'provisional' in the sense that it should not so much attempt to impose a rigid pattern on the facts as we at present see them but rather serve as a device for the better understanding of them. (1953:92-93)

His proposal is set out in full in the final paragraphs, which are worth quoting more or less in their entirety. The proposal is that we consider translation

> ... as a complex act of communication embracing two acts of speech, each with its own structure of speaker and hearer, 'meaning' and medium, and wherein the one speech act stands in some analysable relationship with the other; and that we must then consider what must surely be the chief questions: In *what* ways may an utterance in one linguistic medium be made 'like' another in a different medium, and what things are essentially within and what necessarily beyond the control of the translator?
>
> In recommending a codification and analysis of these activities, in advocating an examination of what translation is and can be rather than what it ought to be but never is, we do no more than urge a measure that

is being increasingly applied in other spheres. [...] Before we can begin to make value judgements about translation, we must know more about its nature, and it is suggested that an analysis of *procedure* – in the belief that translation is as translation does – is the approach that promises best.

[...] That these things will in themselves be complex is inevitable, and an analysis of this kind may seem to many an over-sophisticated, even perverse, undertaking if at the end of it all we merely find ourselves left with a further set of even more forbidding problems: philosophical problems of meaning and communication; aesthetic problems of the function of media in artistic creation; psychological problems of mental patterns and their influence on style; ethnographical problems of national character and its influence on thought. But it will at least be some small achievement if we find ourselves dealing with concepts that have had close scrutiny in other fields of enquiry where there is a coherent structure of thought surrounding them. Inevitably, scholarly caution is at a premium: translation borders on too many provinces for the linguist to remain secure within his own proper territory or to survey the ground from one vantage point alone; a thorough exploration will compel him to make repeated approaches through the territories of his neighbours, and he will rely desperately on their guidance and advice. (1953:93)

There is a great deal here that will surface again in later translation studies. The relevance of distinguishing between referential and emotive meaning, and the dominance of one over the other in specific text types, would be elaborated into a functional model by Katharina Reiss (1971, 1976). The idea of employing different referential symbols to gain similarity on the emotive level parallels Eugene Nida's famous 'dynamic' (later: 'functional') equivalence.

More importantly, the essay prefigures a number of key points in the descriptive paradigm. Translation involves communication, and is a question of concrete speech acts rather than of abstract language systems. The notion that "translation is as translation does" implies a view of translation as a relative, historical concept; it also forecloses glib generalizations and invites scrutiny of the "analysable relationship" between original and translation. The study of translation then becomes "an examination of what translation is and can be rather than what it ought to be but never is", which puts the entire endeavour on a new, 'diagnostic' footing, aware of the provisional nature of its theoretical concepts and constructions. That should make it possible to decide "what things are essentially within and what necessarily beyond the control of the translator" in terms of both the linguistic medium and social and other contextual factors. And translation research will be interdisciplinary in nature - a commonplace today, but thirty-odd years after McFarlane's essay Peter Newmark was still qualifying the philosophers' and anthropologists' contributions as "dead ducks" (1986:48-49).

With its recommendations for a diagnostic, analytical and open-ended approach McFarlane's essay signalled an alternative direction for research. However, it could not be more than a pointer, a sketch of a different orientation, barely a programme, even less a blueprint. McFarlane himself never followed it up. A decade or so later, independently of McFarlane's work, Czech and Slovak researchers began to devise ways to put the study of translation on a systematic footing and analyze relationships between translations and originals. They were building on the theoretical insights of Czech Structuralists like Jan Mukařovský, Felix Vodička and Otokar Fischer, who in the 1930s and '40s had developed a semiotic framework for the study of language, literature and art. The framework proved compatible with what James Holmes was doing and, later, with the polysystems idea.

**Decisions, Shifts, Metatexts**

The programme which Jiří Levý set out in his book *Die literarische Übersetzung* ('Literary Translation', first published in Czech in 1963, translated into German in 1969) contained the kind of detailed investigation McFarlane could only hint at. In opposition both to the unsystematic, essayistic and practice-oriented nature of most work on literary translation at the time, and to the linguistic approach which treated translation merely in terms of differences between language systems, Levý wanted to focus attention on three things. They were, firstly, the role of the translator as a historical and social agent; secondly, translation as an expression of differences in poetics between national traditions or literary periods; and thirdly, methods of translation as resulting from certain norms and attitudes towards translating (1969:25). Individual translations, that is, needed to be seen in context.

Levý's is a relational approach. In his view, understanding literary translations requires the backdrop of prevailing aesthetic conventions, original works of literature, and the historical development of translation criticism. Criticism itself, he points out, is a product of historical evolution and philosophical presuppositions, and cannot provide absolute criteria. As an example of the different demands made on translation he contrasts the French tendency to adapt foreign verse forms to prose or to an indigenous form with the Slavonic tradition, which insists on preserving the formal characteristics of the original (1969:30-31).

For Levý, the value of a given rendering depends on its relation to a historically determined norm. He perceives two norms at work: a reproductive norm which shapes translation as a derived product, and an aesthetic norm which applies to a translation as a text in its own right. A translation is then a hybrid product, a conglomerate, part of which refers back to the original text while other parts reveal the translator's input.

The place of translation in a given literature shows the same duality: translations constitute independent texts while simultaneously reproducing already existing foreign works. Which of these aspects is dominant, and hence in a position to elicit the style of translating most suitable to each particular case, depends on the relations between the cultures involved and on various factors pertaining to the receiving culture. As a result, individual translations, and translation as a genre, may fulfil different functions within the receiving literature. They may supplement or support entire sections of a literature, for example if there is deemed to be insufficient local production in a particular genre, or they may enter into competition with the indigenous production. They may open up possibilities for new developments by introducing novel forms and themes, and in this way foster greater diversity within a literature. During periods when translation is mistrusted or perceived as a negative value, we may see translations being published as if they were original works; when it represents a positive value, original works may be brought out under the guise of translations. But Levý emphasizes that the value attached to translation in certain periods, and the corresponding methods of translating chosen by individual translators, spring from and are determined by "the cultural needs of the time" (1969:76). He quotes Georges Mounin to make his point: when after centuries of polished, classicizing renderings, Leconte de Lisle's 1866 translation of the *Iliad* put into relief Homer's vast distance from us, there were social and political as well as aesthetic reasons for this, as the vigorous post- Revolution French bourgeoisie had learned to celebrate history as a potent weapon against the old order.

In view of McFarlane's call for more analysis and a multidisciplinary approach, it is striking to see Levý, in an English-language contribution to a conference of literary translators in Hamburg in 1965, stating explicitly that he wanted to promote

> ... rational analysis – as opposed to subjective impressions – dealing
> with the problems [of translation] not only by means of linguistics and
> of aesthetics, as we have been used to doing, but by a compound ana-
> lytical methodology including psycholinguistics, structural anthropology,
> semantics, and all the disciplines (and 'interdisciplines') which today
> are used in the research into communication processes. (1965:77)

He went on to give examples of how psycholinguistics, anthropology and semantic theory might not only lead to better insights into translation but be of benefit to translators as well, discussing such things as the tendency of translators to choose superordinate terms, i.e. terms with a broader and less specific meaning than those used in the original, and a similar tendency to be more explicit in indicating logical relations and fill out elliptical expressions. The first tendency would be put forward as a tentative 'law of translation' by Gideon Toury thirty years later (Toury 1995:267-74; see Chapter 7). The second is being tested by research based on corpus linguistics (Baker 1995:236).

Levý began his intervention at the 1965 congress with the emphatic statement that he wanted to study translation as part of a communication process. In transmitting the original message the translator has first to decode and interpret it, then recode it in a different medium. The express reference to translation as communication is also the starting point of what is perhaps Levý's best-known essay in English, 'Translation as a Decision Process', in the three-volume Festschrift for Roman Jakobson (Levý 1967). It represents a bold attempt to cast new light on the process of translating by looking at it from an unusual angle but one which, he says, conforms with the practical experience of translating as problem-solving. The angle is that of game theory, a branch of mathematics first developed in the 1940s and greatly developed since, with numerous applications (Ridley 1996:53ff.).

Levý describes the activity of translating as a series of moves, each of which involves making one choice from among a set of alternative possibilities. In translating the German word *Bursche*, for example, the translator needs to select an English word from a set including such terms as *boy*, *fellow*, *chap*, *youngster*, *lad* and *guy*. The terms are not equivalent for there are differences of meaning, style and register between them. Neither is the translator's choice random, for it depends on his or her memory capacity, aesthetic standards and other such things. In addition, each selection from the paradigmatic set of alternatives will become part of the conditioning factors for the next choice to be made, so that the process has a syntagmatic aspect as well. In this sense, Levý argues, translating can be compared with a game with complete information, like chess, where every next move takes account of all previous moves.

When we study existing translations, however, we can only see the outcome of the translator's choices. The motives, the pattern of instructions which informed the choices, can only be inferred. In this sense studying translation means engaging in what Richard Dawkins today calls 'reverse engineering': confronted with an artifact from the past we make the working assumption that it was designed for some purpose, and we analyze it so as to figure out what problem it might have been good at solving (Dawkins 1996:120). Levý suggests that in encountering two French translations of the phrase 'not a little embarrassed', one which reads

(a)  *pas peu embarrassé*

and the other

(b)  *très embarrassé*,

we can assume that the translator of (a) decided to preserve the stylistic quality of understatement in the English phrase and run the risk of being accused of writing anglicisms, while (b) sacrifices style but writes acceptable French.

We can then assess the relative weight of stylistic preferences and of purist opinion among the readership the translators were addressing, and construct a picture of how their decisions may have been triggered by those factors.

In fact, Levý observes, translators intuitively appraise the way readers are likely to respond to their translation choices. Researchers therefore need to bear in mind such things as the functions which different epochs attribute to certain stylistic and other devices in different types of text, the relative importance of such features, i.e. their place in a hierarchy of importance, and the kind of audience the translators were addressing. This 'generative model of translation', as Levý called it (1967:1182), would operate on the basis of the methods used in defining decision problems. We will meet this idea again later, especially with respect to the notion of convention, which I will discuss together with norms in Chapter 6.

Levý's work goes well beyond McFarlane's first stab. To translation-as-communication he adds the translator as a decision-making agent. He points to the relevance of historically contingent concepts of translation for the practice of translating in a given period. He emphasizes the importance of prevailing attitudes towards translation as the backdrop to practical norms of translating. These norms form part of the environment which conditions the translator's choices, and they help to determine the nature of the end product. The approach is both functional, in that it seeks to explain the occurrence and nature of translation in terms of its function in the receiving culture, and structuralist, in that Levý constantly looks for patterns behind phenomena, the grammar underlying events, the Saussurian *langue* beneath the *parole* of individual translations.

Levý's death in 1967 did not stop his compatriots František Miko and Anton Popovič from continuing along roughly the same track. Miko's specialism was stylistics. His main contribution to become known in the West was a highly abstract methodological essay in French, "rigorously structuralist" as well as "functional" (Miko 1970:73), in which he distinguished different text types and tried to break each type down into a set of expressive features. This should allow us to confront a translation not only with its donor text but also with other relevant texts, and to measure variance and invariance. The aim, in other words, was to supply adequate tools for text analysis, reducing features of style to their smallest constituent units in true structuralist fashion. The fact, however, that Miko stayed at the level of forbidding abstraction and appeared unable to derive a workable methodology testifies to the complexity of the task. We have to wait until the 1980s for practicable models to be developed; I will discuss them in Chapter 5.

Popovič took a broader view. He repeated Levý's point about the dual character of translation, which always reveals "the existence of two stylistic norms in the translator's work: the norm of the original and the norm of the translation" (1970:82). Literary translation involves a confrontation not just between two systems of expression, each with its own stylistic means, but also between two sets of aesthetic conventions. For their analysis Popovič referred to Miko, seeing his stylistic researches into 'shifts of expression' as laying the foundations for "the objective classification of differences between the translation and its original" (1970: 84), which in turn will permit us to determine "the aesthetic theory of translation crystallizing from the literary trends of the time" (1970:81). The ideal of objective measurement and knowledge, incidentally, a constant undercurrent in structuralist thinking, would continue to hover in the background of much descriptive work on translation, especially at times when the reaction against strongly evaluative and prescriptive approaches was at its most strident and the lure of rigorous empiricism and dispassionate scholarship proportionately strong. It would take the impact of cultural studies, deconstruction and more overtly ideological positions like gender-oriented and postcolonial studies to dislodge the spectre.

Of particular concern to Popovič was the attempt to capture the specificity of translation by setting it among and against similar 'metatexts', as he called them. Translation in his view constitutes a form of 'metacommunication'. The term refers to "all types of processing (manipulation) of the original literary text, whether it is done by other authors, readers, critics, translators, etc." (1976a:226). James Holmes shared Popovič's concern; André Lefevere would later speak of 'refracted texts' and then of 'rewriting'.

In his 1976 essay 'Aspects of Metatext' Popovič surveyed the whole range of 'metatexts' and their relations with 'prototexts', from transcription, plagiarism and forgery to parody, paraphrase and translation, including fictitious translations (he called them pseudotranslations) and pseudo-originals. Among the interesting features of his account is the distinction between affirmative and polemical, and between overt and covert ways in which metatexts can relate to prototexts. Translation, for example, is said to stand in an overt and affirmative relation to its source, whereas parody takes up a polemical and covert position vis-à-vis its prototext. Holmes had been working on a very similar classification.

## A Disciplinary Utopia

James Holmes's role in the emergence of translation studies as a scholarly discipline generally, and in the formation of the descriptive 'disciplinary matrix' in particular, is now widely recognized. In the 1960s, when there were no translation studies newsletters and few specialized journals, he maintained close contacts with the Czech and Slovak researchers, and was remarkably well informed about ongoing work elsewhere, both on translation and on literary theory. He played the key part in bringing together the 'invisible college' of descriptive translation studies.

Holmes shares with Popovič the view of literary translation as metaliterature; the idea stems from Roland Barthes' notion of metalaguage, i.e.

language which speaks about language (1988:10, 23). A translated poem is a metapoem. Because it speaks about another poem, it is also like criticism or commentary or glossing. The difference is that a metapoem "interprets [...] not by analysis but by enactment" (1988:11). This approach allows Holmes to delineate the specific nature of translation in terms of Wittgenstein's idea of 'family resemblances' between translation and various more or less comparable forms (1988:23ff.). The distinctive features of verse translation, for example, include the following:

- it uses verse as its medium – a feature shared with, say, a poem loosely inspired by another poem in the same language, but contrasting with prose translation or prose commentary;
- it offers an interpretation of the original – in common with prose translation and commentary, but in contrast with a poem inspired by another poem;
- it is determinate in length and subject-matter – as is a prose translation, whereas commentary or a poem inspired by another poem show no such limitation;
- it is written in a language other than that of the original – like prose translation and some forms of commentary, but unlike same-language commentaries or metatexts.

The procedure sidesteps the problem of defining translation in essentialist terms, pointing instead to a cluster of interlinking phenomena, all of them partly similar and partly dissimilar. Holmes consequently describes a 'metapoem' as a "nexus of a complex bundle of relationships" (1988:24), more or less as a phoneme, for instance, is made up of distinctive features.

In considering the relation between a translation and its source Holmes elaborates Levý's idea of translating as decision-making into a two-plane model. His argument is that translators proceed not only serially, making one decision after another as they work through a source text, but also structurally, on the basis of a mental map of the prospective target text. Discussions of translation issues should therefore take into account the interplay between a whole set of factors comprising language, literary tradition or 'literary intertext' (the term is Julia Kristeva's), and socio-cultural situation (1988:41, 89). He brings these factors to bear, for example, on what he calls the 'cross-temporal factor' in translating poetry from an older period (1988:35ff.). A present-day translator has to decide whether to 'exoticize' or 'naturalize', to 'historicize' or 'modernize' in respect of language (e.g. as regards syntax and vocabulary), literary intertext (e.g. in the choice of a modern or outmoded verse form) and socio-cultural situation (e.g. keeping source-culture symbols and topical references or inventing new ones). The combination of different axes and different levels generates complex and highly flexible descriptive tools which Holmes, with his penchant for complicated diagrams, sets out in impressive visual shape.

Using methods like these Holmes is able to systematize aspects of translation and to place them in a historical setting. Among the best-known applications is a 1968 paper on 'Forms of Verse Translation and the Translation of Verse Form' (1988:23-33). Here he distinguishes between form-derivative and content-derivative form in translation. Form-derivative form in turn comprises two types, mimetic and analogical. An example of mimetic form is an English hexameter to render an ancient Greek hexameter, as in Richmond Lattimore's *Odyssey*; this is the opening of Book 11:

> Now when we had gone down again to the sea and our vessel,
> first of all we dragged the ship down into the bright water,
> and in the black hull set the mast in place, and set sails,
> and took the sheep and walked them aboard, and ourselves also
> embarked, but sorrowful, and weeping big tears.

An analogical form is one which in the receptor tradition fulfils a function similar to that fulfilled by the original form in its context. In eighteenth-century English literature, for example, the heroic couplet is used to translate Greek, Latin or Italian epic poems originally written in various metres. Robert Fitzgerald uses pentameters in his *Odyssey*:

> We bore down on the ship at the sea's edge
> and launched her on the salt immortal sea,
> stepping our mast and spar in the black ship;
> embarked the ram and ewe and went aboard
> in tears, with bitter and sore dread upon us.

If both Lattimore and Fitzgerald used a verse form derived from the original verse form, Ezra Pound chooses a verse form which seems to grow out of the material itself and assumes its own unique poetic shape. This 'organic form' is a type of content-derivative form:

> And then went down to the ship,
> Set keel to breakers, forth on the godly sea, and
> We set up mast and sail on that swart ship,
> Bore sheep aboard her, and our bodies also
> Heavy with weeping. So winds from sternward
> Bore us out onward with bellying canvas,
> Circe's this craft, the trim-coifed goddess.

A fourth type would be 'extraneous form', not derived from either the form or the content of the original, but here, significantly, Holmes does not supply an example; we could perhaps think of exercises in which a text, whatever its topic, is turned into a sonnet, an epigram, a rondeau, etc.

Of more interest is that Holmes goes on to place his various types historically. Mimetic form, for instance, introduces novelty and new formal resources
into the receiving literature; it tends to occur when the need is felt to stress the
strangeness of the original form, when a culture is open to outside influences,
as in Europe in the nineteenth century (Holmes does not elaborate). Analogical form can be expected in a culture with highly developed genre concepts
and a strong sense of its own norms providing the touchstone for other literary
forms, as was the case in the Neoclassical eighteenth century (1988:27-28).

These are crude generalizations, as Holmes readily concedes. Their value
lies in the opportunities they provide for classification and comparison, and in
the invitation to explore broadly-based historical preferences and patterns.
But they also foreground the problematic nature of the relationship between
original and translation. Indeed for Holmes, as for McFarlane, equivalence is
asking too much. Instead he speaks of similarity in overall structure, 'matchings', functions which "in many and appropriate ways are closely akin (though
never truly equivalent) to those of the words etc. in the language and culture
of the original and its reader" (1988:12, 54) and finally of a "network of *correspondences*, or *matchings*, with a varying closeness of *fit*" (1988:101; his
emphasis).

With the examination of such relations in mind Holmes urges those
interested in studying translation to "lay aside prescription in favour of
description"; and more emphatically: "I would like to question whether helping
the translator is really a criterion for translation studies . [...] It need not be a
main aim of translation studies to help the translator" (1988:25, 97). Debates
about what translators should or should not do, and about which mode of
translation is better or worse or more or less appropriate than some other mode
tend, in Holmes's view, to generate "more heat than light" (1988:25, 45).

The idea that the study of translation should seek illumination instead of
handing down rules about how best to translate forms the starting point of
Holmes's most famous essay, 'The Name and Nature of Translation Studies'
(1972). It begins by claiming legitimacy for the study of translation as a scholarly discipline in its own right. With a somewhat heavy-handed reference to
the philosophy of science Holmes notes that a 'disciplinary utopia' requires a
grouping of researchers who share a fascination with a common set of problems together with the channels of communication to permit them to exchange
and propagate views and findings. These conditions, he observes, are now
beginning to be fulfilled in the field of research concerned with translation
and translating.

A couple of impediments to the development of a disciplinary utopia still
need to be removed, though, and Holmes's essay sets out to do just that. First,
the new discipline needs a name. After surveying a number of alternatives
such as 'translatology' or 'science of translation', Holmes opts for 'transla-

tion studies' as the broadest and idiomatically most acceptable term. Another impediment is the lack of consensus as to the scope and structure of the discipline. Holmes will devote the rest of his essay to sorting out this problem.

The way he approaches the issue is of interest. Having claimed that translation studies is not coterminous with comparative or contrastive terminology, lexicography, linguistics or indeed with translation theory, he adopts Werner Koller's view that the field comprises "all research activities taking the phenomena of translating and translation as their basis or focus" (1988:71). From this statement, and presumably from the word 'phenomena' in it, Holmes concludes that translation studies, "as no one I suppose would deny" (ibid.), is an empirical discipline. The philosophy of science is again invoked to identify the two major objectives of such disciplines: to describe the relevant phenomena, and establish general principles to explain and predict their occurrence. As a field of pure research, then, the discipline of translation studies has two main branches. The first, descriptive translation studies, is concerned with describing translation, translations and the activity called translating. The second, translation theory, is charged with explanation and prediction.

From there Holmes proceeds to survey and subdivide each branch. The descriptive branch, for example, consists of a product-oriented division which investigates existing translations, a function-oriented one which looks at how translations fare in their socio-cultural context, and a process-oriented section interested in the mental processes taking place in translators' heads. The theoretical branch is mapped out and furrowed in the same way. It is only after all this careful sorting and categorizing is done that Holmes announces there also exists a branch of the discipline which is 'of use' rather than 'of light' and which is called applied translation studies. It is composed of translator training, the production of translation aids, translation policy, and translation criticism. Two concluding paragraphs stress the interdependence of the various branches, and the relevance of the historical and meta-theoretical dimension of the discipline itself.

Holmes's path-breaking survey of translation studies is remarkable not just for the comprehensive attempt to map an emergent field of study, but no less so for the way in which it foregrounds 'pure research' at the expense of the applied branch. For once Holmes himself did not supply a diagram with his essay. Gideon Toury (1981:181) did it for him, showing a central node called 'Translation Studies' dividing into two main branches, one 'Pure', the other 'Applied'. The 'Pure' branch then subdivides again in 'Descriptive' and 'Theoretical', and so on. The diagrammatic representation puts the 'pure' and the 'applied' divisions at the same hierarchical level; it corresponds also with the numbering system Holmes used to structure his essay and which indeed gives equal weight to 'pure' and 'applied' studies. But – and this is why I do not reproduce Toury's diagram here – it obscures the way in which Holmes's discursive presentation clearly privileges the view of translation studies as an empirical discipline, with description and theory emphatically coming first and the applied branch reduced to little more than an afterthought (Hermans 1991:155-56; Sorvali 1996:26).

The ambivalence looks like a calculated move: translation studies may well consist of two main parts, pure and applied, but whereas traditionally the applied part came first, here that hierarchy has been decisively reversed and the 'pure' branch, which is 'of light' rather than 'of use', has gained prominence. The references to the philosophy of science at the beginning of the essay thus serve a polemical purpose. From now on, the message reads, translation studies will be a field of study in its own right, seeking illumination for its own sake. It is no longer the ancillary discipline that has to be of service to translators or their teachers to justify its existence. In that sense Holmes's 'Name and Nature' constitutes translation studies' declaration of independence.

# 3. Points of Orientation

The ideas we saw being explored in the previous chapter came together in the 1970s in the personal grouping and the series of conferences which resulted in the new descriptive and systemic paradigm. Some lines of investigation, among them Miko's excursions into stylistics, were eventually discontinued. New accents emerged, as the encounter with the scholars from Israel and the Low Countries, each of whom brought their own special emphasis, produced a wholly new impetus and coalesced into a full-fledged programme. Its main features are summarized in the following pages. I will then elaborate individual aspects in the next few chapters.

One of the most frequently quoted statements summing up the new approach is from the programmatic introduction to *The Manipulation of Literature* (Hermans 1985a). I will use that passage to structure the present chapter.

The introduction began by wondering why the study of literary translation in particular had remained such a neglected field. Three reasons were advanced. Firstly, ever since the Romantic period our modern concept of literature had been marked by an emphasis on creativity and originality – what Pierre Bourdieu, in an essay of 1977, called the "charismatic ideology" of art (1993:76). An allegedly derivative form like translation was therefore disdained as second-hand and second-rate. What little attention had been paid to it had never risen above the level of judgmental criticism, which always found translations falling short of the ideal of exactly reproducing their originals in every nuance and detail, and thus constantly pushed translation back into its subordinate place. Secondly, although linguists had in recent decades begun to address issues of translation, they had dealt primarily with non-literary texts and restricted themselves to the level of the sentence instead of tackling larger textual and discursive entities (a charge, incidentally, which might have been appropriate a generation earlier but was hardly fair, let alone informed, in 1985). Thirdly, psychological attempts to probe the human mind during the process of translation were unable to do more than produce speculative diagrams because they could not engage in direct observation, the translator's mind being an inaccessible black box.

The novel approach which was then announced as heralding a 'new paradigm' would operate on the basis of "a comprehensive theory and ongoing practical research" (1985:10). It was being elaborated by a group of researchers who were in agreement on some basic assumptions. The group being referred to was, of course, the collection of individuals who had met at the series of conferences mentioned in the previous chapter (Leuven 1976, Tel Aviv 1978 and Antwerp 1980). The passage summing up the common ground between them runs as follows:

> What they have in common is, briefly, a view of literature as a complex
> and dynamic system; a conviction that there should be a continual inter-
> play between theoretical models and practical case studies; an approach
> to literary translation which is descriptive, target-oriented, functional
> and systemic; and an interest in the norms and constraints that govern
> the production and reception of translations, in the relation between
> translation and other types of text processing, and in the place and role
> of translations both within a given literature and in the interaction be-
> tween literatures. (Hermans 1985:10-11)

Let me take each part of this statement in turn and comment on it. This will
allow us to appreciate the general principles and contours of the approach,
before we go into more detail.

### *'a view of literature as a complex and dynamic system'*

The subtitle of *The Manipulation of Literature* was 'Studies in Literary Translation'. The literary aspect is emphatically present on the title page and in
most contributions to the book. So were the papers read at the Leuven, Tel
Aviv and Antwerp conferences. Just as the work surveyed in the previous
chapter had already been consistently focused on literary translation, the empirical paradigm would continue to be elaborated primarily with reference to
literary texts until more or less the end of the 1980s. True, a number of Gideon
Toury's methodological soundings in his *In Search of a Theory of Translation* (1980), for example, did not presuppose a literary context, or could readily
be applied to non-literary texts, but the book as a whole never strayed far from
literary examples and references. More recent work has opened up the scope
in a more deliberate manner. José Lambert in particular has written about
translation in the media, the business world and international organizations,
and urged research into the social and political importance of translation on a
global scale (see Chapter 9). Today, it is fair to say, theoretical work on such
things as norms of translation or the concept of equivalence, or the case studies which are produced, are no longer predicated on a literary frame of reference
– even though that frame remains close at hand.

The idea that literature can be thought of as a system, a set of interdependent elements, has a respectable pedigree. In the context of empirical
translation studies one term in particular has gained prominence: literature as
a polysystem. More will be said about this below and in Chapter 8. The
polysystem concept, which views literature as a network of elements which
interact with each other, is meant to serve as a tool for investigating why
translators behave in this or that way, or why some translations prove more
successful than others. It forms part of the explanation for what is observed on
the ground.

If we want to understand, for example, why Ezra Pound, writing around the time of the First World War, translated the passage from the *Odyssey* quoted in Chapter 2 as he did rather than in the way, say, Matthew Arnold might have liked to see Homer translated, then it helps to see his action in terms of what he was trying to achieve with his literary criticism and his original poems as well as his verse translations. A plausible scenario can then be constructed which casts Pound as engaging in a sustained campaign to break the mould of Edwardian poetry by introducing or recovering unusual modes of poetic writing. He selected certain source texts, and employed a particular and startling style of translating, as a lever to unhinge the prevailing convention, with a view eventually to replace it with his own preferred kind of poetry. Rephrasing this scenario in system terms means relating the individual instance to a set of other factors which all hang together and are put forward in their totality to account for the particular instance. The point about the systems idea is that it invites us to think in terms of functions, connections and interrelations. Contextualization of individual phenomena is the key. It is worth noting, though, that the explanation remains a tentative construct.

### '... a conviction that there should be a continual interplay between theoretical models and practical case studies'

This idea, apart from being common sense, bears on the way the Manipulation group styled itself to some extent after the Russian Formalists. The Formalists prided themselves on being self-critical and methodologically rigorous as well as radical and innovative. They emphasized the provisional nature of their theories and positions. Theories were means to an end, tools for analysis. If the tools proved inadequate or needed refinement, they were promptly replaced. In 1914, for example, Victor Shklovsky launched the provocative idea that literary works consisted of nothing more than stylistic 'devices' designed to impede the reader's habitual perception of language and the world. The notion of literature and art as 'defamiliarization' was subsequently refined by Shklovsky himself and others, as a result of theoretical speculation and its application to individual works such as Cervantes' *Don Quixote* and Sterne's *Tristram Shandy*. Although the notion of 'device' soon gave way to other concepts, it served for a time to focus attention on specific aspects of literary texts, and generated case studies. It was discarded when better concepts became available. Something of this willingness to revise and adjust the analytical apparatus can be seen in the Manipulation group, notably in Gideon Toury's abandoning the notion of the 'Adequate Translation' when it proved unworkable (see Chapter 5), or in the way André Lefevere toyed with terms such as 'refraction' and 'universe of discourse' (Chapter 9).

The other, more important but less clear-cut aspect of the relation between theories and case studies bears on the philosophy of science. Broadly speaking, no focused observation is really possible without a theory which tells the observer what to look for and how to assess the significance of what is being observed. In this sense a theory provides what Karl Popper would call a 'searchlight'. Case studies are then adduced to test the theory, which may be vindicated as a result but may equally have to be modified or even jettisoned if the findings fail to match the predictions. Such at least is the theory about the relation between theory and practice of research. In practice, things are messier. In the humanities, and especially in areas like history, anthropology or literary studies where experiments are hard to conduct, case studies are rarely chosen with a view to testing specific theories. Instead, theoretical models and problem-solving methods, usually of the fairly general variety Diana Crane refers to as 'orientation paradigms' (1971:137), are projected onto a particular situation or body of texts. The value of the models and methods lies in the fact that they throw new light on old material, bring other than the traditional aspects to the fore, often give rise to different ways of gathering and sorting data, and suggest explanations of a different order from the ones proposed before. The importance of the case studies is then twofold. They illustrate the productivity of the theory and its applicability across a range of situations. In addition, they serve to convince other sections of the scholarly community of the relevance of the theories and models by demonstrating that interesting and illuminating insights can be gained from them in areas which peer researchers also recognize as being of significance.

A good example of this interaction is provided by José Lambert's various reports on a series of research projects dealing with the role of translation in French literature and culture in the first half of the nineteenth century (Lambert 1978, 1981, 1988). Early explorations concerning the reception in France of the German romantic writer Ludwig Tieck took their cue from Jiří Levý's work, but came up against the problem of the erratic behaviour of some translators. Levý's schemes left no room for such apparent frivolity. A much larger project was set up (involving Lieven D'hulst, Katrin van Bragt and several generations of willing students) with a view to delving into the complexities of translation strategies, genre conventions and the unequal distribution of innovative and conservative forces across the different sectors of literary life at the time. In the event Even-Zohar's polysystem theory and Toury's insistence on a target-oriented approach supplied more fitting tools for the treatment of a corpus of this size and intricacy. The theoretical and methodological consequences of operating along these lines led to sets of specific research questions and procedures, which were themselves subject to revision in light of the data they dredged up. Theory and practice of research interacted.

It may be relevant to note in connection with this example that for Lambert, as for Toury, theory has tended to be seen virtually exclusively in terms of its applicability as a research tool. This has led, particularly in Toury's case, to a pronounced emphasis on methodological issues (of the type: on what grounds can I assume I am dealing with a translation? Where do I start my analysis?). The strength of Toury's work (Toury 1980 and 1995) lies in the consistency and rigour with which he draws up practical research procedures. The corollary has been the risk of sliding from rigour into rigidity, and a relative neglect of the theoretical underpinning of some of the methodological stances, which remain vulnerable to criticism for that reason. I will return to this in Chapters 5 and 7.

### '... an approach to literary translation which is descriptive ...'

For 'literary translation' read 'translation', as discussed above. But 'descriptive' is the key word. As explained in the previous chapter, John McFarlane urged a 'diagnostic' rather than a 'hortatory' approach as early as 1953. The Czechoslovak scholars, Holmes and others did the same. The difference between the early calls and the Manipulation group is that now a complete and explicit programme was being elaborated on a resolutely descriptive basis. The programme found its fullest and most forceful – and in some ways its most problematic – statement in Gideon Toury's work.

As was indicated in Chapter 1, the term 'descriptive' was used as a programmatic declaration in opposition to other terms and approaches, and is best understood in that oppositional sense. This also makes it possible to characterize its 'negative heuristic', the things which descriptivists are reacting against and emphatically do not want to do. They do not want to be prescriptive, and they do not want value judgements to be the sole or even the primary aim of the study of translation. In rejecting a prescriptive, or normative, approach to translation, the descriptivists want to conduct research for its own sake and not in order to distil from it practical advice or guidelines for good translating, or rules of thumb which translators should follow when they translate, or criteria with which critics and reviewers can assess the quality of translations. 'Descriptive' thus signals a deliberate shift away from 'applied' to 'pure' research, in a historical context in which the 'applied' tendency had long been dominant. This lends the term 'descriptive' its polemical, oppositional edge.

The 'positive heuristic' of descriptivism redefines the aims of studying translation by claiming legitimacy for research which is 'of light' rather than 'of use', to speak in Holmes's terms. It wants to study translations as they are, and to account for their occurrence and nature. These endeavours may yield insights that turn out to be of practical use to translators and to translation teachers and critics, but such benefits are incidental. In essence, descriptivists regard what translators do and say, and what translation teachers and critics do and say, as their object of study. In this way not only translations but also statements about translation, including prescriptive and evaluative pronouncements, are grist to the descriptive mill.

The way in which the descriptive paradigm was elaborated in practice, and the particular circumstances of its emergence, give rise to some interesting and fundamental but profoundly problematic issues. I will briefly indicate two of them here; a fuller discussion follows in Chapters 7 and 10.

One issue concerns the ultimate goal of translation studies. Toury is clear about the answer to the implied question in the title of his second book, *Descriptive Translation Studies and Beyond* (1995). For him, what lies beyond description is the discovery of 'laws' of translation (see Chapter 7). No one else in the descriptive camp has followed Toury in this quest. For them the aim remains that of gaining insight into the theoretical intricacies and the historical relevance and impact of translation.

Another point bears on the question of whether the descriptive option entails the observer's neutral, objective stance, detached from the object of study. Some descriptive pronouncements undoubtedly gravitate towards this position. It becomes manifest not only in Toury's scientistic jargon and his apparent belief in the possibility of attaining objectivity in cultural and historical research, but also, for example, in the introduction which Delabastita and D'hulst wrote for their collection of essays on *European Shakespeares*. They insisted on the need for "a detached and purely descriptive attitude", "the maximally detached stance of the neutral observer", "the maximally detached position of the historian" and "the researcher's ideal of a maximally neutral and complete understanding" (1993:14-16). Connected with the ideal of 'detachment' is the strict separation between object-level and meta-level: for the researcher, actual translations, together with the statements about translation made by translators, teachers and critics, constitute the object of study, while the researcher's own pronouncements about these texts operate at a meta-level. Detached, scholarly, disinterested observation and meta-level commentary are supposed to remain distinct from the object-level. The polemical context in which the descriptive paradigm came into being partially explains the over-emphasis on dispassionate investigation. It is also true that by no means all descriptive work follows this line of thought. Today, at any rate, the idea of neutral description is generally viewed with suspicion in the human sciences. There are good reasons for this. The very fact that all linguistic utterances, including descriptions, imply modal aspects is hard to reconcile with the idea of neutrality; the translation researcher does not observe or comment from nowhere in particular but from a certain institutional position; the claim to neutrality or objectivity is already an ideological statement in itself; understanding, whether in terms of Popper's searchlight theory or in more hermeneutic terms, is possible only from a given point of view, starting from preconceptions. These, and one or two other reasons for remaining sceptical of descriptive detachment and objectivity will be discussed further in Chapter 10.

## *'... target-oriented, functional ...'*

Here too the historical context of the descriptive stance is relevant. 'Target-oriented' stands in opposition to 'source-oriented', 'functional' to 'essentialist'. Again it was Gideon Toury who gave the decisive push and supplied the most programmatic statement. As Toury has also noted (1995:25), the *skopos* theory of translation which Hans Vermeer and others developed independently of and more or less simultaneously with the descriptive paradigm, puts similar emphasis on a target-oriented and functionalist approach (Vermeer 1990, 1990a; Nord 1997). There are differences between the two schools of thought. *Skopos* theory takes as its ultimate goal the provision of adequate guidelines for translating and sees itself as a form of applied translation studies. It is predominantly concerned with professional translating, whereas descriptivists have tended to dwell in the literary sphere. The other more or less simultaneous development, characterized by Mary Snell-Hornby (1986) as the 'pragmatic turn' of the early 1980s, was concerned mostly with linguistic approaches; like descriptivism and *skopos* theory, it was strongly functionalist in nature and would contextualize translation in similar ways.

The term 'target-oriented' – we could also say 'receptor-oriented' – is used in a more general and a more specifically methodological sense. In its more general application it bears on the perceived status of translation, and here its opposite, the traditional source-oriented approach to translation, is relevant. This latter approach locates the criterion for measuring a translation in the original or source text. Since the translation is seen as a reproduction of the original, as faithful as can be, its quality can be assessed by mapping similarities and deviations. Apart from the overtly evaluative and prescriptive aspects, the procedure is also predicated on viewing a translation as a vicarious object, a substitute which must constantly be referred back to its source. The authority of the original is constantly re-affirmed in the process. As a consequence, the translation is perceived as merely derivative, lacking in substance, and always to be checked against the original for faults and shortcomings. In her account of the social status of translation in Canada, Sherry Simon aptly noted that "historically, the name of the translator is the site of radical insignificance; unlike the author's name, the translator's name is not required for the classification or circulation of a translated book" (1989:14). If translation, as an object of study, lacks substance and therefore also prestige, the scholarly study of translation is bound to be held in equally low esteem.

By contrast, the target-oriented approach could be said to take its cue from the cultural signficance of translation, as it leaps from the very first page of Louis Kelly's *The True Interpreter*: "Western Europe owes its civilization to translators" (1979:1). If translation is of such historical moment, it deserves sustained attention in its own right. Seen from that angle, the target-oriented stance, which begins by focusing attention on translations as separate texts, is a way of claiming legitimacy for studying translation in the first place. One of André Lefevere's more combative essays is suggestively entitled 'Why Waste Our Time on Rewrites?' (1985): spending research time on a low-status object like translation, as on such other forms as summarizing, adapting and anthologizing which Lefevere collectively terms 'rewriting', requires justification in an institutional and ideological context which privileges originality and authorship over mere reproduction and recycling.

However, once the claim for the relevance of translation has been made, on historical, linguistic, philosophical or other grounds, and translations are felt to be worthy objects of study, it is worth asking what the problem was that a given translation was intended to solve. Why did Voltaire translate Shakespeare? Why did he do it in the way he did? The answers to these questions cannot be found by reducing Voltaire's versions to Shakespeare's words. There are too many changes – 'shifts', Popovič would have said – which are clearly not dictated by differences between English and French. Voltaire was perfectly capable of rendering Hamlet's 'To be or not to be' soliloquy in a manner that hugged the exact order and dictionary value of the English words. In 1761 he did exactly that (I have added the English words in italics between Voltaire's lines):

> Être ou n'être pas, c'est là la question,
>> *To be, or not to be; that is the question:*
> S'il est plus noble dans l'esprit de souffrir
>> *Whether 'tis nobler in the mind to suffer*
> Les piqûres et les flèches de l'affreuse fortune,
>> *The slings and arrows of outrageous fortune,*
> Ou de prendre les armes contre une mer de trouble,
>> *Or to take arms against a sea of troubles,*
> Et en s'opposant à eux, les finir? Mourir, dormir,
>> *And, by opposing, end them. To die, to sleep –*
> Rien de plus; et par ce sommeil, dire: Nous terminons
>> *No more, and by a sleep to say we end*
> Les peines du cœur, et dix mille chocs naturels
>> *The heartache and the thousand natural shocks*
> Dont la chair est héritière; c'est une consommation
>> *That flesh is heir to – 'tis a consummation*
> Ardemment désirable. Mourir, dormir (...)    (Voltaire 1879:202)
>> *Ardently to be wished. To die, to sleep.*

He then observed how, despite its undeniable raw beauty, this "rough diamond with faults" ("un diamant brut qui a des taches", 1879:203) could not possibly please the exquisite ear of the French theatregoer brought up on Aristotelian unities, decorum, verisimilitude and a dozen other rules. If *Hamlet* was to have a chance on the French stage, Voltaire suggested, the monologue would have to be cast in dignified rhyming alexandrines, and sound something like this:

> Demeure, il faut choisir, et passer à l'instant
> De la vie à la mort, et de l'être au néant.
> Dieux justes, s'il en est, éclairez mon courage.
> Faut-il vieillir courbé sous la main qui m'outrage,
> Supporter ou finir mon malheur et mon sort?
> Qui suis-je? Qui m'arrête? Et qu'est-ce que la mort?
> C'est la fin de nos maux, c'est mon unique asile;
> Après de longs transports, c'est un sommeil tranquille.
> On s'endort, et tout meurt.   (1879:201-202)

The reasons for Voltaire's rejection of one mode of translation in favour of another, even the reasons for his selecting certain texts for translation in the first place, as when he tackles Shakespeare's *Julius Caesar,* cannot really be traced by checking Voltaire's texts against Shakespeare's. Voltaire translates Shakespeare and chooses to render him in one way rather than another because he uses translation as a means to an end. Without such intentionality, without taking account of the function which the translation is meant to serve or the problem it is trying to solve, the translator's choices appear whimsical, or pointless, or wholly idiosyncratic. In Voltaire's case it is fair to say he was attempting to breathe new life into neoclassical French drama with impulses from the much freer theatrical traditions of England and Spain, while simultaneously retreating in disgust at what appeared to him as the crude excesses and lack of good taste in many of these foreign products.

Looking for possible answers to the question *why* translations turn out as they do means inquiring into their function, or their intended function. As a rule, this also means starting the investigation at the receiving end, the target pole. A target-oriented approach is a way of asking questions about translations without reducing them to purely vicarious objects explicable entirely in terms of their derivation. In countering an ideology which views translation exclusively as replication, this approach contextualizes the translator's activity in functional terms. Respecting the complexity of translation in its cultural, social and historical context, it urges attention to the whole constellation of functions, intentions and conditioning factors.

Of course, the target pole is not necessarily the place where the answers to 'why' questions will be found. From a methodological point of view however it is both a sound and an economical first move. Toury (1995:70-74) insists on the value of initially checking a translation for acceptability in the host environment, comparing its features with original texts of the same genre and with existing translations before bringing the source text into the picture. The methodological rationale for starting at the target and not the source end, and thus for opening up the frame of reference, is ultimately a matter of convenience. Translations tend to be initiated and produced with a consumer in mind, which usually means a consumer in the receiving culture. Translation choices normally result from judgements by the translator – or whoever is in a position to control or override the translator – about perceived needs and benefits, audience expectations, personal and collective motivations. For the researcher it makes sense to start prospecting in the area with the best chances of success. The question of the actual relation between the translation and its source follows in a subsequent move.

Does a target-oriented approach mean that translations are 'facts of the target system only'? Gideon Toury has repeatedly made the claim. In his *In Search of a Theory of Translation* he was emphatic about the restrictive 'only', not in every formulation of the point, but in most. Every translation, he claimed, aimed "to serve as a message in the *target* cultural-linguistic context, and in it alone", and translated texts were "facts of one language and one textual tradition only: the target's" (1980:16, 83); a 1985 essay reiterated "the hypothesis that *translations are facts of one system only*: the target system" (1985:19; his emphasis).

In this exclusive sense the claim is not tenable, and counter-examples are readily available. Bilingual editions to aid foreign-language learning do not fit into a target environment or tradition clearly distinguishable from the source. Whatever the interpretation of 'textual tradition', there is little doubt that authors like Milan Kundera or Peter Hoeg have increased their literary standing at home due to their success in translation abroad. In Ireland some writers working in Irish refuse to have their books translated into English. As the Irish-language poet Biddy Jenkinson put it in 1991, her refusal is "a small rude gesture to those who think that everything can be harvested and stored without loss in an English-speaking Ireland" (Cronin 1996:176). Considering the historical background, the unequal distribution of Irish and English on the island, and the massively unequal power relations between both languages, the publicaton of English translations from the Irish has obvious political and ideological significance for the source culture. Tejaswini Niranjana, who has written about William Jones's projects of translating Indian law texts into English at the end of the eighteenth century, pointed out that Jones's entire effort was designed to reintroduce the translations into India as instruments of colonial domination (1992:11-19). Dryden and many others in the seventeenth and eighteenth centuries translated at least in part for audiences perfectly capable of reading the Classics in Latin or Greek but curious to see with how much grace and skill the translators acquitted themselves. Maintaining a rigid distinction between source and target contexts seems forced in cases like these – and, for that matter, in the context of the multiple interdependencies of the modern world. In answer to points like Niranjana's, Toury argued that translations reimported into the environment of their originals have ceased to function as translations (1995:26), but that will hardly do. It is useful to note, though, that in his *Descriptive Translation Studies and Beyond* Toury took the sting out of his old claim and merely asserted that "translations are facts of target cultures; on occasion facts of a special status [...] but of the target culture in any event" (1995:29). The exclusive qualifier has quietly been dropped.

### *'... and systemic'*

There is no necessary relation between descriptive, target-oriented and functional approaches on the one hand, and the systemic angle on the other. As I mentioned in the section above, *skopos* theory describes itself as functional and target-oriented, but makes no use of systems concepts. Vast amounts of descriptive work on translation are being conducted, in a variety of places, along other than systemic lines. The prominence of system ideas in the Manipulation group is largely a matter of personal accident. Nevertheless, the systemic perspective has proved extremely useful, in more ways than one.

Polysystem theory in particular provided much needed support for translation studies' bid for recognition as a legitimate field of study by granting translation a place in the scheme of things. A concrete idea of the distance that had to be travelled may be gleaned from the successive 'Reports on Professional Standards' of the American Comparative Literature Association (ACLA). In 1965 the first ACLA report, written by a committee chaired by Harry Levin, stressed that university teachers of comparative literature "should have some access to all the original languages involved", and distinguished clearly between courses on "foreign literature in translation" and courses in Comparative Literature proper; about the latter the report observed that if they "include a substantial proportion of work with the originals, it would be unduly puristic to exclude some reading from more remote languages in translation" (Bernheimer 1995:23). Reading texts in translation was tolerated at best, and only as a last resort. The 1975 report, prepared by a committee under the chairmanship of Thomas Greene, still noted with alarm that "the most disturbing trend is the association of Comparative Literature with literature in translation" and called on lecturers to ensure that frequent references to the original texts for the benefit of those with a command of the relevant languages would "make the remaining students aware of the incompleteness of their own reading experience" (Bernheimer 1995:35).

It was not until the ACLA's third report, in 1993, that we can read that "the old hostilities toward translation should be mitigated" and a positive note was struck: "In fact, translation can well be seen as a paradigm for larger problems of understanding and interpretation across different discursive traditions" (Bernheimer 1995:44). Coincidentally, Susan Bassnett published her *Comparative Literature: a Critical Introduction* in the same year. She argued that traditional comparative literature was now dead and the new impulses were coming from such fields as cultural studies, gender and postcolonial studies, and translation studies. Her concluding chapter proposed to turn the tables on comparative literature by suggesting that "[w]e should look upon translation studies as the principal discipline from now on, with comparative literature as a valued but subsidiary subject area" (1993:161). The provocation did not go down well in comparative literature circles.

Given the long-standing distrust of translation in comparative literary studies, a paper like Itamar Even-Zohar's 'The Position of Translated Literature in the Literary Polysystem', presented at the Leuven 1976 conference (1978a; 1990:45-52), supplied welcome ammunition for translation researchers. It firmly located translation, together with all manner of other texts, in the fields of force which govern cultural dynamics. Even-Zohar's outline of the role translation could play in the constant tug of war between the various sections of the complex system of literature highlighted translation's radically innovative potential.

It did more than that. It strengthened the functional and target-oriented approach to translation by stressing that the search for explanations needed to be conducted primarily in the receiving culture if anything like a comprehensive picture was to be attempted. Its appeal lay in replacing the old unilateral relation between a translation and its original with a multilateral matrix anchored in the translating culture. Apart from the relation between source and target texts there were other relations to be explored: between different versions of the same or similar originals, between translations and non-translated texts, and between translation and discourses about translation. In addition, polysystem theory was keen to extend the researcher's horizon to the interaction between the canonized central sectors of the cultural domain and less prestigious, more peripheral areas (I will return to this in Chapter 8). It stimulated research into such genres as popular detective series (e.g. Robyns 1990) and literature for children (e.g. the work of Zohar Shavit).

Polysystem theory viewed literary and cultural life as the scene of a perpetual struggle for power between various interest groups. This focus on interaction and conflict gave the model its dynamic character. It also added a teleological dimension to translation by suggesting that translators' behaviour was guided by ulterior motives. Translation, that is, could now be seen as one of the instruments which individuals and collectives could make use of to consolidate or undermine positions in a given hierarchy. In thus broadening the scope, drawing attention to the impact of translation as a historical force and providing an explanatory frame of reference, polysystem theory gave the descriptive paradigm depth and relevance as well as legitimacy.

André Lefevere's use of system concepts pointed in a different direction. Apart from the internal dynamic of preservation and change within the literary series, he was interested in its control mechanisms. These he described in

terms of poetics, patronage and ideology, which he regarded as more important constraints on translation than linguistic differences (Lefevere 1992a:87).
While, for example, Anne Frank had noted in her diary that there is "no greater
enmity in the world than that between Germans and Jews" ("er bestaat geen
groter vijandschap op de wereld dan tussen Duitsers en Joden"), the German
translation by Anneliese Schütz had: "there is no greater enmity in the world
than that between these Germans and the Jews" ("eine größere Feindschaft
als zwischen diesen Deutschen und den Juden gibt es nicht auf der Welt").
The restrictive addition – "*these* Germans" – was obviously deliberate, and
had the approval of Anne Frank's father. The translator later explained that "a
book you want to sell well in Germany [...] should not contain insults directed
at Germans" (in Lefevere 1992:66). Patronage, which for Lefevere includes
commercial factors, and ideology would seem to combine here in accounting
for the shift.

As Lefevere also pointed out, however, manipulations of this kind do not
occur only in translation. The first edition of Anne Frank's diary, edited by
her father Otto Frank and published in 1947, contained a number of omissions. These included a passage introduced by the question "Why woman
occupies a position so much lower than man's among the nations", and most
references to Anne's awakening sexuality, such as the sentence in which she
asks a girlfriend "whether, as a token of our friendship, we should feel one
another's breasts". Interestingly, these passages, while missing from the Dutch
1947 edition and the 1950 French translation, are there in the 1954 English
translation by B.M. Mooyaart-Doubleday and in Anneliese Schütz's 1955
German version, both of which were made directly from the manuscript
(Lefevere 1992:64-65).

A literary parallel, with poetics providing the motive, may be found in
some eighteenth-century treatments of Shakespeare. Voltaire's French translation of *Julius Caesar* ends less than halfway down Act Three, immediately
after Caesar's murder, because for Voltaire the action in a tragedy was supposed to constitute one indivisible Aristotelian whole. He never got as far as
Mark Antony's 'Friends, Romans, countrymen' speech, delivered over Caesar's dead body (Act Three, Scene Two). In England, the Duke of Buckingham
could obviously not translate Shakespeare into English. So he rewrote him,
correcting Mark Antony's words in fine eighteenth-century style – and entirely in line with contemporary criticism of Shakespeare – as follows:

> Friends, countrymen and Romans, hear me gently.
> I come to bury Caesar, not to praise him.
> Lo here the fatal end of all his glory:
> The evil that men do lives after them,
> The good is often bury'd in their graves;
> So let it be with Caesar. (Quoted in Lefevere 1985a:100)

(Here are Shakespeare's lines: 'Friends, Romans, countrymen, lend me
your ears./ I come to bury Caesar, not to praise him./ The evil that men
do lives after them;/ The good is oft interred with their bones./ So let it
be with Caesar.')

Lefevere's point in cases like these is that editing and redrafting texts, like
translating them, means working with and under certain constraints, whether
they are economic, ideological or aesthetic in nature. This also applies to other
forms of what he calls 'rewriting', from producing summaries or literary criticism to anthologizing and historiography. The obvious implication is that
"translation can no longer be analysed in isolation, but [...] should be studied
as part of a whole system of texts and the people who produce, support, propagate, oppose, censor them" (Lefevere 1985:237).

*'... and an interest in the norms and constraints that govern the production
and reception of translations, in the relation between translation and other
types of text processing, and in the place and role of translations both within
a given literature and in the interaction between literatures.'*

This sums up the practical focus of attention of a great deal of descriptive
work. The orientation on the receptor pole, on the impact of translation and on
its conditioning factors explains the interest in translation norms, which have
been employed as analytical tools in the descriptive paradigm. The concept of
norms is discussed in Chapter 6.

The empirical bias of the descriptive approach, and its primarily literary
ambience, has meant that questions surrounding the production, reception and
historical impact of translation – especially literary translation – have been
prominent. Relatively little attention has been paid to such aspects as the linguistics or the philosophy of translation, or the mental and cognitive operations
of the translation process itself. The main beneficiary of this eclecticism has
been the historical dimension.

Historical case studies, some explicitly set up with reference to norms
and polysystem concepts, cover not only individual translations and larger
corpora, but also the historical discourse on translation. This too is part of the
contextualization of translation. The history of a society's thinking about translation informs us about that society's changing values and beliefs regarding
language, identity and otherness. It further leads to a self-reflexive appraisal
of our own contemporary thinking about translation. Lieven D'hulst, among
others, has questioned attempts to separate traditional from contemporary theorizing in this respect (D'hulst 1995; and see Chapters 7 and 10).

This 'historicizing' of translation and of translation concepts has largely
swallowed up the earlier attempts by Miko and Popovič to codify the relation
between translation and other forms of textual derivation. If translation is con-

ceptualized and delineated differently in different periods and communities, then studying this historical differentiation and its changing relations to other textual practices is preferable to a purported immanent description which can only reflect our contemporary view. The distinction between, say, translation and imitation is drawn very differently in the European Renaissance compared with nineteenth-century or modern usage. That must mean that translation is differently contoured over time.

The historical projection is increasingly being supplemented by a spatial and thematic opening up. Whereas early descriptive work on translation tended to concentrate on canonical West European literature and its past, studies by Maria Tymoczko on Old Irish, by Saliha Paker on Turkish translations, by Theresa Hyun on Korea and by various Israeli researchers on the Middle East applied the polysystem model to other, including non-Western traditions. André Lefevere, Susan Bassnett and José Lambert have all urged expansion along these lines (Lefevere 1992:73ff.,124ff; Bassnett & Lefevere 1998:12-24; Bassnett 1993; Lambert 1995a). So far these ventures have been a matter of applying the descriptive research methodology to new data. They have not yet resulted in a reconsideration of the presuppositions of the model itself, but in a postcolonial world it must be a matter of time before this happens.

The same can be said for Lambert's forays into media studies and language planning (e.g. Lambert 1994). Pointing, for example, to different national policies regarding subtitling and dubbing on television, Lambert highlights not only their social relevance but also the more complex issues behind them: their institutional context at international, national and sometimes regional level, the intricate relations between the public and the private sector, and the globalization brought about by communication technology. He goes on to suggest that empirical translation studies, with their emphasis on systemic interference and norms, may provide a more suitable model for the study of these phenomena than, say, sociolinguistics. It remains to be seen to what extent this is the case. At any rate, the references to Pierre Bourdieu's sociological work in Lambert's essays suggest that empirical description, polysystem theory and norm concepts are already, and increasingly, being supplemented by insights from elsewhere.

# 4. Undefining Translation

At the end of 1814 there appeared in Paris a rather carelessly printed collection called *Vies de Haydn, de Mozart et de Métastase* ('Lives of Haydn, Mozart and Metastasio') by one Louis Alexandre César Bombet. In the preface the author tells us that he had met Haydn in Vienna some time before 1808. The larger part of the book consists of twenty-two letters full of admiring anecdotes about Haydn's life and work, the first one dated 5 April 1808, the last 22 August 1809. Although the book did not sell well at all, a second edition, without an author's name, came out in 1817. Earlier that year an English translation by an unknown translator had been published, of which grateful mention is made in the preface to the new French edition.

In the meantime, in 1815, an Italian named Giuseppe Carpani had published two indignant if rambling open letters written from Vienna and accusing Bombet of plagiarism. Large parts of the Frenchman's letters about Haydn, Carpani claimed, were translated from his own Italian *Haydine* which had appeared in Milan in 1812. It was he and not Bombet, he also declared, who had befriended the great Haydn in Vienna about ten years earlier; Bombet had not only plagiarized and shamelessly pillaged his – Carpani's – book, but also impersonated its author. Attached to the second letter was a statement signed by Antonio Salieri and others to the effect that the *Haydine* was indeed Carpani's work and the French book an unacknowledged translation of it.

In August 1816 the French paper *Le Constitutionnel* carried a notice saying Bombet had written to them turning the accusation of plagiarism against Carpani. It was followed a month later by an acerbic letter from Bombet's younger brother challenging Carpani to have thirty pages of his *Haydine* translated into French and put them alongside his brother's pages. Readers would then be able to judge for themselves. Carpani, incensed, replied in October. He printed the opening paragraph of his *Haydine* in Italian alongside Bombet's French, and showed, among other things, that whereas in his *Haydine* the first document was dated 'Vienna, 15 April 1808', Bombet had actually predated his own so-called letter from Vienna to 5 April 1808. The polemic rumbled on for a little longer and then petered out. Carpani's book was properly translated into French by Domenico Mondo in 1837.

It is now known that Carpani was right all along. The Haydn section of the *Vies de Haydn...* is a free translation from the Italian. As for Bombet and his younger brother, they never existed. The name Bombet is one of the two hundred or so pseudonyms used by Henri Beyle, better known under the penname Stendhal. The *Vies de Haydn, de Mozart et de Métastase* was Stendhal's first published work. In 1831 a third edition appeared (actually the unsold copies of 1814 and 1817 recycled), this time with the name Stendhal on the cover; Carpani's name is not there. Towards the end of his life Beyle half admitted having translated and adapted Carpani without mentioning the original author's name, adding that the publisher had told him in 1815 that a book announced as a translation from the Italian would not find a single reader in France. "In any case", he is reported to have muttered, "how can you be a plagiarist when you're anonymous?" (for details of the case see Stendhal 1970).

The French national bibliography (*Bibliographie de la France*) does not list the *Vies* by Bombet/Beyle/Stendhal as a translation. The near-exhaustive bibliography of French translations 1810-1840 compiled by Katrin van Bragt and her colleagues Lieven D'hulst and José Lambert (Van Bragt 1995), which is based on the *Bibliographie*, does not list it either, although it has Domenico Mondo's 1837 regular translation of Carpani.

Cases like these raise a number of questions. For example, how do we know if a text is a translation? When we have two texts, one of which might be a translation of the other, can we determine on the basis of textual evidence which is the original and which the translation? As open letters flew between Carpani and Bombet, one editorial note in *Le Constitutionnel* sat squarely and smugly on the fence, suggesting that whichever was the original it surely deserved to have been translated into the other language. Should we be able to figure out which is which? And if not, how can translation studies ever determine its object of study? Or was Bombet adapting rather than translating? And should the ethical aspect – Beyle's was undoubtedly a reprehensible act – be part of the picture? In any case, unless we stumble upon it, how can we ever hope to locate such a text if old and new bibliographies alike let it slip through their nets?

Not all these questions are answerable. But they oblige us to think about what it is translation studies is concerned with – in other words, what constitutes the object of the discipline, or how we know a translation when we see one.

Nearly all traditional definitions of translation, whether formal or informal, appeal to some notion of invariance or equivalence. It is also the way we intuitively think about the subject: surely translation means saying the same thing, or something which amounts to the same thing, in a different language? Put differently, and more ponderously: translation means the replacement, or substitution, of an utterance in one language by a formally or semantically or pragmatically equivalent utterance in another language. Definitions or circumscriptions of this sort abound in the literature on translation. They look straightforward enough. But there are at least two major problems with them. One has to do with the concept of equivalence itself, the other with the way it bears on the definition of translation.

The more closely one looks at what constitutes 'equivalence' in translation, the more problematical the notion becomes. In the first edition (1979) of his *Einführung in die Übersetzungswissenschaft* ('Introduction to Translation Studies') Werner Koller devoted fifteen pages to equivalence; the fourth edition has over a hundred pages on the subject, fully one third of the book (1992:

159-272). A strict application of the concept as it is used, say, in mathematics, is obviously unworkable. It would imply reversibility and interchangeability, and we know that translation is a one-directional event involving asymmetrical linguistic and cultural worlds. Weaker definitions suggesting similarity rather than synonymy led to the use of terms like correspondence, congruence or matching. Koller himself broke up the concept into five different kinds: denotative, connotative, text-normative, pragmatic and formal-aesthetic equivalence (1992: 228-65). In doing so he continued a line of thought begun by Katharina Reiss in 1971 when she first distinguished different text types connected with different functions of language (mainly three: conveying information, self-expression, and appealing to someone to do something), each with its own demands on equivalence, which as a result ceased to be an undifferentiated concept. Notions of functional or communicative equivalence contain the same idea: equivalence tends to be valid, not across the board, but in particular situations, for particular participants in a communicative context. In this way equivalence became a fluid, relative concept, never more so than when Mary Snell-Hornby shrewdly pointed out that the English term 'equivalence' itself is not actually equivalent to its German counterpart 'Äquivalenz' (1995:13-22).

Nevertheless, however differentiated or diluted the concept, it continued to be the central notion in determining translation. In Koller's view equivalence represents translation's "constitutive relation" (1992:9), hence the amount of space he grants it. But to what degree should a translaton exhibit this or that species of equivalence? If full equivalence on all fronts is plainly unattainable, what is the minimum equivalence required, and of what type should it be, for a given text to be accepted as a translation of another text? And who decides? Here the connection between equivalence and the definition of translation becomes clear. Equivalence is the aim of translation in that translation is seen as striving towards equivalence, or at least the particular kind of equivalence which suits the occasion. At the same time, equivalence is the precondition of translation in that only a target text which displays the required amount of equivalence, of the right kind, is recognized as a valid translation.

Such a definition of translation is prescriptive. It prescribes what translators should do and what requirements their texts must fulfil to be accepted as translations. It is also ahistorical. What do we do, for example, with a translator like Antoine Houdar de la Motte who renders the *Iliad* into French at the beginning of the eighteenth century and blithely informs us in his preface that he, the "mere translator", reduced Homer's twenty-four books to twelve, "which are even shorter than Homer's", cut out superfluous repetitions, trivial descriptions, anatomical detail and long speeches, and now delivers to us "a better proportioned and more sensible whole than Homer's original" (in Lefevere 1992b:28-30)? There are not many today who would label the fruits of Houdar de la Motte's labour 'translation'. So is it or is it not translation? If it is, we are obliged to revise drastically our criteria of what constitutes translation, not only for this case but for countless other historical cases – until the criteria dissolve entirely? If it is not, we have a problem with Houdar de la Motte calling himself a translator, along with many others at the time who engaged in similar practices.

It was against the background of such prescriptive and ahistorical approaches to translation that Gideon Toury's proposals acquired their revolutionary hue. Toury effectively turned the relation between translation and equivalence on its head. Instead of trying to define translation *a priori* in terms of what it should be, he claimed, we should look at translation empirically. In doing so he elaborated McFarlane's 'translation is as translation does' into a guiding principle. In Toury's own words:

> When one's purpose is the descriptive study of literary translations in their environment, the initial question is not whether a certain text *is* a translation (according to some preconceived criteria which are extrinsic to the system under study), but whether it is *regarded* as a translation from the intrinsic point of view of the target literary polysystem. (1980:43)

> [...] for the purpose of a descriptive study a 'translation' will be taken to be any target-language utterance which is presented or regarded as such within the target culture, on whatever grounds. (1985:20)

It was a bold, decisive and liberating move that launched, if not quite a thousand, at least a few dozen research programmes. It freed them from the anxiety of first having to distinguish translation from non-translation in theoretical terms, and getting hopelessly bogged down in the process. Of course, Toury's stance – a translation is what is regarded as a translation – does not amount to a definition, if only because the term to be defined occurs on both sides of the equation sign. When a four-year-old asks her father, 'Dad, what is a zebra?' and dad replies: 'A zebra? Well, a zebra is what we call a zebra', the little girl is not going to be entirely satisfied. In his second book Toury himself refers to his statement as no more than "a working hypothesis" (1995:32), which is fair enough. Kitty van Leuven-Zwart speaks of it as a way of suspending a definition (1992:31). One of its consequences has been, however, that James Holmes's idea of defining translation by means of a Wittgensteinian set of 'family resemblances' has virtually disappeared from sight, which is a pity.

Equivalence is still part of the picture, though, but in a somewhat unexpected way. Toury's argument was, and has remained, that when a text is viewed as a translation, several postulates automatically follow. He has identified a cluster of three such postulates. The first states that if there is a translation, there must also have been a source text from which the translation was derived. Secondly, the process of derivation must have involved the transfer of something or other. And thirdly, there exists between the two texts a certain relationship, the exact nature of which has to be determined from case to case (Toury 1995:33-35). The notion of equivalence crops up in connection with this third postulate, but let us look at each one in turn. It seems to me that each brings problems in its wake.

The first, which Toury calls the source-text postulate, states that a translation presupposes the existence, and the prior existence, of an original. The original, that is, enjoys logical and chronological primacy. However, Toury takes the point a step further, elevating the target-oriented approach from an issue of pragmatic convenience into a principled position. What matters, he argues, is not so much the actual existence of an identifiable source text but the mere assumption that there is one. This means that texts which are presented and regarded as translations constitute "legitimate objects of translation studies" (1984:84) even if it subsequently proves impossible to trace the relevant source texts. In many cases this is indeed unproblematic. We have plenty of medieval texts, for example, which are believed to be versions of other texts now lost. Things are slightly different when we come to fictitious translations, which Toury calls 'pseudotranslations'. They are deliberate fakes, like MacPherson's Ossian poems, Horace Walpole's *The Castle of Otranto* or Voltaire's *Candide* in the eighteenth century: texts which are in fact original even though they claim to be translations. Toury contends they must be taken as "legitimate objects of study within our paradigm" and "proper objects of the discipline" (1995:34, 46) until the mystification is exposed.

Fictitious translations are fascinating things. They range from Thomas More's *Dialogue of Comfort against Tribulation*, written while More was awaiting execution in the Tower of London and passed off as an English translation of a French version of a Latin dialogue between two Hungarians, to such contemporary instances as Peter Russell's invention of the Latin poet Quintilius, Alison Fell's altogether naughtier but rapidly unmasked *Pillow Boy of the Lady Onogoro* (1994), purportedly translated from the Japanese by one Arye Blower, and the not yet fully resolved case of Jacopo d'Ancona's *City of Light* (1997), almost certainly written by David Selbourne rather than translated by him from a thirteenth-century Italian manuscript as he would have us believe. What makes these texts interesting is that they must mimick the appearance of translation if they are to have a chance of fooling the public. As a result they tell us a great deal about how, at certain times, translations are supposed to look. Instructive comparisons could be made between, say, Alison Fell's *Pillow Boy of the Lady Onogoro* and Kazuo Ishiguro's *An Artist of the Floating World*, the latter a novel also set in Japan but written directly in English by an author of Japanese extraction who has lived in Britain since he was six.

The question whether fictitious translations are 'proper' or 'legitimate' objects of translation studies is immaterial. It can be of relevance only to those who worry about legitimacy or want to patrol the fences separating disciplines. The real problem lies in the fact that Toury's approach to pseudo-translations creates a pseudo-problem (as indeed Frank 1987:xiii and Koller 1992:207 have noted). Fictitious translations are not translations. If, as Toury does, we wish to claim as a postulate correlated with the notion of translation that there must be a source text from which the translation is genetically derived, a discipline which insists on being empirical lands itself in trouble for there is, factually and empirically, no source text and hence there cannot be a translation. The argument that a fictitious translation functions as a translation for as long as the mystification escapes exposure (Toury 1995:34) is perfectly true, but it does not help, for two reasons. First, it can only be deployed after the mystification has been cleared up and the researchers know they are not dealing with a translation. Secondly, it can have no bearing on the language-independent *notion* of translation which Toury is emphatically trying to define by means of his three postulates (1995:33).

One obvious way to resolve the definitional problem is to relinquish the idea of postulates. Fictitious translations remain a source of interest as well as amusement because they appeal to a set of expectations associated with translation. It is precisely a feature like this which Jonathan Culler in his recent *Literary Theory: A Very Short Introduction* highlights as part of his discussion of how a concept like 'literature' could be defined. He treats it as an institutional label that raises certain expectations. For Culler, "[l]iterature [...] is a speech act or textual event that elicits certain kinds of attention. It contrasts with other sorts of speech acts, such as imparting information, asking questions, or making promises" (1997:27). In the same way it may be more profitable to start from the kind of signals emitted by an institutionalized – and therefore also historical and culturally determined – label 'translation'. It would at least sidestep the ontological contortions which postulates tend to lead to.

The problems raised by Toury's second postulate, his 'transfer postulate', can be dealt with more briefly. They are of a more philosophical nature and concern the relation between language and meaning. The transfer postulate refers to "the transference from the assumed source text [to the target text] of certain features that the two now share" (1995:34). The notion of translation as transference is deeply rooted in the very etymology of the word 'translation' (from the Latin 'transferre', to carry across) and its metaphorical associations of ferrying across – and the word 'metaphor' itself means transference, transposition, translation. But it suggests that there is something to be transferred. The idea is also present in the broad semiotic definition of translation which Toury provided for Thomas Sebeok's *Encyclopedic Dictionary of Semiotics* of 1986. There he emphasized that translating involved the transformation of one semiotic entity into another, "providing that some informational core is retained 'invariant under transformation'" (1986:1118). If something can be retained invariant under transformation across semiotic boundaries, it can presumably migrate, and be detached from its carrier.

Now, as Jacques Derrida has argued, this idea presupposes that the informational core – let us assume it could be a 'concept', or 'meaning' – can be separated from language, that it exists, as Derrida puts it, "before or beyond language" (1982:120). The problem is that we cannot identify this entity without using words, other words, more translation, continuing to beg the ever larger question of what exactly is being transferred, what remains invariant, what is being transformed. In other words, we cannot fix what Derrida calls the 'univocality' of meaning or master its 'plurivocality'. If this is so, it becomes impossible to maintain the common notion of translation and translatability as consisting in "the transport of a semantic content into another signifying form" or "the transfer of a meaning or a truth from one language to another without any essential harm being done" (1982:120; cf. Davis 1997). Yet it is to such a notion that Toury's transfer postulate appeals. In positing invariance and transference, it acts out the standard metaphor of translation itself, which is at the same time a particular conceptualization of translation tied to a particular language or group of languages. If the etymology of the word 'translation' had suggested, say, the image of responding to an existing utterance instead of transference, the whole idea of a transfer postulate would probably never have arisen. This undermines Toury's claim that his postulates account for "the *notion* of (assumed) translation [...] no matter what name it goes under" (1995:33; his emphasis).

It should not be impossible to think of translation while avoiding the notions of transfer and invariance. To do that we could return to the way Culler spoke about literature as an institutional label, a speech act, a textual event eliciting certain expectations. Starting from that angle we can envisage translation as promising a representation, and typically a re-enactment, of an anterior text which exists at the other side of an intelligibility barrier, usually a language barrier. A translation is then an operation or a text which invites the perception of relevant similarity (Chesterman 1996) or interpretive resemblance (Gutt 1991). This way of conceptualizing translation may be able to steer clear both of the abysmal difficulty of determining invariance, transformation and the ratio between them in a cross-cultural or interlingual sense, and of Derrida's deconstructionist critique of the idea that translation somehow extracts and transports something which would then have to be imagined as existing beyond language. It is also in tune with recent attempts to define, for example, speech genres in terms of classes of communicative events with a shared public purpose (Bex 1994).

Toury speaks of his third postulate as the 'relationship postulate'. Calling a text a translation means that we posit relationships "which tie it to its assumed original"; these relationships, he contends, are "an obvious function of that which the two texts allegedly share and which is taken to have been transferred across the cultural-semiotic (and linguistic) border" (1995:35). If we remove from this formulation the troubled notion of something identifiable that has been transferred, we could rephrase the statement and say that a translation, which announces an intention with reference to an anterior and differently coded utterance, signals the fact that it stands in a certain relation to the text which it purports to represent or re-enact. The elaboration of the exact nature of this relation will lead us back to the concept of equivalence. Put simply, Toury argues two things. The first links up with the startling reversal of the traditional perspective on translation that we saw above. The second is a matter of patient research.

The first argument runs as follows. If a text is regarded and functions as a translation in a given community, then we agree to call the relation between this text and its original one of equivalence (Toury 1980:39, 65). In other words, equivalence is merely the name given to the 'translational relation' that is posited as existing between two texts from the moment one of them is accepted as a translation of the other. The move is rather more radical than it may seem. It divests the idea of equivalence of any substantial meaning, and demotes it from its central position as simultaneously the goal and prerequisite of translation. As we saw, equivalence was traditionally regarded as the ideal which translation sought to attain, while at the same time the presence or absence of one kind of equivalence or another, to this or that degree, served as the criterion by which translation was judged and, by extension, distinguished from non-translation. Toury's alternative starts from the observation that some texts are apparently referred to as translations, assumes that if something is a translation there must also exist a source text, and proposes that we give the relation between translation and original the name 'equivalence'. If we accept that *A* is a translation of *B*, then we also accept that *A* stands in a relation of equivalence to *B*. In this line of thought the label 'equivalence' is merely the consequence of translation instead of its precondition; or more exactly: it is the consequence of the decision to recognize a text as a translation.

The next step is to investigate what the label actually covers. The main tool for this, which has become a central concept in descriptive studies, is the idea of translation norms. They are the subject of Chapter 6, but let me indicate the basic argument here. It is this. If the process of translating consists of a series of decisions which translators make as they go about their business and select this or that word or phrase in preference to another, then it is reasonable to assume that these decisions and choices are not random but conditioned. The degree of conditioning varies considerably and depends on circumstances. A translator working for, say, the European Union may not have any leeway in the terms used for a particular type of contract or financial transaction, whereas Ted Hughes translating Ovid may feel somewhat freer to follow his own nose in deciding which chapters of the *Metamorphoses* to render and how to phrase and modulate his rendering. Both translators make choices with their own goals in mind, in a context which exerts a certain amount of pressure – explicit and strong pressure in one case, little more than a gentle indefinable nudge in the other – to go for certain options rather than others which in principle were also possible. In both cases it is the sum total of all the choices made which determines the shape of the final text.

Toury's point in this connection is that the exact nature of the relation between original and translation, which results from the translator's choices, needs to be determined from case to case. Whatever actual relation is found, we agree to speak of it as a relation of equivalence. But because this equivalence is the result of choices made by the translator, and because the choices were governed by norms, the role of norms is crucial in shaping the text and colouring in the equivalence relation. In this way the downgrading of equivalence is accompanied by an upgrading of the notion of norms. The reversal provides the study of translation with a new focus. The evaluative assessment of equivalence makes room for a comparative analysis intent on seeking out the norms governing the translator's choices.

Before we look at models to analyze translations in relation to their source texts, let me add a critical footnote about Toury's 'relationship postulate'. The two lines of argument which he developed in connection with his third postulate are complementary. The first, which claimed that if we have translation then we have equivalence, makes equivalence part and parcel of the notion of translation. The other, complementary argument says that in practice equivalence is merely the empty label denoting a 'translational relation', the shape of which is determined by translators' choices which are in turn governed by norms. We thus end up with two uses of the term, one denoting an *a priori* assumption associated with translation as such, the other describing the relative similarities as the researcher construes them between actual texts. This is confusing.

There is another and rather more important criticism to be made of Toury's use of the term 'equivalence'. Like the metaphorical baggage conveyed by the word 'translation' and its cognates and forerunners, 'equivalence' carries its own load. It suggests equality in value, an equitable exchange, one thing being 'as good as' another. No doubt many translations are commonly used in place of original texts which remain beyond the reader's linguistic grasp. No doubt also many translators do their best to deliver products which they hope will be accepted as being 'as good as' their originals. In other words, equivalence may be the effect translation craves, and routinely claims. But the history of translation suggests that, as a rule, translations have not been perceived as equal to their source texts at all and that, in addition, they are deployed in situations involving highly unequal power relations. From that point of view the particular load carried by 'equivalence' makes it a problematic term. I will return to this point in Chapter 7. But judge for yourself: can we really speak of Bombet's plagiarizing translation of Carpani in terms of equivalence?

# 5. Describing Translation

Sooner or later most translation researchers come up against the basic problem of being faced with a text and one or more translations of it, and wondering what to say about the relations between them. It looks simple, but it is not. An approach to translation which styles itself as descriptive and empirical can be expected to address the methodology of describing actual translations.

Systematic attempts at description have indeed been made, and they are presented in this chapter. The main differences between them concern approach and procedure. Some are source-text based, while others treat the source and target text on an equal basis; some but not all make use of a *tertium comparationis*, a hypothetical intermediate construct serving as a point of comparison for both the original and the translation; some proceed from the bottom up, i.e. from textual micro-structures to macro-structural issues, others from the top down; some focus on the texts themselves, others on how readers respond to them.

None of the models to be reviewed here claims to be the be-all and end-all of translation comparison. In fact, all are problematic in one way or another. Their failures can help us appreciate the difficulty of the task. The problems we will encounter bear on things such as the transition from micro-level to macro-level analysis or vice versa, the definition of the unit of comparison, the place and role of interpretation in the analysis, the selection of representative fragments if a text is too long to be analyzed in full, and the sheer practical applicability of the models in question.

## First Attempts

To set the scene, let me start with a brief word about one of the earliest models. Well before descriptive translation studies made their mark, Eugene Nida and his colleague William Wonderly worked out a three-stage technique (Nida 1964:184-92) which Nida suggested could be used for comparing not only translations with their sources but also different translations of the same original. The model starts from the source text. The first stage, that of 'literal transfer', identifies the source text's lexical units and maps interlinear target-text units on them. The second stage, 'minimal transfer', applies obligatory grammatical rules to the interlinear version to obtain a target text that is just about readable as a text. The 'literary transfer' stage takes off from this groundwork and allows the identification of all manner of optional changes and modifications as they occur in actual translations.

The model is strongly source-oriented and rather too rudimentary to provide more than a very crude indicator of the kind of options selected in individual translations. Nida's own examples barely go beyond such broad categories as changes in the order of phrases and clauses, omissions, structural alterations, and additions. More insidious is the unacknowledged presence of various interpretive moments in the actual operation of the model. However, Nida never made any claims for it beyond its usefulness as a rough and ready means of classifying translations as literal, paraphrastic, archaizing and the like. Could a more sophisticated apparatus be constructed on the basis of an explicitly descriptive paradigm?

In his *In Search of a Theory of Translation* (1980) Gideon Toury made an attempt. Although the model was given a good deal of space in that collection, it would be unfair to linger for too long on it here: in his 1995 book *Descriptive Translation Studies and Beyond* Toury himself summarily consigned it to oblivion. I discuss it only as an illustration of a problem.

The 1980 model operates with a *tertium comparationis*. Toury's starting point is the observation that since apples and pears cannot be compared directly, an invariant of the comparison needs to be established first. In the case of translation, he goes on, this *tertium comparationis* cannot be based on a bilateral relation between two equal entities, but has to take into account the unequal status of a translation in relation to its source. The original enjoys logical and chronological priority, whereas the translation is a derived and secondary product. The *tertium comparationis* should therefore be based on the source text (1980:113). Toury's argument here is peculiar as well as traditional, especially in view of his claim that recognizing a text as a translation of another text implies a relation of equivalence between them.

The *tertium comparationis*, which Toury calls the AT or Adequate Translation (with capital A and T), results from an analysis of the source text. It is a hypothetical construct consisting of an "explicitation of [source text] textual relations and functions" (1980:116). As such the AT can be seen as embodying the principle of a wholly retentive, source-text-oriented translation. This principle, which also constitutes a practical translation strategy, is termed 'adequacy' (I will say more about it in Chapter 6). It refers to a mode of translation "which realizes in the target language the textual relationships of a source text with no breach of its own [basic] linguistic system" (Even-Zohar quoted in Toury 1995:56).

In theory Toury's AT represents a full and explicit reconstruction of the textual relations and functions present in the source text. It should ideally be expressed in a formal language, but for reasons of convenience the receptor language will normally be used (even though in the example he gives Toury employs the source text language).The actual comparison then involves, first, the identification of textual relations and functions in the source text and the formulation of the AT; next, mapping target-text units on the AT and on the corresponding source-text units; and, finally, measuring shifts and deviations between target text, source text and AT so as to be able to characterize the overall relation between the translation and its source. By way of example Toury considers two lines from a popular American song:

One thing's sure and nothing's surer
The rich get richer and the poor get – children. (1980:118)

The analysis foregrounds structural features such as phonological, syntactic and semantic parallelisms, the allusion to Shelley ("The rich have become richer, and the poor have become poorer", in *The Defence of Poetry*), and the significance of the non-rhyme 'children' in place of the expected 'poorer' in the second line. This explicitation of textual relations and functions presumably constitutes the AT. The German translation ("Einzig gewiss in der Welt ist nur eins:/ Die Reichen bekommen's Geld und die Armen bekommen – Kinder") is said to be "very close to being adequate", although its structural density is "somewhat poorer" than that of the original (1980:119). The term 'adequate' is here to be taken in the sense of exhibiting 'adequacy' as defined above, even though on the same page Toury also speaks of the lines not being 'adequate' as a song to be sung, where the term bears its standard meaning.

The method, which relies on in-depth analysis of the source text and careful mapping, is obviously labour-intensive. Realizing that the detailed work required by such a procedure means that for longer texts only partial comparisons can be made, Toury suggests selecting passages that are somehow representative and contain textual relations pertinent to the entire text (1980:119-20).

As I mentioned above, Toury eventually jettisoned his AT model. It was the right thing to do. The model is flawed and unworkable. The selection of pertinent textual nodes and of representative passages for analysis clearly requires an interpretive moment which remains unacknowledged. The transcription of source-text textual relations in the form of an AT cannot be done without an operation of translation and a further act of interpretation on the researcher's part. This is bound to render the invariant of the comparison pretty unstable. The fact that this issue is completely glossed over in *In Search* is indicative of the positivistic slant informing much of Toury's project. Not only is it deemed necessary to establish an explicit invariant as the immovable point from which to observe the drift and flux of shifts and deviations (1980:117), but this point, it is assumed, can be fixed objectively, on the basis of formal textual analysis. The invariant is to be worded in language apparently taken to be neutral. The transition from the texts under scrutiny to this meta-language is not felt to be at all problematic.

However, the failure and subsequent dismissal of the AT model left a gaping hole. After all, the AT was the centrepiece of the comparative analysis. It would provide the groundwork for assessing translational shifts and norms, which would in turn lead to a reconstruction of the overall concept of translation underlying individual texts and larger corpora. It had to be replaced with something else. In the course of the 1980s Kitty van Leuven-Zwart, a hispanist at the University of Amsterdam, elaborated another model based on the idea of a *tertium comparationis*.

**Transemes?**

Van Leuven-Zwart's model merits attention because it is the most explicit as
well as the most extensive and detailed ever designed for the purposes of
translation analysis. Its bottom-up procedure compares originals and translations on an equal footing by first identifying the common ground between
them, without privileging either side. In this respect it differs from both Nida's
derivational approach and Toury's AT attempt.

The model (Van Leuven-Zwart 1984, 1986, 1989, 1990) was designed in
the first instance for application to integral translations of narrative texts, such
as novels and short stories. Its terms are grounded in established linguistic
and narratological theories like Functional Grammar, structural semantics and
Mieke Bal's narratology. It is intended to be a relatively neutral, non-prejudi-
cial model; the outcome of the analysis is not known in advance.

Its aim is to describe and catalogue 'shifts' in translation, and to deduce
from these the translator's underlying strategy or norm. In other words, the
model tries to provide a sound basis for statements about what are usually,
and more impressionistically, referred to as 'tendencies' in certain translations.
Its starting point was one such indeterminate impression, a sense of flatness
which struck Van Leuven-Zwart in the Dutch translation of *Don Quixote* when
compared with the Spanish original. When she looked more closely, she could
not detect any radical divergences between the two texts, only very minor
shifts. Suspecting that in one way or another the accumulation of micro-level
differences produced a qualitative difference at the macro-level, she decided
to develop an analytical model to test that assumption.

The model consists of two parts, one comparative, the other descriptive.
The comparative component, which comes first, analyses the micro-structure
of the two texts. The descriptive component takes care of their macro-structure.
The model as a whole is complex, and I will give only a rough idea of it here
to illustrate its structure, main distinctions and procedure. Even this requires a
certain amount of detail.

The first task is to identify and classify micro-level shifts, which means
shifts below the sentence level. Only shifts of a semantic, stylistic or pragmatic nature, that is, shifts which substantially affect meaning, are logged.
The basic unit with which the model operates is called a *transeme*, defined as
"a comprehensible textual unit" (1989:155). There are two types of transeme:
the 'state of affairs transeme', consisting of a predicate and its arguments, and
the 'satellite transeme'. A sentence like 'The colonel was getting ready to go
out when his wife seized him by the sleeve of his coat' contains two state of
affairs transemes: 'The colonel was getting ready to go out' and 'when his
wife seized him', while 'by the sleeve of his coat' is a satellite.

A source-text and a target-text transeme are said to be related when they
show aspects of both similarity and dissimilarity, i.e. of conjunction and dis-

junction. The comparison is carried out in several stages. First, the perception of similarities between two transemes allows the establishment of a common denominator called the *architranseme* or *ATR*, which encapsulates what the two transemes share. Van Leuven-Zwart suggests that in most cases "a good descriptive dictionary" will suffice to identify the ATR (1989:158). Next, each transeme separately is compared with the ATR. When only aspects of conjunction between a transeme and the architranseme are found, the relation is said to be synonymic; when there is both conjunction and disjunction, the relation is hyponymic.

Comparing, for example, the English 'she sat up quickly' with the Spanish 'se enderezó' we can establish the semantic common ground between the two phrases: 'to sit up'. This is the ATR. If we then set 'se enderezó' beside the ATR, we notice a relation of conjunction between the two: they are exactly matched. The English transeme however entertains a relation of disjunction with the ATR because of the qualifier 'quickly'. A rule of thumb for identifying disjunction is to ask if 'x is a form/class/mode of y'.

These comparisons lead to four possible relationships between the ATR and the respective transemes. First, synonymy, which occurs when both transemes are synonymous with the ATR. This is like saying that if 'a=c' and 'b=c', then 'a=b', which means there is no shift in translation. The remaining cases do involve shifts. We have hyponymy when one transeme is synonymous with the ATR and the other hyponymous. Thirdly there is contrast: both transemes are found to stand in a relation of hyponymy to the ATR. And finally when no conjunction at all between the transemes can be detected it is impossible to build an ATR and no relationship can be established.

On this basis Van Leuven-Zwart distinguishes three main categories of micro-structural shift, each of which spawns more finely meshed categories and subdivisions. We speak of *modulation* when we find a hyponymic relation between transemes: one transeme is in conjunction with the ATR, the other in disjunction. If it is the target-text transeme which exhibits hyponymy, then we have specification, as in this case the target transeme is a 'form/class/mode' of the ATR. If on the other hand the source-text transeme exhibits hyponymy, we have generalization. Both specification and generalization can be either semantic or stylistic. Stylistic modulations may concern either a social aspect of disjunction or an expressive aspect; each is further subdivided.

The Spanish noun phrase 'los almendros de la plaza' translated as 'the almond trees in the *plaza*', for example, is classified as 'stylistic modulation/ specification, exotization': the modulation involves 'specification' because 'plaza' and '*plaza*' share the ATR 'square' but the use of '*plaza*' in English introduces a culture-specific element, and 'exotization' on account of the 'exotic' quality of the culture-specific word '*plaza*' here occurring in an English text (1989:164).

We speak of *modification* when both transemes stand in a hyponymous relation with the ATR. For example, English 'lane' and Spanish 'callejuela' have as a common denominator the ATR 'narrow road', but 'lane' is more specific than the ATR in denoting a 'narrow road in the country, bordered by hedges', while 'callejuela' refers to 'a narrow road in a town, a narrow street' (1989:165). Modification can be semantic, stylistic, syntactic, stylistic, pragmatic or a combination of these.

*Mutation* occurs when no aspect of conjunction and hence no basis for comparison can be found. If the sentence 'Oh, how extraordinarily nice workmen were, she thought' is rendered in Spanish as '¡Oh, qué simpáticos son los obreros', then the source-text transeme 'she thought' has no visible counterpart in the Spanish and hence no ATR can be established for that unit (1989:169).

These analyses and classifications constitute the comparative model. Next comes the descriptive model, which is complementary to the comparative one and operates beyond the sentence level. It focuses on such things as action and plot structure, the make-up of characters and the relations between them, the narrator's attitude towards the fictional world, and issues of focalization (or 'point of view'). In other words, this is where narratological aspects are addressed. In moving from stage one to stage two in the analysis, selectivity increases. The assumption is that "only those microstructural shifts which show a certain frequency and consistency lead to shifts in the macrostructure" (1989:171; 1990:70).

The descriptive model combines three general functions of language with three levels of narratological analysis. The three functions of language (borrowed from Halliday) are held to be present in every linguistic utterance and therefore also in narrative texts. They are firstly the interpersonal function, defined as "the way in which the communication between speaker and hearer is established" (1989:172), which in fictional texts covers aspects of the narrator's position and angle on things; secondly the ideational function, or the way in which the information about the fictional world is presented, determining the image which is offered to the reader; and thirdly the textual function, or the way in which the information is structured and organized in language – whether, for example, events are presented in chronological or some other order, certain information is being deliberately withheld, etc.

The model then follows narratological practice in distinguishing three textual levels. 'History', which corresponds to what the Russian Formalists called *fabula*, is the deepest and most abstract level of events and actors, but does not play a part in the descriptive model. 'Story', which the Formalists termed *sujet*, is the level of concrete actions by fictional characters. 'Discourse' refers to the linguistic expression of the fictional world as it is created on the story level. The importance of the distinction between story and discourse levels is that a story may be told, for example, by means of discursive prose or in the form of a comic strip. The key concept of the narrator, as the medium through which communication between the reader and the fictional world is established, belongs to the discourse level.

Functions and levels are meshed together when each of the three functions of language (interpersonal, ideational, and textual) is considered at both story and discourse level. For example, the way in which the interpersonal function operates at the story level determines focalization (or 'point of view'), which may be internal, with the reader seeing the fictional world through the eyes of one of the characteres, or external, when the reader looks at the fictional world 'from outside', as if standing outside the fictional world.

These principles are then applied to individual transemes. One example will do to illustrate what kind of issues are highlighted. In Gabriel García Márquez's novella *El coronel no tiene quien le escriba* (*No One Writes to the Colonel*), the sentence 'Hacía cada cosa como si fuera un acto trascedental' is translated into English as 'He did each thing as if it were a transcendental act'. The differences in meaning between the Spanish 'trascedental' ('very important in view of its consequences') and English 'transcendental' are said to bring about a double shift: one in the ideational function operating at the story level, as the colonel's actions and character acquire a touch of the supernatural, the other in the interpersonal function, because slightly different things are being seen and reported to the reader (1990:75).

At this stage Van Leuven-Zwart brings the modulations and modifications of the comparative model back into the picture, and considers their macro-structural effects. The reason is that shifts like semantic modulation, as we just saw, may cause shifts in the ideational function on the discourse and story levels. In this way the model is able to tabulate such things as implicitation and explicitation in translation, and ultimately, when all the data are put together, the kind and degree of difference between the total 'impression' created by the original text and its translation. Moreover, the density of shifts can be expressed in quantitative terms. If roughly one shift, of whatever kind, occurs in each transeme, we have an average of 100%. Computing various kinds of shifts tells us something about the particular colouring of a translation. As Van Leuven-Zwart admits herself, however, the percentages as such are not very informative, since the macro-structural impact of a shift depends on its quality rather than on frequency (1990:88).

A single illustration will again have to do. In the passages describing the dictator protagonist in Alejo Carpentier's 1979 novel *El recurso del Método* (translated into English as *Reasons of State*) the fictional world is presented to the reader from a generalizing perspective, the language is neutral, distant and impersonal, and the dictator's actions do not appear to result from mere whims or personal motives but from some universal law of nature, which makes him into a prototype of all dictators. The Dutch translation of the novel reveals a high degree of specification (semantic modulation) and explanation (syntactic-semantic and syntactic-stylistic modification). As a result, it exhibits a substantial shift in the way the dictator is presented. The language is subjectively coloured and emotionally charged rather than neutral and impassive. The dictator's behaviour appears to be that of a deliberately acting individual, a specific person rather than a prototype (1990: 90-91). Whether this different overall impression created by the translation stems from conscious or unconscious decisions on the translator's or editor's part is of course a separate question, which the model is not equipped to tackle.

The model can be applied to more than one text, to a whole corpus. This has been done, and the outcome proved interesting. At Kitty van Leuven-Zwart's university in Amsterdam about seventy undaunted postgraduate students turned the method on a range of modern texts and translations, mostly Spanish fiction from the period 1960-1985 and their Dutch counterparts. Not all the results from this corpus of some eighty texts were predictable. In all the translations that were investigated, semantic shifts turned out to be the most common, with semantic modulation and syntactic-semantic modification topping the charts. Within these two categories the frequency of specification was noticeably higher than that of generalization, and there was a clear tendency to explanation, mainly due to the insertion of function words and connectives (1990:88-90). While this latter result was unsurprising, since other analyses had shown a similar tendency to make logical and syntactic relations more explicit in translation, the first finding remains startling, as it runs counter to the widely held belief that generalization rather than specification is a common feature of translation.

What are we to make of the model as a whole? As a bottom-up analytical tool it is the most detailed and systematic there is. It is built on relatively clear and explicit concepts, and provides a solid basis for discussion, or at least a basis more solid than the usual impressionistic or intuitive statements about translations. It has the added advantage of comparability. When different readers come away with different impressions of a translation, the differences can be pinpointed with reasonable accuracy. The extension into the domain of narratology represents a bold move, and more work could be done in this area (and is being done, e.g. Taivalkoski 1998).

But the model has also been severely criticized (for example by Stegeman 1991:79-98 and Linn 1993:172-74), and rightly so. The criticism does not primarily concern the model's intricacy, although working with it requires an induction course and is so labour-intensive that it can hardly be applied to longer texts, in which case fragments have to be selected – but then which fragments, and how representative will they be? The main thrust of the criticism is directed at the fact that the application of the model involves a strong interpretive element, but interpretation is not really given any space in the whole procedure. The problem already surfaces in some of the examples above. Could or should, say, English '*plaza*', compared with an ATR 'square', not be regarded as semantic rather than stylistic modulation? The suggestion that, in comparing transemes, a good dictionary will usually suffice seems inadequate in this context, especially when stylistic shifts are at stake. More complex phenomena like intertextuality, allusion, irony, wordplay, the impact of syntactic differences, certain discourse features like cohesion, the use of genre-specific conventions and such like remain beyond the model's reach. If the model can only accommodate certain shifts in translation, the larger question to be asked is what exactly constitutes a shift?

Other points of criticism concern the fact that it remains unclear exactly how the macro-structure is derived from the micro-structure, or at what point an accumulation of micro-structural shifts makes a macro-structural difference. As Van Leuven-Zwart already recognized, the qualitative importance of some shifts outweighs the quantitative aspects, but the model is unable to tell us which shifts are qualitatively more significant than others. This problem ties in with the model's blindness to such things as intertextuality and genre-related signals. It is a purely formal, even formalistic model, which treats texts as if they existed in a vacuum. And this also exposes its corollary: the model itself is presented as context-free and value-free, one which, perhaps with further refinements, can aspire to deliver an exhaustive description of the relation between a literary text and its translation. But the notion of an exhaustive description of a literary text, let alone of relations between texts, is not one to carry much conviction in contemporary literary or cultural theory.

## Real Readers

Jelle Stegeman's model (1991) takes its bearing from that branch of reader-response criticism which is concerned with how real, empirical readers handle literary texts. In his *Übersetzung und Leser* ('Translation and Reader') he sets out to test the way in which actual readers respond to different translations, and to translations as opposed to their originals. His frame of reference derives from Siegfried Schmidt's model of literary communication. The idea is roughly that a text, as an artefact, only comes to life as an aesthetic object when a reader responds to it, when it serves as a stimulus in an actual communication process. The reader's role is therefore vital. Stegeman uses this stimulus and response approach in an attempt to pin down the notion of equivalence. The claim is that equivalence is obtained when no significant difference can be observed in the way source-language readers react to a source text and target-language readers react to the corresponding target text. Measuring the various responses requires laboratory-type tests using questionnaires which are then analyzed statistically.

Stegeman's tests, which range from multiple choice questions to cloze tests, and were foisted on a total of almost nine hundred real-life students in Amsterdam and Zurich, cover micro-structural, macro-structural and paratextual aspects of literary works and their translations. They concern such things as readers' perceptions of plot structure, of a particular fictional character, or of the humour in a given passage, assessed on a scale with a fixed number of points. The responses which he collected clearly demonstrate the impossibility of defining the exact point where an accumulation of micro-level shifts will trigger a higher-order shift. On the other hand, manipulating for instance the name of a slightly odd character in a novel could change the readers' perception of that figure from well-meaning bumbler to portentous fool.

Of course, Stegeman's questionnaires tell us more about the psychology of reading in artificial laboratory situations than about translation description and analysis. His net has a very coarse mesh. An appreciation of a fictional character in terms of eight character traits (taken from secondary literature) on an eight-point scale yields no more than just that: points on a given scale, incorporating a preselected number of variables. Broader cultural factors, such as the reputation of the original author in the source culture and the preconceived ideas and expectations prompted by this, cannot be accounted for in this type of testing. A historical dimension is also lacking.

## Checklists

The 'contextual' model which José Lambert developed in Leuven (partly in collaboration with Hendrik van Gorp) is very much a top-down model, broadly compatible also with Toury's more recent approach (Toury 1995). Early versions of it go back into the 1970s (e.g. Lambert & Lefevere 1977). Although the model fits in with polysystem theory and later versions are explicitly related to this theory, it originally grew out of a series of ambitious research programmes concerning translated literature in France in the first half of the nineteenth century (more about this in Chapter 8). The scope of these programmes made the researchers appreciate the need to study translation as a cultural phenomenon in a broader setting, rather than as a confrontation of two isolated texts. This opened their eyes to the relevance of other than strictly textual elements. They began to look at interrelations and networks, at series and genre indications, the perceived status of authors and translators, and so on. Studying German romantic prose works and their French translations, for example, Lambert had noticed that many of the German originals lacked chapter divisions, whereas the translations generally did have them, entirely in line with original French prose of the time (Lambert & Lefevere 1977:341). In other words, the scale of the project itself directed the attention to the contextual and historical siting of translations, and beyond translation.

The concrete model took shape when students were drafted into the project. They had to be supplied with checklists aimed at mapping out certain aspects of a set of texts, including such apparently mundane things as, for example, the data on the title pages of translated novels or plays (Is the book identified as a translation? Is the translator's name mentioned? Where and in what typeface? Is there a genre indication? Does this correspond to that of the source text? Are we told the work is 'translated by x' or 'translated from language x by translator y'? etc.), or the general make-up of the text itself (Are there chapter divisions? Do chapters start on a new page? Do they bear titles, roman numbers, arabic numbers? Same as in the original? Same paragraph division within chapters? Is direct speech indicated by means of single/double quotation marks or a dash? etc.). In this way the model became more of a prodding device, a means to generate questions and focus attention rather than a formal protocol.

The model's principles and objectives spring from this practical research context. It wants to be comprehensive but at the same time open and flexible. It seeks to avoid reducing the analysis to a comparison between texts divorced from their context. Instead, it stresses that translation analysis involves the exploration of two entire communication processes rather than two texts. The model consequently needs to account for a range of other factors in addition to the donor and receptor texts. This is why it is conceived as a multi-level operation, based on a communication scheme. It has been expressed in the form of a diagram (Lambert & Van Gorp 1985:43), as follows:

```
author 1 – text 1 – reader 1    ~    author 2 – text 2 – reader 2
   |         |         |                 |         |         |
authors  –  texts  – readers         authors  –  texts  –  readers
   1'...     1'...     1'...             2'...     2'...     2'...
_____            _____
        system 1                              system 2
```

'System 1' refers to the source culture or one of its subdivisions, and 'system 2' to the target culture. The communication chain 'author-text-reader' in the source culture has its counterpart in the target culture; in the case of translation, the 'author 2' slot identifies the translator. The relation between the two communication chains, indicated here by the symbol '~', is supposed to stand for a correlation, the exact nature of which cannot be predicted but has to be established as part of the analysis. The vertical lines linking each element in the top row ('author 1', 'text 1', etc.) with corresponding elements in the second row ('authors 1'...' etc', 'texts 1'...' etc.',...) suggest that in each case a particular author is to be seen in relation to other authors, each text in relation to other texts, each reader in relation to other readers.

The scheme claims to "comprise all functionally relevant aspects of a given translational activity in its historical context, including the process of translation, its textual features, its reception, and even sociological aspects like distribution and translation criticism" (Lambert & Van Gorp 1985:45). The claim stems from the authors' insistence that each relation in the scheme is worth examining separately, generating questions regarding simple and complex relations, such as:

- text 1~ text 2, i.e. the source text and its translation, which is what Van Leuven-Zwart's model investigates;
- [text 1– reader 1] ~ [text 2 – reader 2], i.e. reader responses to a source text versus reader responses to its translation – the subject of Stegeman's model;
- text 2 – texts 2'... , i.e. the position of a given translation among other texts, original and translated, in the receptor culture; Toury's methodology favours a consideration of this relation as a first step in the analysis, as it can shed light on what he calls the 'acceptability' of the translation as a text in a new environment;
- [text 1 – texts 1'...] ~ [text 2 – texts 2'...], i.e. a comparison of the source text's place among other texts in the source culture with the place of the translation among other texts at the receptor pole;
- author 2 – authors 2'..., i.e. the position and status of the translator (author 2) in relation to other translators and original writers, which in turn should open perspectives on interrelations between individual and collective behaviour in the receiving culture.

As Lambert & Van Gorp recognize (1985:50), the various relations and aspects listed in their scheme are routinely investigated in various kinds of translation research. They have now brought them all together in one comprehensive scheme, which stresses the more important point that translations need to be studied as part of a complex web of interrelations. In that sense the scheme is intended as an invitation to look further. Behind the relation text 2 – texts 2'..., for example, we can discern not just sets of similar texts but also genre concepts, textual models, appropriateness or stylistic rules governing text types, and so on. The overall scope is ambitious: "Our object is translated literature, that is to say, translational norms, models, behaviour and systems" (1985:51).

Synthetic as it is, the scheme does not tell the student where to begin and what to do next. For most practical applications Lambert & Van Gorp suggest starting from the immediate context and paratexts of a given translation or corpus of translations, going on from there to textual macro-structures and on to micro-structures, before working up again via the macro-level to the wider sociocultural context. This movement from the general to the particular and back again to the general corresponds to the scheme later proposed by Toury (1995:38) in which 'discovery procedures' spiral down from the translation's outward presentation to the detailed confrontation of source and target texts (or sections thereof), followed by 'justification procedures' which climb up again from translation units and first-level tentative generalizations to overall correspondences between the texts in question, before finally locating the translation in relation to existing texts and concepts of translation.

The practical procedure, as Lambert & Van Gorp envisage it, is captured in a checklist (1985:52-53) which suggests the following steps:

1    *Preliminary data.* This means looking at such things as the outward presentation and packaging of the translation (publisher's list of other titles; perhaps part of a series?; binding; information on the cover or blurb, ...); the data on the title page (name of translator; genre indication; title, date, language of the original, ...); the presence, provenance and content of any paratexts (prefaces, dedications, disclaimers, introductions, footnotes, endnotes, ...), etc.

     In each instance the findings in the case at hand should be checked against other texts or corpora for similarities and differences, and what we can infer from them.

     Ideally these first impressions should provide clues as to the actual make-up of the text itself.

2    *Macro-level.* This involves investigating such things as macro-level omissions, additions or alterations (e.g. different plot or ending); the division of the texts into chapters, acts, sections, stanzas, paragraphs; the use of typographical conventions (for example in signalling direct speech, or the use of italics for emphasis); the overall handling of plot, setting, proper names, culture-specific elements, etc.

     Here too cross-checking with relevant material outside the immediate corpus will be instructive.

     The macro-level findings should lead to hypotheses about what micro-level options the translator is likely to have chosen.

3    *Micro-level.* Here a number of detailed textual comparisons have to be carried out. Longer texts can probably not be analyzed in full. The selection of passages to concentrate on should be informed by the macro-level findings. Analyses could focus on, for example, grammatical patterns and literary structures, vocabulary, modality, certain stylistic features, particular language varieties (register, sociolect,...), or indeed the various types of micro-level shifts treated in Kitty van Leuven-Zwart's model.

     In Toury's approach a central place is given to establishing what he calls 'coupled pairs' of replaced and replacing segments, i.e. source and target text segments that can be mapped on each other. I will return to this below.

     Micro-level analyses should be referred back to the macro-level findings to see if a coherent picture emerges, but they should also be

subjected to counterchecks using random text samples.
4   *Context.* This final step leaves the detail of the individual text and con-
    fronts the patterns that have been found with analyses of other texts
    (e.g. translations by the same translator, in the same series, the same
    genre,... or original writings by the translator, in the same series, the
    same genre,...) and with prevailing models and norms of text produc-
    tion, translated or original, in the host culture. It is at this stage also that
    explanation, as opposed to description, comes into its own, as all the
    tentative hypotheses which guided the analyses in steps 1 to 3 are pulled
    together into a coherent case to account for the findings and place them
    in a broader context.

## Comparative Practice

How useful are these schemes and checklists in practice? No doubt Lambert
would point out, legitimately, that they suggest possible lines of enquiry, not
a blueprint. The model's broad scope necessitates a high level of abstraction.
Even so, by supplying essentially a list of things that could conceivably be
done but offering little guidance as to how to do them, the model leaves an
awful lot to the researcher's initiative. In a Witwatersrand MA thesis of 1993,
Renate Heydorn applied both Van Leuven-Zwart's and Lambert & Van Gorp's
models to a single text, Thomas Mann's *Death in Venice* as translated by
Helen Lowe-Porter. She found Van Leuven-Zwart time-consuming and ardu-
ous, and had problems relating micro- to macro-structures in view of the
restricted number of passages that could be analyzed. The Lambert & Van
Gorp model proved too general, and hence hard to relate to the particular
genre (Snell-Hornby 1995a). Given that one approach is bottom-up and the
other top-down, they complement each other to some extent. In practice, they
are most likely to be adapted to the researcher's particular needs anyway.

This is exactly what, for example, Raquel Merino did in her study of
English-into-Spanish theatre translations 1950-1990: the overall four-stage
approach is that suggested by Lambert & Van Gorp, while the micro-level
analysis takes as its unit the 'replique', defined as the smallest structural unit
of specifically theatrical communication (Merino 1994:41-48). Dirk Delabastita
(1989) elaborated a more ambitious and comprehensive scheme for use with
audiovisual media. It marshals concepts from classical rhetoric (repetition,
addition, deletion, substitution, transmutation) as well as norm concepts, and
provides extensive checklists geared to dubbing and subtitling in particular.

Despite its emphasis on multidimensionality and flexibility, the Lambert
& Van Gorp model remains essentially binary, as its schematic representation
also makes clear. It suggests tidy divisions and clean patterns. Oversimpli-
fication is inevitable at this level of generality, but the scheme's very ease
runs the risk of perpetuating simplicities, for example the assumption that the

translator belongs to the target culture. If we think of the English-language tourist brochures in Izmir or Shanghai, the sixteenth-century European or native interpreters who translated – some willingly, some not, while others refused – for Hernán Cortés in Mexico and Jacques Cartier in Canada, the contemporary United Nations interpreters in New York and elsewhere, or the multiple code-switching and translating practised by Carribean writers to address readerships in different parts of the world, it become clear that neat divisions into source and target poles are not enough. What matters in such cases is the co-existence of different personal and collective agendas in those fluid zones where cultures tangle and overlap, and the translator or interpreter may belong wholly or in part, permanently or temporarily, to one side or the other, or to both, or to nei-ther in particular. My point here is not that these factors should be incorporated in a scheme which was never designed to include them. It is that neat schemes are apt to sustain convenient myths.

Two additional issues should be raised here. The first concerns the intractable question of the unit of comparison, the second that of repre-sentativeness in selecting passages for closer analysis.

Whereas the Lambert & Van Gorp model makes no attempt to specify a unit for comparative micro-level analysis, Gideon Toury has gestured in that direction. His first endeavours, still tied to the idea of a *tertium comparationis* as the invariant of the comparison, sought to work with what he termed the 'coupled pair' of 'problem plus solution' (1985:27, 32). In his 1995 book the *tertium comparationis* has vanished and the coupled pair is now that of 're-placing and replaced' segments (1995:87ff.). In both cases he justifies operating with such a 'pair' on the grounds that a translation always offers a solution to a source-text problem, even if the solution is, for example, omission. Starting not from the source text but from the two parallel texts in tandem bears an obvious similarity to Van Leuven-Zwart's giving equal treatment to source and target text transemes.

But how to justify and delimit the relevant 'paired' segments? Contrary to Van Leuven-Zwart's linguistic definition, Toury suggests they can be chosen in such a way that beyond their boundaries there are no 'leftovers' of the solution to a translation problem which is represented by a source text segment and its corresponding target text segment (1995:79, 89). This presupposes however that there is an unambiguous way of deciding what such a 'remainder' exactly is and how the boundaries of text segments are constituted. In practice such compartmentalization is illusory. Toury offers two justifications for his use of "coupled pairs of mutually determining 'replacing' and 'replaced' seg-ments" (1995:95ff). One is Brian Harris's notion of 'bi-text', the momentary presence in the translator's mind of the two texts fused into one indistinguish-able construct; the other is the occurrence of so-called stock equivalents, standard ways of solving certain translation problems. Neither looks convincing. Whatever the exact status and boundaries of Harris's bi-text, it is a psychological entity, while Toury's 'coupled pair' is a textual, *a posteriori* construction; and stock equivalents are surely a matter of convention and habitual practice. Unless formal criteria à la Van Leuven-Zwart are employed, it seems hard to justify units of comparison on other than purely pragmatic grounds.

Both Van Leuven-Zwart and Lambert & Van Gorp admit that a microscopic – let alone an exhaustive – analysis of a longer text is not practicable. If exhaustiveness is beyond reach, shorter extracts will have to do. Neither model however provides much guidance as to which passages to select for detailed study. Van Leuven-Zwart, for example, merely urges "a certain representativeness" (1992:78) and says she applied her model to "a few passages chosen at random" in Cervantes's novel (1989:155).

Is it possible to make a more motivated choice in picking representative passages? Luc van Doorslaer (1995) has proposed that we distinguish between quantitative and qualitative aspects of representativeness. The quantitative aspect strikes a balance between economy and credibility: the sample should be large enough to be credible in light of the purpose of the exercise, but small enough to permit appropriate depth. The qualitative aspect is a matter of interpretation and judgement. Extra-textual information can help here, Van Doorslaer suggests. When we know that the Flemish writer Cyriel Buysse was extensively translated into German during the First World War, when Germany was occupying most of Belgium and exploiting the linguistic divisions there for its own ends, it makes sense to utilize that knowledge and select for scrutiny passages that might lend themselves to politically inspired readings (Van Doorslaer 1995:253). There is no reason not to select such passages on the basis of separate readings of the original texts and the translations.

The theoretical basis for selecting passages with reference to what Holmes would have called 'situational' elements lies in the functional perspective. The guiding questions for translation research, Harald Kittel once pointed out, are "*who* translated *what*, *when*, *why* and *in what way*, and *why* in this particular way?", and they cannot easily be separated one from the other (Kittel 1988a:160). The questions derive from the ancient discipline of rhetoric. A fuller list, in modern guise, is provided by Christiane Nord: "*Who* transmits *to whom, what for, by which medium, where, when, why,* a text *with what function? On what subject-matter* does he say *what (what not), in which order, using which non-verbal elements, in which words, in what kind of sentences, in which tone, to what effect?*" (Nord 1991:144; Van Doorslaer 1995:255).

One way of making such broadly-based lists more manageable is to tie them to specific corpora and types of investigation. This is the impulse behind the 'concrete theory' which Armin Paul Frank and his colleagues developed at the Göttingen research centre on literary translation. In a project concerned with half a dozen French and German versions of T.S. Eliot's *The Waste*

*Land* (Frank & Bödeker 1991, Frank 1992a), they elaborated a grid which, they claimed, proved at once necessary and sufficient in their attempts to map the translators' handling of cultural references in Eliot's poem (i.e. references to both intellectual and material culture). The grid consists of a number of parameters set out along three axes in a kind of three-dimensional box. The $x$-axis ranges references according to their degree of explicitness in the various texts (including the source text). This is combined with a $y$-axis which places and relates references according to their scope (regional, national, supranational) and their location in particular spheres (religion, art, sports, etc.). The $z$-axis is formed by the historical dimension, as when Eliot's 'City directors' become archaized as 'potentates' in the French version by Pierre Leyris, or when certain translations introduce different text-type elements or integrate references to other existing texts (which may well be the translator's own, as in the case of poet-translators like Eva Hesse).

Frank and his colleagues developed their grid in order to deal with particular aspects of a particular corpus. Other corpora may require different grids. This is precisely what Frank means by a 'conrete theory', one which grows out of working with a specific corpus. The trouble is that if each corpus requires its own theory, we may as well do without.

The lesson to be learned from the models reviewed in the previous pages is undoubtedly that schemes and procedures can help and offer hints and pointers, but they remain ancillary. In the end it will be the questions to which the researcher seeks answers, on whatever grounds, which focus the attention. In this respect the models are most instructive where they most obviously fail. The failures have taught us the utopia of neutral description, of fixing stable units for comparison, of neat divisions, of excluding interpretation, of studying translation in a vacuum. Their positive uses in providing the means to distinguish, classify and tick off checklists are best harnessed within a research project that sets out its own parameters. That may also be the most opportune way to overcome the strongly textual bias in the models: they show little of the human interaction of which translation is the exponent. The next chapter brings that aspect to the fore.

# 6. Working with Norms

The Vensons are a modern American family consisting of Mum and Dad Venson and their two sons Doug (aged 6½) and Larry (aged 8). One day the Vensons bought a game of Scrabble. Dad put the board on the table after dinner. They each picked their seven plastic letters, put them in their letter stands and were ready to play. But then a problem arose. They all wanted to be the first to start the game. They began to argue, tempers flared, doors slammed and the game was abandoned. They tried again the next day, with the same unhappy result. Some days later, as they made another attempt to play, Larry put down the first word in the middle of the board without further ado. No one objected. Mum went next, then Doug, then Dad. They played the whole evening. The following day Larry simply started again, and again the game got under way and went well. The same thing happened the day after that. By now Mum, Dad and Doug were expecting Larry to have the first go whenever they played Scrabble, and Larry knew the others expected him to start. When two weeks later little Doug attempted a pre-emptive strike by quickly putting down a word as the others were still taking their seats, Mum frowned, Dad scowled and Larry screamed. Doug, red-faced, removed his letters from the board, and Larry started the game as usual. After that, Larry always started. The Vensons continued to play Scrabble in this way for many years, a happy family.

The Venson case illustrates how conventions and norms operate, what the difference between a convention and a norm is, and why we have them in the first place. To anticipate: conventions and norms help regulate our lives so as to develop a sustainable form of coexistence. In particular, they solve coordination problems among members of a group – in this case the Venson family. The Vensons could not start their game of Scrabble unless they resolved their coordination problem, which was a social interaction problem. The convention they adopted by letting Larry go first was an arbitrary (it could have been one of the others who started) but effective solution. It meant that they developed a regularity in their behaviour to which they all conformed and to which each expected the others to conform. After a couple of weeks the convention had grown into a norm in that Doug's transgressive behaviour – he wanted to start when they all knew Larry was meant to go first – met with expressions of disapproval, and those who disapproved all agreed that, in the circumstances, voicing disapproval was the proper response.

This is the kind of idea the present chapter is concerned with. Applied to translation it involves a way of looking at translating as social action, and has its origin in the empirical, perhaps even the behaviourist thrust of descriptive work. As we shall see, this empirical thrust has a strong theoretical component and some far-reaching implications. One initial paradox at least need not deter us: in the following pages norms are discussed from a point of view that purports to be non-normative. The descriptive perspective looks at norms as objects of study. It sets out to theorize and analyze their nature and operation as these affect the practice of translation, but it does not itself seek to lay down rules, norms or guidelines for how translators should proceed. This is not quite the end of the matter, but for the moment I will leave aside the theoretical complication which bedevils the descriptive endeavour to deal with the normativeness of translation; I will return to this in Chapter 10.

The concept of norms has become both a key concept and a handy instrument in descriptive translation studies. Although it has proved its durability and usefulness, it has remained a rather more difficult and fuzzier notion than may appear. I will first describe some initial approaches, then explain Toury's and after that Andrew Chesterman's use of norms in translation, go on to sketch the broader theoretical background, and conclude with suggestions on how to study translation norms.

## Decisions and Norms

As we saw in Chapter 2, Jiří Levý's 'generative model' (Levý 1967) characterized translating as a decision-making process. It emphasized that at every level the translator has to choose one option from among a set of alternatives, in the knowledge that every decision will affect all subsequent decisions. The process covers everything from the selection of a text to be translated, via the overall orchestration at macro-level, down to individual sentence constructions, word choice, punctuation marks and even spelling (for example, the choice between the American or British spelling of English).

Of course, some of the decisions which translators make are hardly decisions at all, let alone their own. Already McFarlane urged consideration of "what things are essentially within and what necessarily beyond the control of the translator" (1953:93). The translator's decision-making concerns us here only to the extent that it lies within his or her control. If a language does not possess a passive, then that option is not open to the translator. If the source text uses a plural with reference to two items because it only has a singular and a plural, and the receptor language has a dual to refer to a twosome, the translation must use the dual if it wants to be grammatical. At the other extreme are incidental decisions which the translator makes perhaps once or twice, randomly, without regard for consistency; but it is unlikely that an entire translation will consist of such random choices.

Levý's decision process was concerned with the area between the two extreme poles of total predictability, such as decisions constrained by strict grammatical categories, and total unpredictability, such as wholly gratuitous one-off choices. The relevance of such decision-making will be obvious. The entire complex set of decisions, and of alternatives considered and rejected, determines the final shape of the text. The matter extends to the reader's point of view. If a text comes to a Western, non-Chinese-speaking reader as being a translation of Lu Xun, it may be the only means available to that reader to obtain an impression of the writer Lu Xun. As this impression results in large measure from the translator's decisions, Levý's focus on decision-making also highlights the translator's power and responsibility.

If there is a whole swathe of decisions which translators make and which are neither fully predetermined nor totally idiosyncratic, what is it that leads translators to opt for certain choices rather than others, and to do this not just once or twice but regularly? What is it, for example, that made so many eighteenth-century European translators decide to disambiguate words or passages in the texts they rendered? The answer which Anton Popovič gave in 1970, with reference to Levý, was that translation involves a confrontation of two sets of linguistic and discursive norms and conventions, those which reside in the source text and those which prevail in the target culture, or in that section of the target culture where the translator hopes to make an impact (Popovič 1970:79; 1968:73). In other words, when non-compulsory choices are concerned, translators will decide in favour of one option rather than another because they are aware of, and respond to, certain demands which they derive from their reading of the source text, and certain preferences and expectations which they know exist in the audience they are addressing. Because such decisions are made regularly across a range of texts, patterns will establish themselves which in turn will affect the expectations readers bring to translated texts. In this way norms become fixed. Norms, that is, are part of the answer to the question why translators tend to make certain decisions rather than others.

Both Levý and Popovič, as we saw earlier (Chapter 2), worked along Structuralist lines. In the 1930s the leading theorist in the Czech Structuralist tradition, Jan Mukařovský, had explored the role of norms in the context of literature and art, especially in his monograph *Aesthetic Function, Norm and Value as Social Facts* of 1936 (Mukařovský 1970) and in the essay 'The Aesthetic Norm' (first published in French in 1937; in Mukařovský 1978). Mukařovský saw a norm as "a regulating energetic principle" with a regulative or sometimes no more than a vaguely "orientational potential" (1978:49; 1970:26). The idea of taste, he argued, boils down to a system of aesthetic norms (1978:55). Norms, which are not to be confused with their formulation or codification, limit the individual's freedom of action, provided the individual agrees to be so constrained. They are also historical entities, and hence subject to change as they adjust to changing circumstances. Some norms, though, are more robust and durable than others. The norms of modern art in particular tend to be regularly breached and thus change rapidly through a combination of application and violation. An individual work can be thought of as a "complex tangle of norms" and a "confrontation of heterogeneous

norms" (1978:52). One important consequence of this is that different specta-
tors or readers may evaluate the same work differently by projecting on it
certain norms rather than others – and not necessarily the ones initially observed by the author or artist. At the same time, norms are tied to shared
values in a community, and in turn values are stabilized by norms (1970:25).

**Toury's Norms**

Building primarily on Levý and Popovič, Gideon Toury firmly installed the
concept of norms in the study of translation and devised practical ways to
identify and classify them (1978; 1980:51-70; 1995:53-69). His initial approach was behaviourist: when we observe regularities in a translator's conduct,
we may go on to inquire how to account for them. If we disregard regularities
attributable to structural differences between the languages involved and focus on non-obligatory choices, we can look for external, socio-cultural
constraints to explain the recurrent preferences which translators show. These
constraints Toury calls norms. They are seen as "performance instructions"
(1980:51; 1995:55), both in a general sociological sense and, with reference
to communication and translation, in the sense of controlling linguistic usage.

Norms, that is, operate at the intermediate level between competence
and performance, where competence stands for the set of options translators
have at their disposal and performance refers to the options actually selected.
The idea goes back to the linguist Eugenio Coseriu, who distinguished the
underlying system of language (Saussure's *langue*), actual speech (Saussure's
*parole)* and a linguistic 'norm', which pertains to language as a social institution, the level of conventional models and of appropriate, socially acceptable
ways of employing language in contact with other speakers. At this level other
people's expectations of what is 'proper', in what circumstances, play a crucial part. Failure to meet these expectations may result in sanctions such as
correction, a reprimand or even the end of a conversation (Snell-Hornby 1988
and 1995:49-50; Poltermann 1990:118).

Toury distinguishes three kinds of translation norms. Although they are
relatively obvious in reflecting successive stages of the translation process,
listing them has proved quite helpful to students of translation. The three kinds
are:

- *preliminary norms*, which concern such things as the choice of the text
  to translate, or the decision to work directly from the original language
  or from an existing translation in another language (the point about this
  latter decision is that the rules permitting or forbidding translation from
  an intermediate language rather than form the original source language
  vary over time as well as cross-culturally and in relation to particular
  genres and source languages); perhaps one could add here the decision

to translate into the native or into a second or third language;
- the *initial norm*, which governs the translator's choice between two polar alternatives regarding the translation's overall orientation, one which leans as far as possible to the source text, the other subscribing to usage in the receptor culture; the first pole Toury calls that of 'adequacy', the other that of 'acceptability' – I return to these terms below;
- *operational norms*, which guide decision-making during the actual business of translating; here Toury distinguishes between
  (a) *matricial norms*, which help determine the macro-structure of the text and govern decisions concerning, for example, translating all or part of the source text, division into chapters, acts, stanzas, paragraphs and the like, and
  (b) *textual-linguistic norms*, which affect the text's micro-level, the detail of sentence construction, word choice, the use of italics or capitals for emphasis, and so on.

The list makes it clear that norms affect the entire process of translation, including source-text selection (and, we might add, the decision to translate in the first place, in preference to, say, importing or exporting a text as it is, or paraphrasing or summarizing it, etc.).

Its most problematic aspect concerns the polar alternatives 'adequacy' and 'acceptability' mentioned under the 'initial norm'. The problems are conceptual and terminological. As we saw in Chapter 5, Toury took the notion of adequacy from Even-Zohar, who defined an 'adequate' translation as one which "realizes in the target language the textual relationships of a source text with no breach of its own [basic] linguistic system", as Toury (1995:56) translates Even-Zohar's Hebrew. The upper limit of such a translation would be the hypothetical (and capitalized) 'Adequate Translation' or AT of the previous chapter, a reconstruction of all the pertinent textual relationships of the source text. It is odd that the demise of the 'Adequate Translation' did not pull the 'adequate translation' down with it, as it should have done. The same objections apply: reconstruction of 'the textual relationships' of a text is a utopian enterprise, and who decides pertinence? The only adequate 'adequate translation' would appear to be the original itself . Even that is questionable, for texts are invested with meaning by readers. It is the reader who establishes textual relations. But, in Roland Barthes' words, "the 'I' which approaches the text is itself already a plurality of other texts, of codes that are infinite, or better: that are lost (whose origins are lost)" (1970:16). Andreas Poltermann (1992:23-24) raised similar objections, pointing out that the identification of 'textual relationships' presupposes a process of socialization, of learning to interpret texts in certain ways. Moreover, as Borges's story of Pierre Menard reminds us, the arrow of time moves in one direction only, so that the attempt by the nineteenth-century Pierre Menard to rewrite *Don Quixote* exactly as it stands, in Spanish, word for word, results in words that have acquired meanings very different from those in Cervantes's time (Borges 1981). Not even verbatim repetition, it seems, guarantees adequacy.

Another objection to the terms 'adequate' and 'acceptable' is simply that they are unfortunate because hopelessly confusing, as already mentioned in Chapter 5. Not only are both terms frequently used in their standard sense, but even writers following Toury's lead have been led astray (Zlateva 1990 is one instance). I share the reservations which Andrew Chesterman (1997:64) expressed in this respect, and will avoid the terms. If alternatives are required, we could replace the pair 'acceptable' versus 'adequate' with 'target-oriented' versus 'source-oriented', 'prospective' versus 'retrospective' or a similar set. An even better solution would be not to think of the 'initial norm' as forcing a choice between two poles only, but as involving multiple factors, depending on how the source text is viewed, whether it or similar texts have been translated before, whether the translation is made for import or export, by a speaker of which language, for what audience or purpose, and so on. If translating is a socio-cultural activity, as the norms concept suggests, there seems little point in trying to conceptualize it in terms of a choice along a single axis.

## Chesterman's Norms

Andrew Chesterman's treatment of norms in translation (1993; 1997:64-70) takes into account recent discussions of the concept in a range of other disciplines. His approach, like Toury's, is descriptive in that he considers the way in which norms and even 'normative laws' appear to operate in the world of translation, without necessarily wishing to recommend or impose them.

Chesterman's discussion covers social, ethical and technical norms of translation. The social norms regulate interpersonal coordination along the lines we saw with the Venson family. Among the ethical norms to which translators appear to subscribe, he singles out their wish to uphold the values of clarity, truth, trust and understanding (1997:175-86). It could be argued that these are pertinent to most communicative interaction between people and therefore not specific to translation. However, Chesterman also relates each of these four values (clarity, truth, trust, understanding) to his central category of technical norms. Under this term he ranges what he calls product norms and process norms.

*Product norms*, also termed *expectancy norms*, reflect "the expectations of readers of a translation (of a given type) concerning what a translation (of this type) should be like" (1997:64). These expectations are governed by the prevalent translation tradition, by the form of other texts of the same genre, and by various other (ideological, political) factors. They ultimately determine what 'counts' as a translation, i.e. what a particular community will accept as a translation. In that sense we could regard product or expectancy norms also as 'constitutive norms'. If translators abide by them, then their products will be classified as (genuine, proper, legitimate) translations. These norms thus stake out the perimeter of translation. Failure to observe them means that the product is likely to be called something other than translation – adaptation, paraphrase, travesty, parody, whatever. As Chesterman points out, even translations qualified as 'bad' are ostensibly translations (1997:60).

*Process* (or *production*) *norms*, which operate at a lower level than expectancy norms, regulate the translation process itself. They issue typically from the world of accredited, professional translators whose behaviour is regarded as norm-setting, which is why Chesterman also speaks of them as professional norms. Chesterman (1997:67-70) distinguishes three such process or professional norms:

- The *accountability norm*, which is ethical in nature, assumes that translators owe loyalty to the original writer, to the commissioner of the translation job, to themselves (!) and to their clients and/or prospective readers. It prescribes that translators should act in such a way that the demands of loyalty are appropriately met with regard to all concerned. The point has also been made by Christiane Nord (1991) and was anticipated by Popovič's observation about the 'affirmative' relation which translation normally entertains with its source (Popovič 1970; see above, Chapter 2).
- The *communication norm* is social in character and stipulates that translators should act in such a way as to optimize communication, as required by the situation, between all the parties involved. Its practical demands correspond broadly to the maxims (be truthful, be clear, be relevant, etc.) which Grice derived from the cooperative principle underlying the pragmatics of all communication (Chesterman 1997:58, 69). This means, as Chesterman (ibid.) also recognizes, that neither the accountability norm nor the communication norm is specific to translation. But the third one is.
- The *relation norm* urges the translator to ensure that "an appropriate relation of relevant similarity is established and maintained between the source text and the target text" (1997:69). Here the translator must make a judgement in view of "the text-type, the wishes of the commissioner, the intentions of the original writer, and the assumed needs of the prospective readers" (ibid.). The relevant similarity to be achieved might be primarily formal, as with legal contracts, or stylistic, as with literary texts, or semantic, as with scientific articles, or a matter of overall effect, as with tourist brochures or advertisements, and so on.

Together, Chesterman's product and process, or expectancy and professional norms cover a wider area than Toury's process norms. Do they get us much further? The first two process norms apply to any form of communication, while the third only takes us back to the question of what counts as a translation. In this latter respect Chesterman thinks that "[at] the most general level, we can perhaps say that the required relation must be one of *relevant similarity*" (1997:62). If this is the case then the requirement is part of the expectancy norm, which, as we saw, embodies "the expectations of readers of a translation (of a given type) concerning what a translation (of this type) should be like" (1997:64).

In this respect Christiane Nord's distinction seems clearer. Nord speaks of constitutive and regulatory norms (or conventions, as she calls them), terms which themselves derive from Searle's speech act theory. For Nord, *constitutive conventions* "determine what a particular culture community accepts as a *translation* (as opposed to an *adaptation* or *version* or other forms of intercultural text transfer)" (1991:100). The sum total of these conventions constitutes "the general concept of translation prevailing in a particular culture community, i.e. what the users of translations expect from a text which is pragmatically marked as a translation" (ibid.). Embedded within the constitutive conventions are *regulative conventions*, which govern the "generally accepted forms of handling certain translation problems below the text rank" (ibid.). These norms, in other words, are helpful when we want to determine what criteria readers or critics are using to evaluate translations.

To the extent that Chesterman's product and process norms correspond to Nord's constitutive and regulative conventions, they are a clear advance on Toury's list. They bring other perspectives apart from the translator's into the picture. More importantly, they allow us to conceptualize a domain of translation, or a translation tradition, in terms of constitutive norms/conventions, and to think about ways of describing its boundaries, how they are kept in place or changed, and what exactly happens inside them. But before we look at ways of studying norms, let us review the theoretical background to the whole concept of norms and conventions.

## Norm Theory

In the descriptive paradigm norms provide the first level of abstraction and the first step towards an explanation of the choices and decisions which translators make. Seen in this light it is surprising that Toury, who systematically foregrounds the role of translation norms, has not explored the theoretical side of the norms concept further. In practice he approaches the issue very much from the translator's point of view. He views norms as constraints, ignoring their role as templates in offering ready-made solutions to particular types of problem. Looking at norms in a wider context will allow us also to set their regulatory aspect against the translator's intentionality, and thus to balance constraint with agency. After all, translators do not just mechanically respond to nods and winks, they also act with intent.

Fortunately, theoretical reflection on the nature of norms in the context of translation and translation studies has not been lacking (see Chesterman 1993 and 1997; Frank & Schultze 1988; Hermans 1991 and 1996a; Nord 1991a). It has an interdisciplinary aspect to it in that norm concepts are widely used in the social sciences, from law and ethics to social psychology and international relations. But while the literature on the subject is substantial, there is no unanimity on terminology or on the exact distinctions as regards the cluster of concepts that includes norms, conventions, rules, constraints, and so on. The collection *Rules and Conventions: Literature, Philosophy, Social Theory* (Hjort 1992) provides a good orientation.

The term 'norm' refers to both a regularity in behaviour, i.e. a recurring pattern, and to the underlying mechanism which accounts for this regularity. The mechanism is a psychological and social entity. It mediates between the individual and the collective, between the individual's intentions, choices and actions, and collectively held beliefs, values and preferences. Norms bear on the interaction between people, more especially on the degree of coordination required for the continued, more or less harmonious coexistence with others in a group, as the Venson case illustrates. Norms contribute to the stability of interpersonal relations by reducing uncertainty. They make behaviour more predictable by generalizing from past experience and making projections concerning similar types of situation in the future. They have a socially regulatory function.

Looking at the world of translation from this perspective implies that we view translation, like other forms of communication, as social interaction, even if it occurs at a distance (as in your reading this page: we share a language, I have written these sentences in such a way that I hope you will continue to read, but you at your end must agree to go on reading my words and refrain from closing this book here and now). Translation involves a transaction between parties who have an interest in the transaction taking place. As one of the parties actively involved, the translator is an agent whose actions are neither entirely free nor predetermined – nor are they necessarily conscious or rational. Moreover, translation is deployed in the context of existing social structures, which are also structures of power, both material and what Pierre Bourdieu would call 'symbolic'.

In this social context, the norms and conventions of translation guide and facilitate decision-making. The basic premise is that translation, as a communicative act, constitutes a form of social behaviour. For communication to succeed those engaged in the process need to coordinate their actions. To appreciate the role of norms and conventions in solving such recurrent interpersonal coordination problems, we may start from the definition of convention provided by the American philosopher David Lewis (1969). The definition is chosen here for convenience only. It is not the last word on the subject but it has been highly influential (see, for example, Fokkema 1989, Huntemann 1990). The main ingredients are as follows: conventions are regularities in behaviour which have emerged as arbitrary but effective solutions to recurrent problems of interpersonal coordination. Because they have proved effective, these solutions become the preferred course of action for individuals in a given type of situation. Conventions grow out of precedent and social habit. They do not have to be explicitly agreed, but they presuppose common knowledge and acceptance. They imply mutual expectations: the expectation of others that, in a given situation, I will adopt a certain course of action, and my expectation that others expect me to do just that. In 1975 Lewis put it as follows:

> conventions are regularities in action, or in action and belief, which are arbitrary but perpetuate themselves because they serve some common interest. Past conformity breeds future conformity because it gives one a reason to go on conforming; but there is some alternative regularity which could have served instead, and would have perpetuated itself in the same way if only it got started. (quoted in Fokkema 1989:4)

Douwe Fokkema and others have pointed out that conventions are not entirely arbitrary. The choice of one convention rather than another has a historical aspect in that the success of previous selections is taken into account (Fokkema 1989:3). However, they are arbitrary in the sense of being contingent: another convention could also have done the job.

Conventions are not norms, although the distinction is not always made and conventions are sometimes regarded as implicit norms, or 'quasi-norms' (Lewis 1969:97; Hjort 1990:43). At any rate, conventions can become norms, as they can fall victim to their own success. If a convention has served its purpose sufficiently well for long enough, the expectation, on all sides, that a certain course of action will be adopted in a certain type of situation may grow beyond a mere preference and acquire a binding character. At that point we can begin to speak of norms.

Norms can then be understood as stronger, prescriptive versions of social conventions. Like conventions, norms derive their legitimacy from shared knowledge, mutual expectation and acceptance, and the fact that, on the individual level, they are largely internalized. There are many social, moral and artistic norms and conventions that we constantly observe while hardly being aware of them, from the way we queue at the bus stop to table manners and answering the telephone.

Unlike conventions, norms have a directive character. They tell members of a community not just how everyone else expects them to behave in a given situation, but how they *ought* to behave. They imply that there is, among the array of possible options, a particular course of action which is more or less strongly preferred because the community has agreed to accept it as 'proper' or 'correct' or 'appropriate'. The intersubjective sense of what is 'proper' or 'correct' or 'appropriate' constitutes the *content* of a norm. More about this below. First a few words about the operative aspect of norms, their executive arm, as it were.

Since norms imply a degree of social and psychological pressure, they act as constraints on behaviour by foreclosing certain options and choices, which however remain available in principle. At the same time they single out and suggest, or prescribe more or less emphatically, a particular selection from among the range of possible courses of action: 'You should learn to say *please*'; 'For God's sake don't swear all the time'. The directive or normative force of a norm is a matter of social pressure, backed up with inducements and rewards or the threat of sanctions. Strong norms are strongly felt to be appropriate, or backed up by strong sanctions, often spelled out explicitly. At that point it might be better to speak of a 'rule'.

Norms can and will be breached. Provided the breaches do not occur persistently and on a large scale without effective sanction, norms are able to cope with a relatively large amount of discrepant behaviour. It is in this sense that the German sociologist Niklas Luhmann speaks of norms as "counterfactually stabilized behavioural expectations" (1984:437). The conventions and norms of polite conversation at a dinner party are not invalidated because one of the guests fails or refuses to observe them. In other words, norms do not preclude agency, or erratic conduct. Which norms are broken by whom will depend on the occasion, on the nature and strength of the norm and on the individual's position and motivation. To the extent, however, that norms become integrated into an individual's routines, they are internalized as dispositions, propensities to act in certain ways. In the actual occurrence of norm-governed behaviour, structure and act correlate. External pressures are interiorized, and in turn the individual's practices which are adjusted to them keep the social system of norms in place.

As the prescriptive force of norms increases from the permissive to the mandatory, they move away from conventions in relying less on mutual expectations and internalized acceptance, and more on codified rules in the form of explicit obligations and prohibitions. The term 'rule' is used here as meaning a strong, institutionalized norm, often issued by an identifiable authority armed with the power to impose sanctions for non-compliance. Here we recognize the hierarchical power structures of most social and socio-cultural systems. Power relations are inscribed in all the multiple networks of norms and conventions operative in societies. As regards language use we can say that this is also what lends all speech a certain performative force: whether it obeys prevailing norms or not, it actively contributes to the modification or maintenance of the power relations which those linguistic usages sustain.

Norms can be strong or weak, and more or less durable. Their scope may be narrow or broad. They may be positive or negative, i.e. tend towards obligations or towards prohibitions. In a 1942 essay on 'The Normative Structure of Science', Thomas Merton spoke of the 'ethos of science' as "a normatively toned complex of values and norms" which was expressed "in the form of prescriptions, proscriptions, preferences and permissions" (Merton 1973:168-69). Dirk de Geest (1992) mapped these 'modalities of normative force' in the form of a so-called semiotic square, as follows:

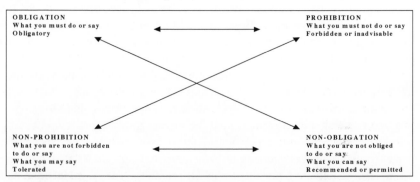

The upper half of the square contains strong, clearly recognized and well-defined norms and rules, formulated as requirements and interdictions (prescriptions and proscriptions), which may be backed up by sanctions or supported by strong attitudes and belief systems. The lower half indicates areas of greater permissiveness (preferences and permissions), where norm-breaking, experimentation and innovation are therefore more likely. On the whole, more permissive norms are also more malleable and hence more open to re-interpretation and adjustment in response to changing circumstances, whereas stronger norms tend to stabilize over time and become institutionalized. If the world of poetry translation is an example of the former, the European Union's translation department is an example of the latter. The very act of observing a norm confirms and reinforces its validity. In practice, following a given set of norms may be a matter of acquired habit, indeed of 'habitus' in Bourdieu's sense of a 'durable, transposable disposition' (see Chapter 9). Such dispositions are not inherited but inculcated. Learning to translate involves a socialization process: it means learning to operate – and perhaps manipulate – the norms of translation. In this way the translator training institute continually anticipates and reproduces – and may work to change – the dominant norms of translation, ensuring their canonization and continuity.

Complications soon arise. In any society a multiplicity of different, intersecting and often conflicting norms coexist. As it happens, the very first extended piece of writing on translation in the Western tradition is already entangled in norm conflicts. Saint Jerome's letter to Pammachius, around AD 395, was written in anger as a response to the charge that Jerome had

shown himself to be either incompetent or unethical in not translating abso-
lutely literally a text on a doctrinal matter. The attack must have reflected an
existing norm, if only because in his counterblast Jerome does not disclaim it
outright. Instead he discredits it by suggesting it lacks intellectual prestige,
and then he defiantly posits his own sense-for-sense norm, invoking august
authorities to legitimize it, but making an exception for a single text (the
Bible, his own life's work) where literalism was called for. Ironically, the
exception would be taken up as a norm by a number of early-medieval Christian translators in the name of the plain unadorned truth, in direct opposition
to what they condemned as the rhetorical lure of the non-Christian writers
(Copeland 1991:37ff.; Schwartz 1985). The internal history of translation could
be written as an unfolding series of norm conflicts.

The multiplicity of translational norms also constitutes the main repository
of the potential for change. Particular communities or groups may adopt certain
norms or discursive models in opposition to other groups. Individuals may
weave their way through and around these configurations, take up positions
and build alliances, in order to achieve their own goals and ambitions. The
marked intertextuality which results from these strategies has a social relevance.
In translating detective novels or popular romances, for example, adherence
to a particular textual model or translation norm may well make a political
point or mark the translation as 'literary' or 'non-sexist' but it may also spell
the end of a lucrative contract. Many of the literary translations prepared in
Germany at the end of the eighteenth century served a national political agenda
in rebutting the polished neoclassicism of the dominant French tradition.

Norms change because they need to be constantly readjusted so as to
meet changing appropriateness conditions. Different groups may judge particular norms more or less relevant or appropriate in certain circumstances.
While non-professional readers are perhaps content to read Thomas Mann in
Helen Lowe-Porter's translation, academic readers may deem it inadequate
and insist on certain standards of linguistic accuracy. The changes may be
played out as part of history. Before the rise of feminism there were no feminist critics to argue against sexist bias in translations. As circumstances and
expectations change, so do notions of what constitutes a well-formed text of a
given type, in a given social or cultural circuit. Translators can follow suit, or
swim against the current.

In themselves, norms are neither true nor false, for they do not represent
assertions. Rather, they stipulate what ought to happen, how things should be.
The content of a norm is a notion of what is 'proper' or 'correct'. It may be
posited as an ideal or be derived from particular models seen as deserving
imitation. The directive force of a norm serves to delimit and secure these
notions of correctness. The notion of what constitutes 'correct' behaviour, or
'correct' linguistic usage, or 'correct' translation, is a social, cultural and ideological construct. Compliance with the set of translation norms regarded as

pertinent in a given community or domain means that the product, i.e. the translation, is likely to conform to the relevant correctness notion. That means it accords with the expectancy norm (Chesterman) or constitutive convention (Nord) of translation. When translators do what is expected of them, they will be seen to have done well. But note: the emphasis in the previous sentence is on being seen, by certain groups, to have done well. There may be more ways than one of producing a correct translation. And what one section or community or historical period calls correct may be quite different from what others, or some of us today, may call correct. Correctness in translation is relative – linguistically, socially, politically, ideologically.

## Studying Norms

If norms can be of use in helping us to understand translation as a social, communicative practice, how do we identify, map and account for them in actual translations, in particular corpora or historical periods? The task is far from simple, for fairly obvious reasons. Norms are not directly observable. The formulation of a norm is not the same thing as the norm itself. There may be a gulf separating declarations about norms from actual norm-governed behaviour. Discrepant behaviour may not be quite so easy to distinguish from conformism. Tracing regularities in texts and reading them as the outcome of a translator's choices and decisions does not tell us *why* the choices and decisions were made. Given a bewildering multiplicity and diversity of norms, it is not always easy to know which are the most relevant ones.

Evidence of norms may be collected in a variety of places. Both Toury (1995:65-66) and Nord (1991:103-106) mention likely sources. First of all there are the translations themselves. A text may have been translated more than once, throwing up differences worth looking into. Bibliographies of translations may suggest preferences and exclusions in selecting texts for translation. Then we have all manner of paratexts and metatexts (paratexts are prefaces, footnotes and the like; metatexts are texts presented independently but dealing with other texts), including such things as: statements and comments by translators, editors, publishers, readers and collectives such as translators' associations (their 'codes of conduct' make fascinating reading); reviews and appraisals of translations as well as other reception documents; theoretical and programmatic statements. Toury adds rather broadly "the activity of a translator or 'school' of translators, and so forth" (1995:65), which includes just about everything, and Nord speaks of language teaching in schools (1991:105).

We could certainly throw in textbooks used in translator training; law suits (what constitutes an 'error' in translation, by whose definition, and who is liable for damages?) and texts dealing with copyright law; and such things as data about the distribution of translations (which ones are reprinted, for example, perhaps with alterations), and translation prizes – not only who receives them, but also who awards them, and on what grounds. With reference to the tumultuous history of Emile Zola's novels in Victorian England, Graham King (1978) analyzes translators' self-censorship and editorial censorship, but also the influence exercised on the publishing world by the powerful public lending libraries, the National Vigilance Association and the courts, with in the background the famous statement by Thomas Bowdler (yes, he of the word 'bowdlerized') that "if any word or expression is of such a nature that the first impression which it excites is an impression of obscenity, that word ought not to be spoken, or written, or printed; and if printed, it ought to be erased" (King 1978:228; Merkle 1994).

The actual move from texts to norms, however, remains a matter of interpretation and inference, the kind of reverse engineering mentioned in Chapter 2. There is no obvious starting point – texts, paratexts, metatexts, extratexual data, it depends on the case. The general ideas presented in the previous chapter on describing translation should be of help in devising an approach. Beyond this, let me offer a few additional pointers.

1   Canonized models and borderline cases. If norms secure notions of correctness, it will pay to figure out which translations are held up as examples to follow. The solutions to specific problems recommended in textbooks on translation, and the kind of translations that are reprinted, anthologized, awarded prizes or otherwise singled out for praise, are likely to embody what is regarded as 'proper' or 'correct' translation – by a particular group, at a certain time and for a certain time. "The version which the general judgment pronounces to be the best obtains possession of the field", G.K. Richards observed in his translation of Virgil's *Aeneid* in 1871 (in Lefevere 1998:46), and that version then serves as a point of reference, perhaps as the supreme challenge, a model to be not only imitated but emulated and eventually dethroned and replaced.

Easier to handle may be conflicts over borderline cases. They tend to lay bare the constitutive norms of translation, and hence what is taken to be the difference between translation and adjacent fields like adaptation, imitation or burlesque. Chesterman (1997:60) quotes the amusing case of the French *Mots d'heures: gousses, rames*, with lines like:

> Un petit d'un petit / S'étonne aux Halles
> Un petit d'un petit / Ah! degrés te fallent [...]

which become transparent when the following English lines are read with a strong French accent:

Humpty Dumpty / sat on a wall
Humpty Dumpty / had a great fall [...]

but which not everyone everywhere might be willing to call translation. Another well-known case in the same vein is the version of Catullus
by the American poet Louis Zukofsky and his wife Celia (Lefevere
1975:19ff). They rendered the Latin line "tum Theditis Peleus incensus
fertur amore" ('Then is Peleus said to have caught fire with love of
Thetis') as "T'my Thetis this Peleus incandesced fair thru his armor",
which bears little semantic resemblance to the Latin but mimicks the
sound (try reading the Latin with an American accent). The Zukofskys
defended their version on the grounds that in poetry sound matters as
much as sense and that they had done no more than adjust the usual
norm of translation which privileges sense. The debate with the critics
over whether this was a translation or something else is instructive.
Interestingly, in 1975 Lefevere did not think the Zukofsky version could
pass as a translation.

A more distant example. The seventeenth-century French Academy member and classical scholar Nicolas Perrot d'Ablancourt
translated a range of historical and other works in a defiantly free manner, resolutely rearranging for instance Tacitus' notoriously compact
and elliptical style into smoothly measured French cadences which
'breathed the air of the Louvre'. He conceded that not everyone might
be prepared to call his versions translations but, he remarked, 'they are
better than translations' and continued to speak of them as translations,
as did his numerous followers for over a hundred years. In England,
Perrot's contemporary Abraham Cowley was equally indifferent to
whether or not 'the grammarians' would admit his renderings of Pindar
as translations. Later in the century Pierre Daniel Huet in France and
Dryden in England objected to the latitude claimed by the libertine
translators (T.R. Steiner 1975). Debates like these concern what is
deemed permissible under the label 'translation', and bring into view
the boundaries of what counts as translation in particular historical
configurations.

2   Selectivity and exclusion. The examples just mentioned also make it
clear that, in choosing particular options, translators adopt certain positions in a context of existing expectations. Whether they go with the
flow or row upstream, both their programmatic declarations and their
actions represent one selection from a menu of available possibilities.
Picking one option means that the alternatives are excluded, although
they remain latent as a store of future possibilities. For the researcher it
pays to have an idea of which options are realistically available to a
translator, for instance because they have been chosen before by other

translators in comparable cases, or are routinely recommended. Reading texts oppositionally by highlighting the exclusions, the paths that were open but that were not chosen, may allow us to glimpse the agenda behind the choices that are made. The exclusions can be quite literally exclusions. Harish Trivedi has noted that in the two and a half decades stretching either way of Indian independence the most eloquent "translatorial response" to Shakespeare in India was silence: whereas fourteen translations had appeared in Hindi alone in the last two decades of the nineteenth century, and twenty-three between 1901 and 1931, there was only one between 1932 and 1956 (Trivedi 1995:19).

Speech act theory has argued that the meaning of an utterance is not just a question of the semantics of the words that are used, but also of illocutionary force, stemming from the fact that a certain statement is made at a certain moment, in certain circumstances. This is why it will be useful to hold individual translations, together with other texts, against the grid offered by the semiotic square (above) and to ascertain what apparently must be said, what must not be said, what may be said, and what can be said in certain circumstances. In the early 1670s Spinoza did everything he could to prevent a Dutch translation of his *Tractatus theologicopoliticus*. The book contained an explosive mix of scriptural criticism and radical republicanism, and Spinoza knew he could say things in learned Latin which the authorities, even in the tolerant Dutch Republic, would not permit being said in a vernacular accessible to all who could read. The choice of a text for translation, the actual mode of translating that is chosen and the response which translations meet, all gain in significance against that background. By focusing on selectivity, on choices as being oppositional, and by thus keeping an eye on those readily available options that were rejected but remain latent, the norms concept can serve as a probe, a heuristic tool.

Zohar Shavit works along these lines when she shows how in the early nineteenth century the children's books of Joachim Heinrich Campe were translated from German into Yiddish and Hebrew by Jews belonging to the Haskala movement (a movement close to the European Enlightenment). Since fictional narrative was not a permissible genre for these groups, Campe's narratives were recast as geography books or historical narratives; the selections made by Haskala translators from the available range of German books for children were deliberate and severe, based on religious, philosophical and educational criteria (Shavit 1992, 1997).

3   Discursive stances. Shavit's material illustrates the intermingling of different spheres and different categories of norms affecting translation. A translation is never a translation *per se*. It is a translated tourist brochure, or computer manual, or comic play. Translation is enmeshed

in all the discursive fields for which it caters. Continuing that line of thought, Clem Robyns (1992) has proposed the term 'sociosemiotics' to mean the study of all manner of discourses and 'discursive practices' in their social and ideological context.

Since translation operates in and on existing discourses while fashioning new texts after models belonging to other discourses, individual cultures or groups may develop different attitudes with regard to these potentially disruptive new arrivals.

Robyns distinguishes four basic attitudes, depending on whether the 'otherness' of the foreign (and hence the identity of the self) is or is not viewed as irreducible, and on whether or not the receptor culture adapts the intrusive elements to its own norms. When one culture sees another as compatible and translation is not a cause for concern or alarm, he speaks of that culture adopting a 'transdiscursive' stance. When a culture reckons it lacks something which is available elsewhere and can be imported, we have a 'defective' stance. When a culture wards off imports and tries to contain their impact because it feels they may threaten its identity, the attitude is 'defensive'. And when a culture only allows imports if they are thoroughly naturalized because it takes the value of its own models for granted, Robyns terms this, not very logically, an 'imperialist' stance (Robyns 1992, 1994a, 1995).

The four stances are emphatically presented as points of orientation only, and 'cultures' covers subdivisions and smaller sections or groups. The advantage of the grid lies in directing attention to ideological factors which bear on self-images and self-perceptions as they find expression in a wide range of discursive practices, not least in the mass media. Robyns has looked at popular detective stories in French translation and at policies to protect and promote the French language in France and abroad in this light (1990, 1995), and pointed to other work which interprets, for example, policies on TV and film dubbing and subtitling in different countries as expressions of underlying ideological positions. In countries like Germany, France, Italy and Spain, where dubbing is the norm, import quotas used to be imposed on American films. Dubbing, Martine Danan notes, can be read as "an assertion of the supremacy of the national language and its unchallenged political, economic and cultural power within the nation's boundaries" (1991:612). The case also makes it clear that translation needs to be seen in conjunction with other fields of discourse, and with questions of power. This is where translation studies blend into cultural studies, as indeed they must.

4   Codes, and a note of caution. The distance separating normative statements from actual behaviour may vary from a hairline crack to a yawning chasm. As we shall see in the next chapter, translation practice does

not necessarily proceed in step with theorizing about it. On the whole, the more frequent and emphatic the statements telling translators what they should be doing, the more likely it is they are not doing it. One consequence of this is that we should distinguish between what in literary studies is called an external from an internal poetics. The external poetics is the cluster of ideas which the researcher constructs on the basis of statements about literature, or in our case about translation. The internal poetics is the researcher's attempt to figure out the principles underlying the primary texts, in our case the translations themselves. Both can be represented in the form of a 'code', understood (e.g. by Fokkema 1985, following the Russian semiotician Yury Lotman) as a set of elements together with rules for their combination.

Codes however cannot simply be equated with norms and conventions. This is because, as Fokkema (1989) has also pointed out, norms and conventions are sociological constructs, whereas codes are semiological constructs. Codes, that is, "describe systems of signs used in communication and conventions refer to (tacit) agreement among a particular population" (Fokkema 1989:11). One requires the other to make communication possible, but they are not the same thing. Neither, as it happens, is directly observable. They are arrived at by inference and interpretation on the researcher's part. One important consequence of this is that we do not 'reconstruct' codes or norms or conventions 'as they really are'. Rather, we construct them. In translation studies, as in other disciplines, 'facts' are not given but made.

# 7. Beyond Norms

What comes after norms? After norms the road branches. One path leads towards possible universal laws of translation. Another path takes us into history and ends up asking questions about translation and cultural identity, why we think about translation the way we do, and how we can trace the provenance of these ideas. Let us explore both directions.

## Laws?

For Gideon Toury, the study of norms is only an intermediate stage in a larger programme. The overall outline of the programme looks as follows. You start by picking a text which you argue can be taken to constitute a translation. You study its composition and its relation to surrounding texts. Then you map it on a text in another language which you have reason to believe is its source. This is where norms come in. Because norms govern the choices which translators make, they determine the receptor text and hence the relation between the translation and it source. This relation Toury calls equivalence, but more about that below. Establishing the relation between translation and original serves as a stepping stone to the next stage, which is that of figuring out the overall concept of translation underlying a given corpus of texts. After that you are ready to "move on to the formulation of general laws of translational behaviour" (1995:69). Or, in a fuller statement:

> the cumulative findings of descriptive studies should make it possible to formulate a series of coherent *laws* which would state the inherent relations between all the variables found to be relevant to translation. Lying as it does beyond descriptive studies as such, the formulation of these laws may be taken to constitute the ultimate goal of the discipline in its theoretical facet. (1995:16)

Toury here takes an expansive and evolutionary view of the discipline of translation studies as a whole. Via the "establishment of regularities from an ever growing (and ever variegating) series of case studies" we work our way towards "a set of laws of translation behaviour" (1991:186) – although he foresees we shall be forever travelling hopefully, lest translation studies come to an end. The programme itself was announced in the editorial to the first issue of *Target*, where the editors spoke of "the gradual progression towards the establishment of a coherent set of laws of the form 'if X, then the greater/the smaller the likelihood that Y'" (Toury & Lambert 1989:6).

For Toury, then, the 'beyond' of his *Descriptive Translation Studies and Beyond* (1995) consists in the formulation of laws of translation. The laws are to be probabilistic in nature. The reasoning which leads to them moves in three steps. First (*1*) we consider what, in theory, translation can involve. Then (*2*) we compare this with what, under particular conditions, translation has apparently involved. Finally (*3*) we deduce what, under conditions to be specified, translation will probably involve. The progression has a logic to it (compare: we begin by imagining everything cobras are capable of doing, given their physical attributes and brain size; then we observe what they do in a number of specific situations; we conclude by predicting what they will probably do in situations yet to be specified). Equipped with the comparison between the possible and the actual we project the probable. Steps (*1*) and (*2*) are seen as the domains of translation theory and of descriptive translation studies, respectively, while (*3*) represents a more elaborate form of theory (Toury & Lambert 1989:6; Toury 1991:186; 1995:265).

Let me pause here and confess to a pervasive degree of scepticism regarding a quest for laws along these lines. It strikes me as being at odds with itself. It assumes that *all* the variables relevant to translation (but relevant from what point of view?) as well as the relations between them can be known. And 'translation' here means *all* translation. The programme announced in the first issue of *Target* wants translation studies "to account for every phenomenon regarded as translational in the world of our experience and to establish general principles for not only explaining, but also [partly] predicting them" (Toury & Lambert 1989:5; square brackets in the original). A tall order. It assumes either that translation is an immanent category, an experiential given, or that its historical and geographical diversity can be gathered and reduced to a common denominator. The former assumption runs counter to Toury's own starting point that we take translation to be what counts as translation whenever and wherever, and the latter rests on the reduction of all translation to a single concept of translation. But such a reduction requires a single theoretical position from which to look at translation, or at the very least a procedure which would make the results of different approaches commensurable and which would therefore involve a form of translation between different paradigms. In addition, what is called translation in different cultures covers various operations with various labels attached to them in the relevant languages – with the consequent need to translate those foreign-language concepts of 'translation' (but they do not call it 'translation', they call it 'tirgum' or 'fanyi' or whatnot) into 'our' (?) concept of 'translation' (or 'Übersetzung', 'vertaling', 'traducción', etc.) – and vice versa. The proliferation of inverted commas and brackets in the previous sentence, together with the one-directionality of translation, suggests we are in a tailspin – or an upward spiral – towards a formidable aporia.

At any rate, as Gregory Shreve has argued (1996:82; 1997:53), while the initial statements of some of Toury's 'laws' look like propositions, the predictions he aims at are better seen as hypotheses. Hypotheses take the form 'if x, then y', and they can be tested. In the final chapter of his 1995 book Toury formulated two such propositions/hypotheses. As an example, let us look at one of them. It comes in stages. This is the first stage:

(*a*) "in translation, source-text textemes tend to be converted into target-language (or target-culture) repertoremes" (1995:268).

A repertoreme is defined as a sign forming part of an institutionalized repertoire, and a texteme is an element of a text standing in a unique relation to other elements in that text. Although these definitions are unsatisfactory (any language is an institutionalized repertoire of signs, and any word in a sentence a texteme), what is meant becomes somewhat clearer with the fuller version of the proposition. We are apparently dealing with habitual, stereotyped options:

(*b*) "in translation, textual relations obtaining in the original are often modified [...] in favour of [more] habitual options offered by the target repertoire" (ibid.; second set of square brackets in the original).

Toury's commentary suggests this is an inherent feature of the mental operation of translating: a text is decomposed into its constituent parts, then transferred at a deep level and reassembled in the target language. The reconstruction however does not go all the way and is content to stop at the more standardized patterns. The proposition takes the form of a hypothesis when a new factor is added:

(*c*) "the more peripheral [the status of translation in a given culture], the more translation will accommodate itself to established models and repertoires" (1995:271).

This hypothesis is correlated with the following proposition (*d*), which logically comes before (*c*):

(*d*) "translation tends to assume a *peripheral* position in the target system, generally employing secondary models and serving as a major factor of conservatism" (1995:272).

'Secondary', like 'repertoreme', means stereotyped, habitual, non-innovative (we shall meet the term again in the next chapter). The claim is that translation tends to be a peripheral activity because it is by nature – see (*a*) and (*b*) – given to using more stereotyped forms of expression. Translation will never be non-secondary to any great extent; and the more peripheral it is, the more stereotyped. This should make it possible to test the converse: in cultures or at historical moments when translation is not peripheral, it should show less stereotypical language, fewer repertoremes. Even though translation generally cannot rid itself of a higher level of repertoremes than original writing because according to (*a*) and (*b*) high repertoreme levels are inherent in translating, we should be able to compute relative repertoreme levels in peripheral and non-peripheral translation. The problem here is that the linguistic make-up of texts is being conflated with the status accorded to them by critics or scholars. While corpus linguistics can measure the first in terms of type-token ratios and the like, status is not measurable in the same way. The cluster of 'laws', it seems to me, is muddled even when we limit ourselves to translations in the more recent Western tradition, let alone if we were to go beyond it.

Andrew Chesterman (1997:71-72) has taken a kinder view of Toury's laws. For him the behavioural 'laws' of translation can be read as hypotheses to be tested. He sees three such hypotheses: (a) the law of interference (which is Toury's second law), according to which source texts leave traces in target-text linguistic structures, even with "competent professional translators" (Chesterman 1997:71); (b) the law of explicitation, which says that translations tend to be more explicit than originals in presenting information; and (c) the law of stylistic flattening, which corresponds to Toury's first law (above), that of growing standardization. As Chesterman also notes, this third law appears to run counter to the first. The issue can be left with corpus linguistics, which is at least able to crunch huge amounts of text. The social, literary or cultural status of texts is an altogether different matter.

Chesterman has also formulated his own 'normative laws' (1997:76-77), which purport to be descriptions of professional translators' behaviour. According to these laws professional translators tend to conform to the product and process norms of translation. This does little more than state the blindingly obvious (it is like saying that professional teachers generally behave in a way we associate with professionals in the teaching profession), but has the modest advantage of explicitating sociological patterns, tying these 'laws' to particular communities and their concept of translation.

## Translation as Index

At the beginning of the previous chapter I suggested that a concept of norms helps in understanding translation as social practice. The conventions, norms and rules which govern translation also define it: they delineate and police the boundaries of what counts as translation. In that sense the expectations we bring to translation are both cognitive and normative. That could be one way of assessing the relevance of norms for translation. But there is more.

It may well be part of a given concept of translation that some people – women, for instance – are held to be more suited to translating than to original writing or to speaking in their own name. It may also be that translation is conceptualized in terms of, say, a demand for quasi-matrimonial fidelity on the translator's part, or of such metaphors as the humble maidservant of progress or as 'belle' but 'infidèle', meaning that translations, like women, can be either pretty or faithful but not both. All these ways of thinking about translation and translators are historical. They were common during the Renaissance and long after, when it was held, for example, that women should not take part in public discourse unless it was in the form of translation or prayer.

The wisecrack that gendered translations as 'belles infidèles' dates from around 1654, and was first applied to the work of Nicolas Perrot d'Ablancourt. All these things are well known (see Krontiris 1992, Simon 1996, Von Flotow 1997). They say as much about the cultural and ideological construction of 'translation' as about the construction of 'woman'.

The point about raising these issues here is that they serve as a reminder that translation is bound up with value. The correctness notions which norms keep in place are not neutral but cultural. The 'correct' translation, I noted earlier, is a translation which accords with expectations about what a good translation should be. But these expectations are loaded. When they are formulated, the metaphors give away the ideological load. Of course, the metaphors do not have to be gendered. Translation has been described in terms of bringing home treasures, taking the original captive, following in its footsteps, building bridges, transplantation, appropriation, portrait painting, migration of souls and a hundred other ways. Most of these metaphors and similes translate effortlessly into rules and norms for translation practice. The results are translations which project the underlying value systems into their representation of the source text. In that sense we can say that translations construct or produce their originals; speaking from a postcolonial perspective Tejaswini Niranjana says translations 'invent' their originals (1992:81).

Paradoxically, this ideological slant is precisely what makes translation interesting as a cultural and historical phenomenon. If it were a matter of technical code-switching only, translation would be as exciting as a photocopier. Translation is of interest because it offers first-hand evidence of the prejudice of perception. Cultures, communities and groups construe their sense of self in relation to others and by regulating the channels of contact with the outside world. In other words, the normative apparatus which governs the selection, production and reception of translation, together with the way translation is conceptualized at certain moments, provides us with an index of cultural self-definition. It would be only a mild exaggeration to claim that translations tell us more about those who translate and their clients than about the corresponding source texts. Or as Goethe observed in a letter of 1828, looking at the issue from a different angle: "the relations between an original and its translation most clearly express the relations of one nation to another" ("eben diese Bezüge vom Originale zur Übersetzung sind es ja, welche die Verhältnisse von Nation zu Nation am allerdeutlichsten aussprechen"; in Frank 1992:384).

The idea was fleshed out in a number of case studies conducted as part of the Göttingen research project on translation anthologies (Essmann & Schöning 1996; see also Kittel 1995). In a long and perceptive essay on nineteenth-century German anthologies of world literature, for example, Ulrich Beil (1996) showed that the universalist aspirations of these collections also served a national, emancipatory agenda. They aimed, in complex and paradoxical ways, to overcome the 'trauma' of cultural dependency, reflecting the self-perception of German culture as always having to rely on foreign models – even as it endeavoured to free itself from them by means of universalist anthologies.

It is worth pointing out in this context that the very notion of translatability already contains culturally significant assumptions about the commensurability of languages and cultures. The way in which, for example, Romantic theories of translation stress the bond between language and thought, and language and nation, is revealing – especially when contrasted with, say, Renaissance and Enlightenment ideas that differences between languages are surface phenomena compared with the universal nature of all human speech and thought. Claims to untranslatability, or indeed active resistance to translation, are as informative as the occurrence of this or that mode of translating. And when translation occurs, the whole normative context discussed above reminds us that it always does so as a particular type of translation, culturally and ideologically circumscribed and often institutionally transmitted. Translators never 'just translate'.

If this is so, then the nature of the relation between translations and their donor texts has to be re-examined. While Niranjana holds that translations 'invent' their originals, André Lefevere (1992) has argued that they create an 'image' of their source, and the image is always slanted, manipulated. The power of translation, as of the other forms of 'rewriting' with which Lefevere constantly links translation, is that it routinely replaces its originals. For most of us, the children's version of *Robinson Crusoe* becomes *Robinson Crusoe*, the TV serial of *Pride and Prejudice* becomes *Pride and Prejudice*, the English Penguin Dostoevsky *is* Dostoevsky. But at the same time we know that the Penguin Dostoevsky, being a translation, norm-governed and all that, is *not* Dostoevsky. There is a tangle here that needs unravelling.

## Equivalence?

As we saw in Chapters 4 and 6, Gideon Toury introduced the idea of translation as a norm-governed activity in an attempt to redefine the vexed notion of equivalence. Instead of taking equivalence as the central criterion for judging translations, he argued that the relation between a translation and its source was determined by the choices which the translator had made along the way. These choices were governed by norms as 'performance instructions'. As a result, "norms [...] determine the (type and extent of) equivalence manifested by actual translations" (1995:61). But equivalence now no longer means equivalence. It has been downgraded to a mere name, a blank label to be filled in. For each translation it needs to be documented in terms of "the balance between what was kept invariant and what was transformed" (1995:86). In other words, equivalence has been reduced to a "historical concept" or "a *functional-relational* concept" (1995:86, Toury's emphasis) denoting "any relation which is found to have characterized translation under a specified set of circumstances", or more fully: "that set of relationships which will have been found to distinguish appropriate from inappropriate modes of translation performance for the culture in question" (1995:61, 86). Reviewing these and other moves to deplete equivalence Andrew Chesterman not unreasonably speaks of "the notion's gradual approach to apparent vacuousness" (1997:10).

Having thoroughly hollowed out the notion, Toury nevertheless hangs on to it. Indeed he expresses "a clear wish to retain the notion of equivalence" (1995:61). The study of individual translations, he explains, will "proceed from the assumption that equivalence does exist between an assumed translation and its assumed source", adding again that "[w]hat remains to be uncovered is only the way this postulate was actually realized" (1995:86).

I have two problems with this. One problem stems from the reference to "the balance between what was kept invariant and what was transformed", which views equivalence as tainted, but only in terms of variance and invariance. As I indicated in Chapter 4, variance and invariance strike me as dubious concepts, due not only to the asymmetry between languages and cultures but also to the intervention of a norms concept which draws attention to the colouring, the slant, the ideological weighting of translation.

Secondly, stripping equivalence down to a mere label and then re-introducing it by the back door without further questioning the term's implications seems unwise because it blurs precisely the aspect of non-equivalence, of manipulation and displacement which the norms concept did so much to push into the foreground. This is not just a matter of norms and values slanting perception, but also of translation taking place in a context of power differentials. Postcolonial studies have shown again and again that relations between communities and cultures are rarely relations between equals. As was mentioned in Chapter 3, the refusal of some contemporary Irish poets to have their work translated into English, an obvious instance of the political significance of non-translation, occurs in a context in which languages like English and Irish are not on an equal footing. In the years following 1513 the 'Requerimiento' which informed the American Indians of their place in the Spanish empire was read to them in Spanish only; any translations into local languages faced not just the linguistic and cultural displacement that translation brings with it, but also their lack of status and legal validity.

The suggestion of equal value in the term 'equivalence' renders it inappropriate in such contexts. Of course, equivalence has become part of the way we habitually think of translation. For those of us without Russian the Penguin Dostoevsky *is* Dostoevsky. But hauling the same tainted concept, even in diluted form, into the theoretical discourse without problematizing it destroys the possibility of critical interrogation. If we want to replace it, Chesterman's proposal of 'relevant similarity' (see Chapter 6) might be a candidate, allowing translations to be seen as 'models' of their prototexts (Hermans 1993).

There remains the point, however, that we routinely associate translation with equivalence. How come? The question takes us back to culturally defined notions and images of translation. As Anthony Pym (1997) and others have argued, equivalence may be understood as a belief structure, the creation of a pragmatically necessary illusion. Our standard metaphors of translation incessantly rehearse this idea in casting translation as a transparent pane of glass, a simulacrum, a replica. A translation may be a derived product, a mere copy and therefore secondary, but as long as there is nothing to jolt us out of our willing suspension of disbelief we assume that to all intents and purposes the replica is 'as good as' and therefore equivalent to the real thing. Coupled with this is the image of translation as delegated speech or as direct quotation. Translators do not speak in their own name, their words are someone else's words. Brian Harris (1990) once formulated it as the universal 'true interpreter' norm: interpreters – and translators – should re-state the original exactly, without interfering with it. It means that translators, like their products, should become transparent, spirit themselves away in the interests of the original's integrity and authority (Hermans 1996c).

Karin Littau (1993, 1997), arguing from a poststructuralist perspective, has pointed out that we can read metaphors like these as part of a historical conceptualization of translation. Just as Michel Foucault suggested that the notion of the 'author' can be reduced to an 'author function' as an ideological figure, so in her view we could speak of a 'translator function' which serves to control translation, to keep it in its place, in a hierarchical order. Lori Chamberlain made a similar point from a feminist angle: translation is so over-regulated because "it threatens to erase the difference between production and reproduction which is essential to the establishment of power" (1992:66-67). In this way cultures construe translation as an ideological category, just as they construe, for example, gender distinctions. Equivalence could be seen as part of that construction. That is why a critical discipline of translation studies would do well to keep the term at arm's length, or, as Deconstructionists would say, use it 'under erasure'.

## Historicizing Theory

Explorations and speculations of this kind take us into the history of thinking about translation – a history which sooner or later brings us back to our own time. What do we actually know about the history of theory? Is there continuity or rupture between past and present theorizing on translation? Is the use of metaphorical language a sign of pre-scientific or unscholarly thought? And if the metaphors employed in past thinking reveal strong normative and evaluative aspects, can or should our own metalanguage try to do without them? In several pioneering essays Lieven D'hulst has tackled the issue of why and how to write the history of theoretical thinking about translation (1991, 1995, 1995a, 1996).

D'hulst's starting point is sharply critical of contemporary attitudes in the field. He dismisses the common assumption of a pre-scientific followed by a scientific era, with an abrupt change of gear occurring shortly after the Second World War when traditional translation theory was supposed to have donned properly scholarly methods. The relative lack of interest in historical issues he blames on the arrogance and "selective amnesia" (1995a:28) of contemporary translation studies: we imagine we have made such momentous progress – what with all our new paradigms – that past thinking has become an irrelevance.

The history of translation theory matters, D'hulst argues, because our current thinking stems from it. But it also holds its own interest, and its complexity. D'hulst is sceptical of the view which takes past theorizing to be a mere offshoot of translation practice, an incidental by-product confined to technical problems and found mostly in translators' prefaces and the odd scurrilous open letter. On the contrary, translation theory is closely tied up with thinking about language, interpretation, public discourse and identity. In any case, it is another fallacy to assume that the history of translating and the history of translation theory run parallel. In fact there is little evidence of a close correlation between the two. Worse, the idea of a seamless web linking theory and practice is a fiction which actually censors the complexity of history.

That complexity becomes apparent when we reflect on the multi-disciplinary nature of historical translation theory. It is embedded in such fields as linguistics, philosophy, rhetoric, religion (for example, biblical exegesis and commentary) and education (especially books on grammar and foreign language teaching, particularly, in the West, the teaching of Latin). This makes gathering data difficult, as the researcher is looking for a needle in a haystack.

Interpreting the texts presents problems as well. We often have to read the *unsaid* into the texts, as writers tend not to make explicit the presuppositions that do not need stating because they are part of what Foucault calls the 'episteme' of a period. But it would be naive to think that historical texts can be taken at face value. In this respect anthologies of historical texts, which often present truncated statements out of context, can be dangerous instruments. Statements fit into argumentative contexts, they respond to existing views and positions and constitute one stage in complex ongoing debates. Here it may be good, incidentally, to recall what was said in the previous chapter about the illocutionary force of an utterance. We need to try and assess the significance of why this statement was made at this moment; as Luhmann would put it, it helps if you know to what question a given utterance was the answer. The construction of a plausible context is also the best remedy against the common lament that the history of translation theory is repetitive and revolves only around the dilemma of free versus literal. Statements about translation come alive as soon as their backdrop is painted in.

A good illustration, though not one discussed by D'hulst, would be the short treatise called 'The Way to Translate Well from One Language into Another' ('La manière de bien traduire d'une langue en aultre') which Etienne Dolet published in 1540. Its five points are easily summarized: the translator should know the relevant subject-matter, have a good grasp of both languages involved, avoid translating literally, be sparing with loanwords, and use a pleasing style. Time and again Dolet's text has been presented by modern scholars as giving a piece of rather obvious practical advice, a few rules of thumb – the kind of thing anyone with common sense can dream up in five minutes. However, as Glyn Norton has argued at length (1984:203-17), the treatise takes on a wholly new complexion when it is read as the first state-ment in French of a set of distinctly Humanist translation principles, polemically opposing to the widespread practice of literalist translation the exacting ideal of a learned, rhetorical translator. It underwrites a nationalist cultural agenda, as Dolet's preface to his project (which consists of more than just the treatise on translation) makes abundantly clear. His five points fit those listed in Latin by the Italian Humanist Leonardo Bruni a hundred years earlier. They are anything but pedestrian. The first three points, for example, are about total intellectual command of the topic in hand and expert linguistic skills, while the fifth point requires profound familiarity with  rhetoric.

Norton's argument gains further strength when we reflect that contem-poraries (Jacques Peletier, for example, or Joachim du Bellay) use a term like the 'law' of translation to mean literal translation, and that Dolet's rhetorical programme finds a contemporary echo in prefaces by the English Humanist John Christopherson (Hermans 1997a). There is, in other words, more than meets the eye in these seemingly innocuous texts. And we could go on. Within ten years of Dolet's treatise, Du Bellay vehemently denied that translation could fulfil the role of cultural enrichment which Dolet saw for it. Instead, Du Bellay recommended imitation, which to him was obviously very different from translation. Yet by the mid-seventeenth century the so-called libertine translators in France and England (Perrot d'Ablancourt, John Denham, Cowley) were talking about translation in exactly the way Du Bellay spoke about imi-tation. Texts answer to other texts.

But how to order them? If we want to do justice to historical complexity, D'hulst points out, we need to think carefully about methodology. The historiography of translation theory, and for that matter the historiography of translation, can learn a great deal from the current debates in the philosophy of history. As regards translation theory specifically, D'hulst sees the his-toriography of linguistic ideas as an example to follow. But not all problems can be resolved by looking at other disciplines. What periodization is best for translation theory, when theory is not necessarily aligned with practice, and when it remains to be seen to what extent translation theorizing falls in with the broad period divisions of intellectual history? And should we adopt a semasiological or an onomasiological principle, that is, should we take a given term and trace its range of meanings over time, or start from a given concept and figure out what terms were used to name it in different periods? D'hulst does not pretend to have the answers to these questions, but he feels it is a matter of scholarly integrity that we address them.

Not afraid to handle Russian-doll-type complexities, D'hulst also raises the question of the historiography of the historiography of translation theory. This leads him to comment, for example, on recent surveys of contemporary translation studies and the way they present their material (e.g. Gentzler 1993, Stolze 1994), and on such things as the perception by others of the so-called Manipulation group. He ends on a bright note. Research into historical translation theory, he claims with a large dose of irony, may end up as the main beneficiary of the increasing fragmentation of translation studies, the lack of dialogue between the various schools of thought and the growing doubts about the possibility of a unified translation theory. "The less chance there is of a general theory of translation, the better the prospects for translation historiography", he concludes (1995:19). The brightness is only marginally dimmed by the awareness that, in time, the historiographers of translation and translation theory will no doubt also break up into warring clans and sects.

# 8. Into Systems

Description is not enough. It has to serve a purpose, such as explanation. This requires that phenomena are put into a context, and that we have an apparatus to bring that context into view. That is where, in the descriptive paradigm, the notion of system comes in. In the previous chapters I have deliberately avoided the term 'system'; from now on it will be on every page, beginning with 'polysystem'. As I pointed out in Chapters 1 and 3, Itamar Even-Zohar's polysystem theory took shape simultaneously and in close association with the descriptive paradigm in translation studies. It offered a comprehensive and ambitious framework, something researchers could turn to when looking for explanations and contexts of actual behaviour. A significant amount of empirical and historical work on translation, and especially on literary translation, is directly or indirectly indebted to polysystem theory.

The notion of literature as a system has its origin in Russian Formalist thinking and is very much present in Prague Structuralism. It has been widely applied in literary studies, as Tötösy de Zepetnek's 1992 bibliography illustrates. Itamar Even-Zohar's polysystem theory goes back directly to Russian Formalism, with the deliberate inclusion of translation. André Lefevere subsequently elaborated a systems concept of literature and translation along somewhat different lines and with more emphasis on social and ideological factors. More recent revisions in sociological terms seek inspiration in Pierre Bourdieu's writings on the sociology of culture or in Niklas Luhmann's idea of social systems. I will explore some of these lines in this and the next two chapters. However, two things should be made clear before we launch into polysystem theory.

Firstly, there is no necessary connection between polysystem theory (or any other system theory) on the one hand and, on the other, descriptive or empirical translation studies or viewing translation as manipulation or cultural practice. You can study translation along the lines set out in the preceding chapters and never encounter a single system, let alone a polysystem. You can also work with polysystem theory and never study translations. If you do use polysystem theory to study translations, you can do so in ways different from what has come to be called the descriptive or Manipulation paradigm; you can, for instance, use Vermeer's *skopos* theory, or Pym's intercultural regimes (Pym 1997), or another approach.

The close association between polysystem theory and the descriptive or Manipulation line is a matter of historical accident and conceptual convenience. As Even-Zohar developed his theory of literature as a polysystem in the early 1970s, he was already collaborating with Gideon Toury. The Russian Formalists were also known to people like James Holmes, José Lambert and André Lefevere. In other words, the polysystem hypothesis, as it was then called, came at the right moment. As a theory about the way literatures behave and develop, it made room for translation, explicitly so, at a time when literary studies generally ignored the subject. It seemed flexible and promising as an explanatory frame; it legitimized research into translation as part of literary studies; and it was available through personal contact. In subsequent years it proved sufficiently broad to be applied beyond the strictly literary domain to such things as theatre translation (Sirkku Aaltonen, Romy Heylen, Marta Mateo, Raquel Merino) and the audiovisual media (Martine Danan, Patrick Cattrysse, Olivier Goris, Dirk Delabastita).

Secondly, there are no systems. Systems exist only in system theory. They have no ontological status. The decision to view, say, literature, art or translation, or for that matter education or politics, as a system is made on the grounds that doing so will provide a certain kind of insight into that world – into its internal structure and evolution, and its relations with the outside world, for instance. As we will see, Even-Zohar stresses the hypothetical nature of polysystems in his definition. Perhaps the most famous instance in this respect is the opening sentence of Niklas Luhmann's *Soziale Systeme*: "Die folgenden Überlegungen gehen davon aus, dass es Systeme gibt" (1984:30; "The following considerations assume that there are systems", 1995:12). While the statement appears to assert that systems exist, the claim to reality status is demolished in the book's closing chapter. As Luhmann slyly pointed out elsewhere (in Krawietz and Welker 1992:381), the first part of the sentence prefigures this 'epistemological dissolution'. I will return to this issue in Chapter 10.

## Polysystem's Sources

The main source for polysystem theory, as Even-Zohar has always fully acknowledged, lies in Russian Formalism. The Formalists, a group of vociferous and sharp-witted academics including Victor Shklovsky, Boris Eikhenbaum, Roman Jakobson and Yury Tynjanov, came to the fore in Saint Petersburg and Moscow around the First World War and remained active until the Stalinist regime silenced them at the end of the 1920s. Their work would be continued, with a different emphasis, by the Czech Structuralists (Jan Mukařovský, Felix Vodička and others) and was taken up again in Russia in the 1960s and '70s by semioticians like Yury Lotman. Around that time Formalist writings also reached Western Europe in French, German and subsequently English translations.

The Formalists revolutionized literary studies. Reacting against impressionistic criticism and positivistic fact-finding, they took the defining characteristic of literature to be the specific way in which it moulds its own material, language. Shklovsky's early essays, for example, treated the literary work not as the expression of a writer's personality or the spirit of the age, but simply as an amalgam of devices, tricks designed to make language and perception new, strange, unfamiliar, de-automatized. In poetry, rhyme and metre could fulfil this role; plot construction, unusual points of view or other techniques could serve similar purposes in narrative prose. The Formalists would have been delighted with a novel like Martin Amis's *Time's Arrow* and the way its story is told going relentlessly backward rather than forward in time; or with, say, Georges Perec's decision to write a full-length novel in French without once using the letter 'e' (*La disparition*); or with the distinctive, jerky camera technique in a TV series like *NYPD Blue*.

From these early notions there grew the idea of a literary work as not just a heap of devices but an ordered heap, a hierarchically structured set. If literature wants to be constantly new, it has to keep foregrounding new devices while decommissioning others. What matters, then, is not so much the device itself as its place in relation to everything around it. Projected onto a diachronic plane this means that defamiliarization can only be effective against the backdrop of the prevailing and the familiar. The driving force of literary evolution, in the Formalist conception, lies in this constant urge to replace the familiar with the unfamiliar, the traditional with the innovative. The literary series thus possesses its own momentum and obeys its own autonomous laws. And just as individual works and genres are structured wholes, literature in its entirety is a hierarchically organized, self-renewing whole. The need for self-renewal however brings constant instability. A synchronic snapshot may give the impression of a harmonious equilibrium, but it conceals the vying for position, the reshuffling of priorities and the generation conflicts being acted out on the diachronic axis.

For Even-Zohar's polysystem theory the work of Yury Tynjanov is particularly relevant. Two of Tynjanov's essays, 'The Literary Fact' and 'On Literary Evolution', from 1924 and 1927 respectively (1982:7-30; 1978:66-78), are worth mentioning here. They sum up the Formalists' mature views.

As Tynjanov sees it, a 'literary fact' is a relational entity. What we call a 'literary work', a 'genre', a 'period', a 'literature', or 'literature' *per se*, represents an aggregate of features which all derive their value from their interrelations with the other elements in the network. It is, in each case, a system – indeed Tynjanov is credited with being the first to have spoken of literature as a 'system'. The whole constellation, moreover, is never still but constantly changing. Literary phenomena therefore need to be studied in a relational way, on the synchronic (relations with elements of the same system and of other systems) as well as on the diachronic level. What is individual and distinctive in a particular work, period, genre or literature, can only be determined in the context of such relations. Synchronic and diachronic cross-sections will show shifting relations of dominance and dependence. A literary system can be thought of as consisting of a dominant, prestigious and canonical centre which, over time, petrifies and is replaced by new and more dynamic forms which come crawling out of the woodwork of the system's periphery. The centre/periphery opposition is one of Tynjanov's key concepts. Literary evolution consists in "the mutation of systems" (1978:67); mutation here means a change in the interrelationships between elements of a system, typically the centre and periphery changing place. This process however is not one of gradual development or growth but a matter of pushing and shoving, of rupture, struggle and overthrow.

In a short position paper which Tynjanov wrote jointly with Roman Jakobson in 1928, the authors observed that if literature is a system, then in turn the history of literature may be seen as a system, since "evolution is inescapably of a systemic nature" (1978:80). Furthermore, if literature constitutes a system with a systemic evolution, it is reasonable to view other cultural and social series also as systems. The correlations between these various systems then form "a system of systems" (1978:81). Exactly how these correlations are to be determined is left open. Tynjanov had noted earlier that while the literary system may not be wholly self-sufficient it must be granted a degree of autonomy and will not necessarily evolve in synchrony with other systems. Boris Eikhenbaum would point out a year later that the relations between literature and the extra-literary world cannot be causal but are at best relations of "correspondence, interaction, dependency, or conditionality" (1978:61).

After the Formalist era, the Prague Structuralist Jan Mukařovský tried to come to grips with the interaction between literature and its environment by positing an 'aesthetic function' which in literary texts coexists with various other, pragmatic functions. Readers bring both aesthetic and non-aesthetic expectations and judgements to bear on literary works, and thus integrate them into their everyday lives. Literary change then stems from a combination of intrinsic evolution and extrinsic intervention. In the cultural semiotics of Yury Lotman, culture as a whole is treated as a vast multi-level system, a 'semiosphere' (a term calqued on 'biosphere') which organizes our existence at a conceptual level. Lotman, like Tynjanov (and Even-Zohar), thinks of individual systems as consisting of tightly structured nuclei and more fluid peripheries, and of change as involving shifts in constellations of elements. His work however stresses not just relations between systems and their environment, but the need to look at what a particular system, from its internal point of view, regards as being within or beyond its boundaries. This makes accounting for relations between systems and their environments even more complicated. Lotman observes, for instance, that the self-description of a system, in the form of a poetics, say, or a literary history, is not only more organized than the reality which it presumes to treat but is also instrumental in regulating that reality (Lotman 1977). The position from which one speaks, whether internal or external, affects the thing spoken about – and Lotman realizes that his own descriptions have the same effect.

## Polysystem's Terms

Polysystem theory is best thought of as a latter-day manifestation of Formalism with a dash of Structuralism, general systems theory and cultural semiotics. Envisaged as a tool for writing literary and cultural history, the theory was elaborated by Even-Zohar in the early 1970s, and restated with only minimal revision in the Spring 1990 issue of *Poetics Today*. Considering the scale and nature of developments in literary theory generally during the intervening two decades, the relative immobility of polysystem thinking and the absence of dialogue with other theories are perplexing. No wonder polysystem theory has begun to look long in the tooth. Even-Zohar's recent work suggests he is now applying his ideas to a wide range of issues in cultural history while still keeping his polysystem concept unchanged.

Even-Zohar originally thought up the term 'polysystem' in connection with language rather than literature. In his doctoral dissertation he spoke of "the polysystemic nature of language" (1971:vii), meaning that heterogeneous sets of linguistic means such as high and low registers, and diverse stylistic modes, all co-exist within one language. The idea of a polysystem of literature, "parallel to the linguistic polysystem" (1971:xv), put into relief a similar diversity in the literary domain, with 'high' and 'low', canonized and non-canonized forms as the main divisions (ibid.; 1978:11).

In 1990, when what had begun as a 'polysystem hypothesis' had graduated to a theory, Even-Zohar still claimed the term was more than a terminological convention: 'polysystem' was meant to foreground "the conception of a system as dynamic and heterogeneous" (1990:12). However, it seems to me that, since all literary and cultural systems of any size may be assumed to be dynamic and heterogeneous, they are all polysystems. And if all systems are poly-, the 'poly-' in 'polysystems' is redundant. In what follows I will speak simply of 'systems', and use 'polysystem' only to refer specifically to Even-Zohar's notion.

For Even-Zohar, polysystem theory forms part of a broader current of thought which he calls 'dynamic functionalism' (1990:2), stressing the complexity, openness and flexibility of cultural systems existing in a historical continuum. He favourably contrasts this 'dynamic functionalism', presented as continuing the Russian Formalist tradition and encompassing also Lotman's cultural semiotics, with 'static' French Structuralism, said to be in hock to Saussurean linguistics and given to merely 'synchronistic' research (1990:11, 89). A contrast between 'dynamic' and 'static' functionalism along these lines seems forced – a way of donning the Formalist mantle while elbowing out a competitor. It is anyway beyond dispute that Even-Zohar's ideas grew out of the expressly structuralist circle around Benjamin Hrushovsky and the Tel Aviv journal *Ha-Sifrut* (Ben-Porat & Hrushovsky 1974).

The central idea of polysystem theory, as of all system theories, is relational. Not only are elements constantly viewed in relation to other elements, but they derive their value from their position in a network. The relations which an element entertains with other elements are what constitutes its function or value. In that sense such theories are functionalist. They are also constructivist: they recognize that the network, and the relations within it, are a matter of the researcher perceiving a network in the first place.

Even-Zohar's definition of the concept of 'system' reflects these relational and hypothetical aspects. He describes a system as "the network of relations that can be hypothesized for a certain set of assumed observables ('occurrences'/'phenomena')" (1990:27); or, more fully though perhaps not more clearly: the "network of relations which can be hypothesized for an aggregate of factors assumed to be involved with a sociocultural activity, and consequently that activity itself observed via that network. Or, alternatively, the complex of activities, or any section thereof, for which systemic relations can be hypothesized" (1990:85). A literary system can then be defined as "the network of relations that is hypothesized to obtain between a number of activities called 'literary', and consequently these activities themselves observed via that network" (1990:28). Other cultural systems would be defined along the same lines.

After the formal definition, the toolbox required to inspect the literary system's internal workings consists of a handful of binary oppositions harking back to the Formalist arsenal. Three of these pairs are particularly useful. They are:

1   The opposition between canonized and non-canonized products or models (i.e. works, forms, genres, but also conventions and norms), roughly corresponding to 'high' versus 'low' literature. 'Canonized' means "accepted as legitimate by the dominant circles within a culture" and hence preserved and transmitted as part of the cultural heritage, while 'non-canonized' is described, rather infelicitously, as "norms and texts which are rejected by these circles as illegitimate" (1990:15). As Even-Zohar points out, canonicity is not an inherent feature of texts but is attributed by individuals, groups and institutions. These attributions can change. We may also note that a term like 'the dominant circles within a culture' cries out for specification: circles dominant in one area, say performance poetry or the opera, are not necessarily dominant in other areas.

2   The opposition between the system's centre and its periphery. As a rule, Even-Zohar observes, "the centre of the whole polysystem is identical with the most prestigious canonized repertoire" (1990:17). The term 'repertoire' stands for "the aggregate of laws and elements [...] that govern the production of texts" (ibid.), or in a more recent formulation: "the aggregate of rules and materials which govern both the

making and handling, or the production and consumption, of any given product" (1997:20). The centre or nucleus of the system can be regarded as its centre of gravity or seat of power. It is institutionally stronger than the periphery, and more organized. Rakefet Sheffy (1990) has corrected Even-Zohar's association of canons with repertoires on the grounds that canons, which are made up of texts rather than of instructions for good writing, do not usually serve as models for new text production but act as exemplars or structured reservoirs providing medium and long-term stability. Miguel Gallego Roca (1994:152) has suggested in similar vein that polysystem theory underestimates the actively shaping role of a collective cultural memory.

3    The opposition between 'primary' and 'secondary' activities, where 'primary' means 'innovative' and 'secondary' equals 'conservative'. This opposition injects a dynamic and diachronic quality into the model as it produces conflict and change which are acted out over time. 'Primary' activities bring about "augmentation and restructuration" of a repertoire (1990:21), whereas 'secondary' production leads first to consolidation but eventually to mummification and ineffectiveness.

The three oppositions interact to yield a picture reminiscent of the Russian Formalist conception of literary history, including its metaphors of warfare and palace coups. Typically, 'primary' models arise in the less regimented periphery of a system and campaign to oust the comfortably entrenched models in the canonized centre. Greater complexity is generated by permutations of the basic oppositions. A system's periphery may itself be differentiated, harbouring its own primary and secondary models, for example. Cultural systems are correlated with the social and the political. Relations between systems tend to mirror those within systems, i.e. the intersystemic parallels the intrasystemic. Also, 'system' does not have to mean, say, 'Italian literature' or 'postwar French cinema', but can refer to the poetry scene in *fin de siècle* Berlin, the multilingual culture of colonial North Africa, intellectual life in Beijing's Forbidden City during the Ming dynasty, or public oratory in Ancient Rome. The unit of investigation can be large or small, from the Petrarchan love sonnet in Renaissance Venice to the interdependent art scenes of the Western hemisphere today. This is worth pointing out because very often, even in Even-Zohar's own work, the idea of a (poly)system is simply equated with a national literature or culture. It is more flexible than that.

Translation can play a part in cultural systems in a variety of ways. Although Even-Zohar's discussion is mostly geared to literary translation, broader applications may be drawn from it. He conceives of translation as a system within the literary polysystem, i.e. as having its own canonized centre and periphery, its own innovative and more established models. Translation, like other forms of transfer, is essentially an instance of 'interference', which Even-

Zohar defines as "a relation(ship) between literatures whereby a certain literature *A* (a source literature) may become a source of direct or indirect loans for
another literature *B* (a target literature)" (1990: 54). If we amend this definition to include not merely the potential interference which it ostensibly bespeaks
but also actual contact, we can view translation alongside various similar operations by means of which cultural goods migrate between systems.

Individual translations or certain modes of translating may play a primary or a secondary role in a polysystem. Which of these roles they play
depends on the condition the system happens to be in. The vast majority of
translations, Even-Zohar observes, are of the secondary or conservative type.
He sees three kinds of situation when translations can be primary (i.e. innovative) and contribute to the elaboration of new repertoires. This is the case
(*a*) when a literature is still 'young' and has not yet crystallized; (*b*) when a
literature is 'weak' and/or peripheral within a larger group of literatures; and
(*c*) when a literature contains a vacuum or finds itself in a state of crisis or at
a turning point (1978:24-25; 1990:47).

This is clear and straightforward. It is also deeply troubling, not only
because it looks "somewhat crude", as Susan Bassnett recently put it (in
Bassnett & Lefevere 1998:127), but because it points to a lack of clarity regarding the vantage point from which the comments are being made. The
value judgement in characterizing a literature as young or weak or in crisis or,
even more puzzling, as containing a vacuum (a culture with a disability?),
requires a criterion to ascertain such things as the youth or strength of a culture or the presence of a 'vacuum' in it. It also suggests critical involvement,
as the qualification affects the situation that is being described. Calling, say,
Israeli literature 'young' may be read as a programmatic declaration; at the
very least it suggests certain points of reference as relevant (the year 1948, for
example), but not others (every literary form in today's Israel has its pred-
ecessors; cultures do not arise *ex nihilo*). A similar blurring of viewpoints
may have been observed earlier when I quoted Even-Zohar's definition of a
literary system as meaning all activities which are called literary – presumably by those within the system who see themselves as entitled to distinguish
between literature and non-literature; but since these are likely to be the people or institutions who will dismiss certain forms of non-canonized literature
as non-literature or as 'illegitimate' literature, it is not easy to see how the
polysystems concept of literature can be inclusive without a deliberate intervention on the researcher's part.

Even-Zohar's statements about typical situations when translations are
likely to fulfil a primary role make more sense if we take them as referring to
perceptions from within a system. We can then think of such cases as the
Renaissance assessment of vernacular cultures as needing translations from
the Classics to enrich the vernacular languages and build 'national' cultures;
or the way in which, in certain periods, countries like Turkey, China and

Japan imported Western technology by means of translation. A striking example is that of the Dutch Neoclassical society Nil Volentibus Arduum ('Nothing is hard for those who have the will'). They changed the face of Dutch theatre in the 1670s by savagely attacking any and all non-classicist plays and translations that crossed their path, and by producing their own versions, sometimes in unseemly haste, with the express aim of keeping rival translations off the Amsterdam stage. They triumphed in 1678: of the ten new plays performed in that year, six were by NVA, including four translations made in order to stop competing versions that did not conform to Neoclassical principles. Neoclassicism would dominate Dutch theatre for generations to come (Hermans 1988a:14-15). Note, though, that on the ground, as seen by the participants, all we have is the changing complex of interaction, networking and competition in which different parties pursue their own interests, without being able to predict the outcome. In that tangle, consolidation, augmentation and innovation are not that easily unpicked. Only hindsight permits the qualification 'primary' – but that robs the concept of its explanatory power.

As these examples indicate, Even-Zohar concurs with other researchers in the Manipulation paradigm in viewing translation as typically initiated at and by the receptor pole. This does not exclude other possibilities. Just as Toury remarks that the target end is where, as a rule, research can most profitably begin without having to be restricted to it (1995:36), Even-Zohar realizes that translations may be exported as well as imported, and that colonial domination, for instance, may mean the imposition of translations on a population that never asked for them (1990:68-69).

Polysystem theory has benefited translation research by placing translations squarely in a larger field of cultural activity. Even though the theory prefers to operate at the abstract level of repertoires and textual models rather than that of actual texts, writers or translators, it draws attention to the practical and intellectual needs which translations might be trying to fill. It thus provides a way of connecting translations with an array of other factors in addition to source texts. In other words, it integrates translation into broader sociocultural practices and processes, making it a more exciting object of study and facilitating what was subsequently hailed as the 'cultural turn' in translation studies. The relative simplicity of the key ideas allows applications in very different contexts. Historical research in particular received a boost. In the next section I will look at two extended examples of such research.

Before I do that, a brief digression. For Even-Zohar, polysystem theory is about writing cultural history, but not only that. Like Toury, he is in search of universal laws and principles. The boldness of the abstract thought here has as its flip-side an eagerness to rush into generalizations. Already in his first book Even-Zohar made a stab at "universals of literary contacts" (1978:45-53). Twenty-odd years later he restated them, with only minor changes, as "laws of literary interference", proposing ten such "governing laws" (1990:59-

72). Most of them have a bearing on translation. As was the case with Toury's laws of translational behaviour in the previous chapter, Even-Zohar's quest leaves me unconvinced. His laws, it seems to me, take the form of pronouncements that are either trivial because self-evident, or problematic.

Among the self-evident ones are the first law, which states that "literatures are never in non-interference", i.e. literatures and cultures do not exist in complete isolation; and the second one, which says that the pattern of contact between two cultures will not be exactly symmetrical in both directions; from this follows the third law, that "literary interference is not necessarily linked with other interferences on other levels between communities", meaning that literary contacts do not of necessity go together with contacts at other levels – which is merely a way of saying that grain imports, for instance, do not automatically generate literary imports.

If these are platitudes at best, the law stating that "a source literature is selected by dominance" strikes me as problematic. Even-Zohar here refers, among other things, to colonial powers dumping literary items on a colonized population. For example, "the fact that English and French dominated many literatures under their political influence is simply due to this influence" (1990:68). This is undoubtedly true. However, apart from the inept suggestion that the colonized 'select' the colonizer's literature as a source, the observation contradicts the previous 'law' which claimed that economic, political and military interference need not result in literary interference. According to the next law, "interference occurs when a system is in need of items unavailable within itself". In his comment Even-Zohar indicates, for once, that this unavailability is a matter of people within the culture perceiving such a need, rather than the researcher deciding the 'need' is an objective state of affairs. Still, it is hard to square this law with the comment provided with the previous one which explicitly allowed for the possibility of items being imposed on a community even against its will.

The final law takes in translation and related activities: "Appropriation tends to be simplified, regularized, schematized". Even-Zohar explains that this applies to "peripheral activities using a secondary repertoire", but then pulls the rug from under his own law by conceding that "the opposite is also true" and that relatively simple textual models borrowed from elsewhere may be elaborated upon "in a non-simplified, non-regularized, non-schematized context". In its original formulation this alleged universal was followed by a self-doubting question-mark (1978:53). Throwing caution to the wind in the later version has made for entertaining but either vacuous or highly questionable generalizations. Like Toury's probabilistic laws, Even-Zohar's universals do not set the blood racing, except with irritation.

Using polysystem theory as a toolkit for historical research seems a more profitable line. Here good use can be made of the theory's relational instincts. It invites the researcher to tease out relative positions, correlations, sites of conflict and competition leading to changes of position within a constellation and eventually to changes affecting entire constellations. As an illustration, let us now look at two related projects.

**Polysystems in Action**

The projects I have selected are among the most determined applications of polysystem theory. Both are concerned with French literature, in adjacent periods. Shelly Yahalom's work (1980, 1981) focuses on the eighteenth-century novel. Lieven D'hulst's book (1987) deals with French poetry before and during the Romantic era, and fits into the larger Leuven University research project to which I have referred in previous chapters. To do justice to these analyses we have to engage with them in some detail. This will take a little perseverance.

Yahalom, who acknowledges critical debts to Lotman as well as to Even-Zohar, seeks to account for changes in the French novel during the Neoclassical period. She does this by positioning the novel in relation to the canonized centre of the literary system and that system's multiform, frayed edges. The metaphor which underlies her analysis is that of a strategic military campaign: the novel and its practitioners – writers and publishers, mainly – first retreat from the powerful centre and then find ways to infiltrate and eventually destabilize it. The means chosen to wage this campaign, however, will also change the novel itself.

The point of departure is an imbalance, as Yahalom perceives it, in French Neoclassical literature. The most prestigious literary forms are serious drama and epic poetry, both of which are tightly regulated. Indeed the substantial increase in normative critical works at the time (think of Boileau's *Art poétique*, 1674) goes hand in hand with a canonized literary production consisting almost exclusively of norm-confirming, conservative, 'secondary' works. In addition, those who control the cultural centre-ground are directly associated with the political and ideological corridors of power in Paris. The result is the closure of social access to the cultural centre, with a corresponding narrowing of the social functions of canonized literature.

The simultaneous contraction and hyperstructuration of the centre stands in marked contrast to the rapid growth and the formal and ideological free-for-all of non-regulated works in the system's periphery. This is where the potential for renewal resides, as the periphery largely escapes regulation and remains open to outside influences. For Yahalom the imbalance between an increasingly rigid centre and a sprawling, dynamic periphery points to a system in a state of crisis.

The negative value judgements raining down on the novel from the strong-holds of the established poetics locate the novel in the periphery of the system. Viewed from the centre the novel is bad, even pernicious, in a moral as well as a literary sense. The novel stands for the opposite of literature, for 'anti-literature'. In the face of such hostility, writers and publishers of narrative prose fiction present the novel as 'non-literature', as existing not in the margins but altogether outside the literary system and thus beyond the reach of the centre's literary jurisdiction. This gesture creates an ambivalent inside-outside position which will allow the novel to tunnel its way back into the system's central parts. Translation plays an important role in these manoeuvrings, but always in tandem with other operations.

As regards translation Yahalom focuses on novels translated from English, and suggests two reasons why they present a useful option for French writers. One is that the foreign provenance of translated works means that the centre can adopt them, selectively, as constituting a 'natural' complement to its own carefully trimmed order. In this way translations remain relatively immune to the centre's norms. The other reason is that the periphery itself soaks up all manner of English texts, mostly novels, in large numbers and in a variety of ways. They significantly increase the pool of diversity there, and their foreign status facilitates acceptance into the more canonized areas of the French system. Pseudotranslations bear this out: by carrying the label 'translated from the English' a text may escape being perceived as a threat to the centre's prevailing norms and sneak into a more sheltered position.

Among the other strategies used to avoid censure is the presentation of fiction as authentic memoir and thus free from the norms of verisimilitude and decorum which apply to fiction. Various textual markers can be employed to stress authenticity and hence non-literariness: titles with the phrase 'written by *x* him/herself', paratextual statements condemning embellishment and stylization in the name of the plain truth, and so on. Yahalom notes that the significance of such markers lies not in their accuracy as descriptors of actual features of the works in question, but in their appeal to criteria distinguishing literature from non-literature (criteria such as fiction/non-fiction and natural/artificial). These techniques lend a substantial body of texts their ambivalent status, as genuine non-literary memoirs intermingle with semi-literary pseudo-memoirs or texts such as Rousseau's *Julie ou la Nouvelle Héloise* (1761) which send out signals in both directions at once.

The cross-overs between epistolary novels and (non-literary) manuals for letter-writing offer a good illustration of the overlap between the periphery of the literary system and other cultural systems. When letter-writing manuals present a range of different types of letters in a narrative sequence, they approach the model of the epistolary novel. At the same time the contents tables of some epistolary novels read like those in the manuals. Actual cross-overs occurred. The Abbé d'Aubignac's *Roman des lettres* of 1667 was re-issued in 1673 as a letter-writing manual; both editions, as it happens, appeared outside France.

The changing relation between the periphery and the centre of the literary system can be illustrated with reference to the integration of moral discourse into narrative texts. From the point of view of the prevailing canon the moral requirement is strong. One solution consists in introducing a moral element into a text in the form of meta-narrative comments, a series of separate moral reflections interrupting the story. This has a double advantage: the narrative now meets one of the centre's requirements, and it no longer needs to be exemplary or semi-allegorical itself. In this way the incorporation of moral commentary into prose fiction will open up new possibilities for plot and character development in narrative prose. Other narratives assimilate moral instruction by being modelled directly on the argumentative schemas of ethical guidebooks, sometimes virtually copying their tables of contents. In yet other cases the moral commentary is tied to the situation of a particular narrator, which renders its impact more relative because it is made to arise out of the particular circumstances of a particular individual. As a result, moral discourse itself will begin to show differentiation, which will have ramifications in other fields.

The point of Yahalom's analysis is that it documents and explains the emergence of textual models as part of a process of cultural semiosis. The admission of narrative prose fiction into the literary system will eventually transform the entire system when the novel captures the system's centre a century or so later. The analysis is conducted in terms of the relative position of various literary and non-literary text types and their struggle for the centre-ground. Yahalom envisages literature as consisting of a highly organized, prestigious centre and a more permissive periphery which is both more flexible than the centre and more likely to absorb a variety of extraneous models and features often via translation. In the examples she gives, such neglected forms as letter-writing manuals and moral guidebooks are shown to be directly relevant to the literary series. Change in a literary or cultural system occurs when new models manoeuvre themselves into new positions and the web of relations is altered. That process never stops. The attention to what happens in the margins of the literary system also means that a systems approach reaches parts other theories seldom reach, concerned as they mostly are with canonized texts only. Another point worth noting is that Yahalom's analysis makes no distinction in principle between intrasystemic relations, i.e. relations between various sections of one literary system, and intersystemic relations, whether these are within one language and culture (e.g. the literary system versus other cultural systems such as education or religion) or spanning different languages and cultures (e.g. French literature and English literature).

My second illustration, Lieven D'hulst's *L'évolution de la poésie en France (1780-1830)* (1987), is focused on poetry, and on a slightly later period. This is a detailed and demanding book, which comprises not only poetry and translation but also relations between poetry on the one hand and music and historiography on the other. I will pick out only a few moments which bear directly on translation but nevertheless shed light on the method of analysis as a whole.

D'hulst's approach, like Yahalom's, is rooted in Russian Formalism, with Even-Zohar's emphasis on multiple systems and Lotman's cultural semiotics as its modern extensions. The analysis is conducted in terms of binary oppositions: between canonical and non-canonical genres, dominant and non-dominant modes and models, the centre and periphery of a system, and innovative ('primary') and conservative ('secondary') forces. Their combination makes for complexity, while the preoccupation with models and positions rather than with actual texts and authors creates a daunting level of abstraction.

The focus is on intrasystemic conflict and 'intersystemic interference', processes seen in terms of interrelations between various strata of the poetic domain, between French and foreign poetry, and between literature and other cultural and social fields. Translation has its place in the context of these multiple and shifting relations. The aim is to understand how genres and entire literary systems develop. But D'hulst also realizes that his own point of view largely determines the selection of items he regards as relevant to his project, and that his description therefore remains partial. Since he wants to trace evolutionary processes, he directs his attention to ambivalent text types and peripheral models (1987:17, 21).

D'hulst conducts his analysis by means of a series of synchronic cross-sections, separating the translation of canonical from that of non-canonical foreign texts, and distinguishing in each case a dominant model of translation from a non-dominant model.

In the years 1780-1810, for instance, a relatively stable period, translations of canonical source texts furnish the larger part of the corpus and attract most critical comment by contemporaries. The dominant model for rendering these texts into French, verse translation, can be broken down into a series of hierarchically ordered rules. At the top of the list we find prescriptions to secure the use of regular alexandrines, periphrasis and rhyming couplets, all of which are designed to harness the translations to endogenous and canonical verse forms. Jacques Delille's verse translations of Milton's *Paradise Lost*, of Pope's *Rape of the Lock* and of Virgil's *Georgics* all faithfully resemble the genre of the French descriptive poem. Further down the list are less binding rules concerning, for example, the desirability of keeping the foreign original's generic label, or the insertion of linking phrases to tie a narrative together. Hesitations frequently occur in this area. Pierre Daru, who translates Horace, leaves the label 'Odes' in place but remarks that they are really songs or conversation pieces. The 'rudeness' of Homer's characters may be eliminated or recast after the more civil heroes of Virgil's *Aeneid*. On the whole, through both the selection and the particular handling of foreign texts, the dominant norms of verse translation reinforce the principles buttressing the canonical system of indigenous French poetry.

Prose translation of poetry constitutes the other, non-dominant model, and obeys its own rules. The prose translators aggressively champion 'literal exactitude' and insinuate that verse translation is imitation or paraphrase rather than proper translation because of the liberties it requires.

The translation of non-canonical source texts, less strictly regulated, exhibits more heterogeneity, especially in the verse translations. An unstable genre like the ballad is rendered in a variety of ways. Letourneur, who translates MacPherson's poems of Ossian into prose in 1777, says he omitted many of the comparisons, which he found tiresome, but refrained from assimilating the poem to French taste. In 1801 another translator, responding to Letourneur's version with his own in verse, speaks of mixed feelings for an original which strikes him as powerful and raw but also incoherent and repetitious; he claims that whereas Letourneur translated Ossian, he will now imitate him, attenuating the original's faults yet without changing its character (D'hulst 1987:67-68).

In surveying these various modes D'hulst points out that the model of verse translation clearly has its place within the canonical zone of the poetic system. It forms a parallel and contiguous canonical field, and offers the centre not only support against the ambitions of the periphery but also a 'dynamic reserve' (the term is Lotman's) which imitators can dip into. The verse translators of canonical texts enjoy prestige; many of them turn out to be leading poets. Prose translation on the other hand is correlated with canonical non-literary systems such as language and literature teaching or philosophy. Translations of non-canonical source texts fulfil contradictory roles. The verse renderings tend to tone down unacceptable aspects of the foreign texts, but especially the prose translations leave a gap between the imported texts and the endogenous poetic models. Here too a 'dynamic reserve' piles up, but this one contains many elements that cannot be assimilated into the French system. From this reserve new poetic models will spring.

After about 1810 translations of the newer, non-canonical foreign texts such as ballads, romances and popular songs become increasingly different from the endogenous models. Prose translation considerably strengthens its position when its norm of literal exactitude is rephrased as a demand for historical accuracy and authenticity, bringing a relaxation of the requirement to submit the foreign text to French stylistic norms. Translations now preserve repetitions, epithets and other such things which earlier verse translators found objectionable. In his version of Spanish romances Abel Hugo observes in 1822 that these "petits poêmes historiques" possess their own charm and so he must be excused the use of unusual idiom for the sake of faithfulness; an anonymous translator of popular Greek songs likewise holds that "their artlessness is their charm" (1987:102, 103). In the course of the 1820s verse translation loses prestige, prose translation becomes the dominant mode and the entire constellation is shifting. What used to be the non-canonical periphery of the poetic field has now gained so much weight and diversity that its innovative force propels it into open competition with the established centre. The next stage will come when this new dynamic 'primary' centre will develop conservative reflexes and another cycle can begin.

In D'hulst's summary of the changes in French poetry and poetic translation over the whole period (1987:159-60) we can taste the flavour of this type of analysis. He sees three stages. First, through the double mechanism of assimilation and rejection of non-canonical elements at the end of the eighteenth century the poetic centre retains its dominance vis-à-vis the periphery. This strategy produces fissures within the periphery, where non-canonical models develop; it also leads to contacts between these non-canonical models and other (non-literary and non-French) systems. In other words, intrasystemic oppositions trigger intersystemic contacts. The second stage witnesses the renewal of the non-canonical field, hesitant and heterogeneous at first, but showing more determination in the 1820s when the periphery produces ambivalent models at the intersection of different interfering systems, so that an intermediary system gradually takes shape. Around 1830, finally, the canonical poetic field is still intact, but it now has to reckon with the increasingly central position of the systems associated with the non-canonical periphery. However, the periphery, having grown into a dynamic primary centre, regenerates intrasystemic oppositions through a partially receptive attitude as regards ambivalent models which have become competitive, while at the same time it emphasizes the autonomy of the poetic system by attributing only subsidiary functions to intersystemic contacts.

Looking back on his method and its findings D'hulst observes that the systemic viewpoint, and the identification of different strata in the poetic field through it, has allowed him to disentangle such complex problems as the evolution of genres, the tension between tradition and innovation, and the connection between various oppositions and dislocations within the system. This means we can perceive poetic evolution as a structured process. Intrasystemic and intersystemic strategies are connected in the same way. Openness or closure to intersystemic interference is a function of the structure of the endogenous field; or, put differently: translation serves the needs of the recipient system or a particular section of it.

## Polysystem's Limitations

What are we to make of analyses like those of Yahalom and D'hulst, and of the underlying theory and methodology? As far as the analyses themselves are concerned, I think it is fair to say they are ingenious, intricate, wide-ranging, and bloodless. Several things spring to mind.

1    The approach via polysystems and cultural semiotics throws the field

of study wide open. By systematically placing canonized products and models in relation to a more fluid and pluriform periphery, a range of traditionally neglected texts and forms comes into view. Translation is recognized as a cultural practice interacting with other practices in a historical continuum. The workings of translation norms, the manipulative nature of translation and the effects of translation can all be slotted into a broader sociocultural setting. The study of translation becomes the study of cultural history. Broadly speaking the theory seems able to cope with this expansion, indeed it invites it.

2    However, as the last few pages have shown, studies of this nature are not only ferociously abstract and depersonalized, they also run the risk of being ultimately deterministic. There are two reasons for this. One is that polysystem theory is aware of the social embedding of cultural systems but in practice takes little heed of actual political and social power relations or more concrete entities such as institutions or groups with real interests to look after. For all its emphasis on models and repertoires, polysystem theory remains thoroughly text-bound. Literature and culture in general are described as sites of conflict, but the stakes remain invisible, and the struggle is waged by competing norms and models rather than by individuals or collectives who stand to gain or lose something by the outcome. As a result, the processes of change and reversal become self-propelling and cyclical: the canonized centre does what it does, and when it is overrun a new centre repeats the pattern, as if the whole thing were on automatic pilot.

The other reason follows from this. Polysystem theory invests heavily in classifications and correlations but shies away from speculating about the underlying causes of such phenomena as changes in genres, norms, and the concepts and collective practices of translation. As a result it is left with description and explanation both inhabiting the same space, creating the suggestion of literature and culture as autonomous series – an old Formalist idea. It is paradoxical that polysystem theory and cultural semiotics were instrumental in fostering the much-vaunted contextualization of translation, but that its applications have tended to refrain from locating the factors motivating literary or cultural developments, including developments in translation, in that context. The unwillingness to identify an engine which drives the historical machine means that what the researcher describes as the abstract structures and evolutionary changes determine each other, as if they existed in a free-floating bubble. Pierre Bourdieu's criticism of Russian Formalism and its polysystemic avatar is directed at precisely this point (1993:34-35).

3    The one opposition which injects historical dynamism into the system, that of 'primary versus secondary' models and activities, proves the

most problematic. It is based on an objectivist logic which interprets changing situations and competing practices as predetermined by their outcome. Whereas the 'centre versus periphery' and the 'canonical versus non-canonical' oppositions are, in principle at least, deduced from statements by actors in the system and from the control they wield over means of production and distribution, the 'primary versus secondary' opposition resembles the researcher's self-fulfilling prophecy. Primary (i.e. innovative) is what the benefit of hindsight permits us retrospectively to label as primary. This is, in Bourdieu's words, a way of "sliding from the model of reality into the reality of the model" (1990:39).

4  The pattern of binary oppositions with which polysystem theory operates, and their multiplication when a more complex field is studied, leads to highly structured accounts of systems which are themselves shown to be highly structured. The optical illusion is that the structuredness of the method produces the structuredness of the object. This is to a large extent inevitable, and D'hulst, for example, explicitly recognizes that the method creates its object. However, the fact that both Yahalom and D'hulst are obliged to acknowledge the ubiquity of ambivalent models and in-between systems suggests that the either/or logic of binarism can wrap itself around its object, envelop it, and still fail to accommodate it. In other words, the intricate picture which the method brings about is not only its own creation, it is at the same time reductive in its inability to discern anything except dual structures and oppositions. To the extent that translation research inspired by polysystem theory operates with mutually exclusive terms (something is either canonized or non-canonized, centre or periphery, source or target, etc.), it remains blind to all those ambivalent, hybrid, unstable, mobile, overlapping and collapsed elements that escape binary classification.

Of course, polysystem-inspired work comes in many shades and variations. The various essays which Maria Tymoczko, for example, has devoted to translations into English of Early Irish texts take account of their political and ideological environment at every step. The essays, now reworked into a book (Tymoczko 1999), recognize that translation is both shaped by and in turn helps to shape that environment. Rather than being a direct application of polysystem theory, though, this type of research takes off from it, and is in tune both with theorizing in a field like postcolonial studies, and with the way in which André Lefevere and others have tried out other system concepts more receptive to the social realities and ideological contexts of translation. These developments, which take us beyond polysystem theory and its literary ambience, are reviewed in the next chapter.

# 9. More Systems?

System theory is more than polysystem theory, and the Manipulation paradigm also operates with system concepts of more recent and more flexible manufacture. Some of the developments described in this and the next chapter attempt to overcome the limitations of polysystem theory, while others take on board concepts, issues and ideas employed in other branches of the human sciences.

I will sketch four such lines of development. The first is a matter of identifying new areas of research, which call for newer models and methods of investigation. As José Lambert became attracted to the modern mass media, where translation flourishes in weird and wonderful ways, he realized that the theoretical concepts of text-based, binary translation studies were proving increasingly inadequate and that additional tools might be needed. André Lefevere, for his part, channelled his unease about some key aspects of polysystem theory into an alternative construction which emphatically placed translation alongside other forms of 'rewriting' and attempted to deal more directly with the social and ideological overdetermination of translation.

The other two developments draw on models coming from sociology rather than from literary or translation studies. Both the French sociologist Pierre Bourdieu and his German colleague Niklas Luhmann have written at length on the sociology of culture – on literature in Bourdieu's case, on art and aesthetic theory in Luhmann's. Both characterize their way of thinking as relational, and both have inspired extensive research in cultural history and related subjects. While Bourdieu does not describe himself as a system theorist, citing his empirical impulse as the main obstacle, his concepts of 'field' and 'habitus' have been taken up in translation studies. Luhmann's work, resolutely theoretical and less widely known in the English-speaking world, represents a consistent application of modern systems theory to a range of social and cultural questions, taking account of what he regards as the 'new paradigm' in systems theory itself. For this reason I will give it slightly more space, and present it in a separate chapter.

## Mass Communication Maps

Although in the 1970s José Lambert initiated the Leuven research project of which Lieven D'hulst's book on French poetry translations was a product, he always remained more interested in asking questions than in supplying answers. Over the years the project spawned a number of larger and smaller case studies (see the Bibliography under Van Bragt, D'hulst and Lambert), followed by a 1,000-page bibliography (Van Bragt 1995), but despite several announcements (e.g. Lambert 1995a:98, 115) the grand synthesis is still to be published.

The project's complexity revealed both the strong points and the restrictions of polysystem theory. Nonetheless, Lambert has not been especially intent on shifting his theoretical base, and has distanced himself from the polysystem approach. When he voices criticism, he tactfully omits names. However he has consistently raised awkward questions, pointed to novel phenomena, and insisted on the need to remain undogmatic in tackling them. Perhaps his major contribution in this respect has been in drawing attention to the significance of translation in the mass media.

The subject is worth highlighting here, partly because of its sheer size and social relevance, partly because it has implications for theory and methodology, and partly because Lambert's publications in this area have not attracted as much notice as they perhaps deserve. As regards this latter point Lambert is his own worst enemy. Many of his articles are marred by woolly phrasing, circuitous statements and tortuous lines of argument. However, we can sum up his main points concerning translation, public discourse and the modern media with reference to a series of essays and papers published in different places in English, French and German (Lambert 1989, 1991a, 1993a, 1994, 1995a and 1995b; also Lambert & Delabastita 1996); the most important of these is the essay in German on 'literary and translational world maps' (1993a).

The opening of descriptive translation studies to audiovisual communication began in the 1980s and originally concentrated on such things as dubbing and subtitling in films and on TV (see Delabastita 1989; and above, Chapter 5). Lambert's contributions break new conceptual ground in two major respects. Firstly, he points to the complexity of contemporary international communication and to the range of translation phenomena occurring in it. Our traditional methods of studying translation, he argues, are not adequate to deal with this complexity. We need to push beyond binary oppositions, the idea of national cultures, or the neat equation of cultures with monolingual territories coinciding in turn with nation states. Secondly, he proposes that cartography may be better suited to the task than historiography, and offers suggestions towards a sociocultural geography of language processing in the modern world.

The kind of communication Lambert focuses on is characterized by its international nature, its use of multimedia technology, its relentless penetration into people's daily lives, and the fact that a relatively small number of senders reaches a very large number of receivers worldwide. Overall, Lambert advances four reasons why modern mass communication and international discourse matter to translation studies:

1   They make much more, and more varied, use of translation than is commonly thought. These texts and images enter our lives on a daily

basis, via the media, from newspapers and magazines to television and computers. Their sheer volume and their social and cultural impact are such that we cannot ignore them.

2    They often conceal the intervention of translation. For commercial or other reasons many translated texts do not want to flaunt their status as translations. This is fairly obvious in the case of advertisements, which may want to avoid being labelled as 'exogenous', or in, say, voice-overs in TV documentaries. But it also occurs, to an extent, in dubbed films, where dubbing can serve as an effective means of obscuring the foreign origin of a film or TV programme. This means not only that the volume of translation in the media is greater than may appear at a first glance, but that it is worth inquiring into when, where, why and by whom translations are consistently rendered so discreet as to escape the consumer's notice.

3    They do not necessarily translate entire texts, but may use a combination of partial translation and original text production, so that translation occurs in dispersed and fragmented form. As a result, all kinds of snippets and remnants of translation percolate from public into private discourse. Think, for example, of the vocabulary of European Union directives or of international finance, the terminology of fashion and psychoanalysis in English, computer and sports jargon in numerous languages other than English, all of them shot through with translations, calques, borrowings and loanwords. Translation studies should deal with such fragmentary translations as well as with complete texts.

4    They often produce translations via numerous intermediate stages and make no clear distinction between translation and operations like adaptation, editing, imitation and so on. Documents in several languages may be drafted simultaneously and in mutual consultation rather than with reference to a single identifiable source text (Schäffner 1997 traces a set of EU documents illustrating this procedure). These techniques call into question the traditional concepts of translation studies, and even its object of study.

If we want to analyze phenomena of this type and calibre, Lambert argues, we need to rethink our concepts and methods. A Toury-style empiricism which regards as translation what is called translation or what we have reasonable grounds to assume is translated, becomes inadequate when confronted with systematically concealed and fragmented translations. When texts are moulded and manipulated via any number of intermediary versions and stages, it is no longer relevant to speak in terms of 'source' and 'target', let alone that translations could be 'facts of one system only'. Binary models, postulates, neatly delineated systems and the idea of translations as complete texts cannot cope with the hybrid nature of many of the operations in these types of discourse. Perhaps cartography can.

In an earlier essay Lambert (1991a) had derided the association of national cultures with homogeneous national languages and nation states. They reflected a nineteenth-century Eurocentric view, kept alive only by the fact that to this day most research is still organized and financed along national lines. If we begin to map languages and language use, including so-called minority languages, we obtain a very different territorial picture. If we go on to design multiple maps showing in some detail where, in a city like Brussels, for instance, French and Dutch and English and Arabic are spoken by which community, in which environment (workplace, school, shops, home), for what kind of transaction and even at what time of day, we start to see differentiation, complexity and shifting patterns. Parts of India and Africa, where multilingualism is the norm, would lend themselves to similar but vastly more complex mapping, on a macro-scale.

This type of multiple map-making, Lambert claims, has been put to good use elsewhere, by sociologists, sociolinguists, social geographers, anthropologists and others. He suggests cartography is in fact more flexible than historiography. Whereas historians tend to privilege single story lines, mapmakers can stack, multiply and combine maps. He mentions other advantages. We can design maps to show the material channels of distribution for translated and other texts, the financial flows, the part of translation versus non-translation in written and spoken, public and private communication, in short the economic as well as the sociocultural geography of translation. For Lambert, non-translation matters in this context. If we want to know what kind of problem is being solved by translation, we also have to ask what other solutions are available – solutions such as bilingualism, selective multilingualism, or the reliance on a lingua franca or on pictorial symbols, for example.

In discussing the relevance of textual imports and exports, Lambert draws attention to questions of power, control and dependence. He formulates several general hypotheses. One of them states that a society which exports non-translated texts is in a position of power vis-à-vis the receiving society. Also, the more a society imports without a counterbalancing volume of exports, the more it tends to be unstable; and vice versa, the more a society exports, the more stable it will be, at least with respect to the receiving system or systems. But the more a society imports from a single source, the more it will find itself in a position of dependency vis-à-vis that source.

These are social and political issues. For Lambert, the importance and urgency of conducting research into mass communication systems is a matter of recognizing that this form of communication substantially re-draws what he calls 'discursive identities', the often multiple and complex sense of identity built up in and through discourse when we speak of politics, of education, of art, sports, religion and so on. Different and overlapping international media discourses infiltrate our usage and speech patterns all the time. That process entails the importation of values. As we watch imported films, videos, advertisements and TV programmes, Lambert observes, "we don't just import stories, we also import culture, language and values" (1993:102). Since the mass media affect and alter value systems, the occurrence of translation in this context is also of political and ideological relevance.

Lambert's mapping proposal would be worth trying out in practice. But we should perhaps see cartography as a supplement to rather than as a replacement of historiography. Maps can show distributions, quantities and flows, but not motives, reasons or causes. They can visualize but not explain. More thought will also need to be given to the practicalities of mapping techniques, about which Lambert has had nothing to say. Social network analysis may be of use here. It has already been applied in empirical literary studies to explore such things as relations between material production centres (publishers, magazines), personal connections, and groupings around literary programmes and styles (De Nooy 1991 provides a first orientation). Anthony Pym's *Method in Translation History* (1998) uses network concepts in connection with translation but, surprisingly, without any reference to the theoretical literature available on the subject. Another line of research, closer to the world of mass communication, might take its cue from models of gate-keeping between and within organizations (Vuorinen 1997).

Lambert's comments on the mass media explicitly recognize the complex conditioning factors of translation and various similar operations, things the polysystem approach was aware of but rarely managed to lift into view. André Lefevere's articles and books show a more pronounced emphasis on the ideological and sociocultural conditioning of translation – which may explain why his work has found more resonance with contemporary researchers in literary and cultural studies. Lefevere, like Lambert, presents a world in which texts are constantly being remoulded, overhauled and recycled for various purposes and under various constraints. The picture does not quite amount to a postmodern hall of mirrors and simulacra without a trace of any 'originals', but it certainly highlights both the quantitative and the qualitative significance of these 'refractions' for the perception and transmission of cultural goods.

## System, Ideology and Poetics

In Lefevere's work the frame of reference is again primarily literary, although broader applications can be derived from it. His essays and books, breezier than most, proved eminently readable, bristling with well-chosen, lively examples. A mercurial personality, he was prolific, polemical, provocative and ready to experiment. His work is also frequently superficial, inconsistent, and sloppy (Hermans 1993).

Lefevere's first book, *Translating Poetry: Seven Strategies and a Blue-*

*print* (1975), fleshed out the forms of verse translation and the translation of verse form which James Holmes had cast into formulae and diagrams in the 1960s (Holmes 1988:23-33; see Chapter 2). It was unashamedly prescriptive, viewed literary translation in terms of losses and gains, and sought to identify a minimum-damage option from a range stretching from phonemic translation to imitation. Of interest with regard to his later views was Lefevere's insistence that language is merely one of the problems translators have to contend with; other problems are rooted in what he abbreviated as 'tpt', or 'time, place and tradition', the sociocultural positioning of the original and its subsequent dislocation in translation.

His contribution to the seminal 1976 Leuven colloquium was peculiar. In 'Translation Studies: the Goal of the Discipline', a one-page Appendix tagged on to the published proceedings, he declared that "[t]he goal of the discipline is to produce a comprehensive theory which can also be used as a guideline for the production of translations" (1978a:234), which ran exactly counter to the non-prescriptive, historicizing direction the colloquium generally had been taking. His actual paper sought to demonstrate that "translation, as a meta-literary discipline, is better suited to make literary products accessible, and can claim a higher degree of scientificity, than the other metaliterary activity, commentary" (1978:7). It brought Stephen Toulmin and Karl Popper, inter-subjective testability and a critique of logical positivism and hermeneutics to bear on that unprepossessing thesis. He repeated the exercise in his *Literary Knowledge* (1977), a slight and bizarre book, ill-tempered, barely known and best forgotten.

He turned a corner in the early 1980s. His theoretical interests made him receptive to Even-Zohar's polysystem proposal, but he soon moved on to other propositions, taking in General System Theory (Von Bertalanffy 1971) as he went along. He criticized polysystem theory on several grounds: it tended to be essentialist, i.e. to behave as if systems really existed; it was too fond of jargon and diagrams and the rest of the "scientistic panoply"; the opposition between 'primary' and 'secondary' activities was superfluous; and its abstract categories were not sufficiently amenable to concrete research (1983: 193-94).

As a consequence, Lefevere consciously differentiated his own systems concept from Even-Zohar's, and devised his own categories and terms. The most important of these are patronage, ideology, poetics and 'universe of discourse'. Terminology apart, the main difference between Lefevere's and Even-Zohar's concepts lies in Lefevere's greater emphasis on interaction between system and environment, on the system's internal organization and on control mechanisms. A further feature of Lefevere's thinking is that he insists on viewing translation as a particular mode of a broader practice which at first he termed 'refraction' and subsequently 'rewriting' – terms which were meant to correspond roughly to what Anton Popovič had called 'metatexts' (1992a:13; see Chapter 2).

Lefevere developed his ideas about systems and the place of 'rewriting' in them over a period of about fifteen years. The first full presentation occurs in 'Why Waste Our Time on Rewrites' (1985), which was taken further in 'The Dynamics of the System: Convention and Innovation in Literary History' (1989). He summed up his position and demonstrated its potential to guide research in *Translation, Rewriting and the Manipulation of Literary Fame* (1992). Throughout, he remained emphatic that the concept of 'system' should be taken as no more than a heuristic model, a cognitive metaphor (1983: 191), "a map to make sense of a territory" (1984:91).

The broad idea is that society can be viewed as a conglomerate of systems, of which literature is one. Leaving the nature of the overarching social system for what it is, Lefevere concentrates on the literary subsystem. This literary system possesses a double control mechanism. One mechanism governs it largely from the outside, and secures the relations between literature and its environment. Here the key words are patronage and ideology. The other keeps order within the literary system, and here the operative terms are poetics and a somewhat less well defined group referred to variously as 'experts', 'specialists', 'professionals' and also 'rewriters'.

Patronage is defined as "the powers (persons, institutions) which can further or hinder the reading, writing and rewriting of literature" (1992:15). Power, Lefevere reminds us, is to be understood in the pervasive Foucaultian sense. Patronage can be exerted by individuals, groups, institutions, a social class, a political party, publishers, the media, etc. As a regulatory body, patronage sees to it that the literary system does not fall out of step with the rest of society. It consists of three components. The ideological component determines what the relation between literature and other social systems is supposed to be. By means of the economic component the patron assures the writer's livelihood. The status component means that the patron can confer prestige and recognition. Patronage is undifferentiated when all three components are concentrated in one hand or institution, as under totalitarian regimes; it is differentiated when they are not, for example when commercial success does not necessarily bring status.

Patronage is mostly interested in ideology, understood as the dominant concept of what society should be, or can be allowed to be (1992:14). Earlier Lefevere had defined ideology simply as 'world view' (1985:226), but he also refers approvingly to Fredric Jameson's concept of ideology as "that grillwork of form, convention and belief which orders our actions" (1992:16), which itself is so wide as to comprise everything Yury Lotman's cultural semiotics might term 'culture'. In one of his last essays he described ideology as "the conceptual grid that consists of opinions and attitudes deemed acceptable in a certain society at a certain time, and through which readers and translators approach texts" (1998:48). Definitions were not Lefevere's forte. Anyway, being interested primarily in ideology, patronage rarely intervenes directly in the literary system. Instead it tends to delegate control of the literary field to groups which operate within it. They consist of 'experts' such as critics, reviewers, teachers, anthologists and also translators (1985:226). Their task is to secure the system's ideology and its poetics.

For Lefevere, poetics is the dominant concept of what literature should be, or can be allowed to be, in a given society (1992:14). He also thinks of it as a code which makes literary communication possible (1985:229). A poetics consists of an inventory component (devices, genres, motifs, prototypical characters, situations and forms) and a functional component. The latter is described as "an idea of how literature has to, or may be allowed to, function in society" (1982:6) or "a concept of what the role of literature is, or should be, in the social system as a whole" (1992:26). This definition makes the functional component identical with the poetics as such. It may be better to think of a poetics along the lines proposed by Douwe Fokkema and Elrud Ibsch (1987), as consisting of an inventory of elements, a syntactic component (rules for combining elements from the inventory) and a pragmatic aspect, which tells writers when certain elements can or should be deployed. This is entirely compatible with Lefevere's concept.

Patrons and literary experts, ideology and poetics control the literary system, and therefore the production and distribution of literature. Not only literary texts are produced under these constraints, so are 'refractions', or 'rewritings', including translations. Lefevere first took 'refraction' to mean "the adaptation of a work of literature to a different audience, with the intention of influencing the way in which that audience reads the work" (1982:4). Later it was

> any text produced on the basis of another with the intention of adapting
> that other text to a certain ideology (the fascist Schiller, for example, as
> a 'brother in arms of the Führer', or the Hamlet who suffers from an
> Oedipus complex) or to a certain poetics (Voltaire's *Othello* in alexan-
> drines and minus Desdemona's offensive handkerchief) and, usually,
> to both.  (1984:89)

As the reference to Hamlet shows, ideology is taken in a very broad sense. 'Refraction' gave way to 'rewriting' in 1985.

Rewriting includes such operations as translation, criticism, reviewing, summary, adaptation for children, anthologizing, making into a comic strip or TV film, and so on, in short any processing of a text whether in the same or another language or in another medium. Subsuming translation under other forms of text processing, and insisting that they ought to be studied together, Lefevere recognizes that a great deal of cultural transmission, and hence much of our cultural knowledge, is based not on direct contact with 'originals' but on the various 'rewritings' in circulation. As he puts it: "In the US he or she will tell you that *Moby Dick* is a great novel [...] because he has been told so in school, because she has read comic strips and extracts in anthologies, and because Captain Ahab will forever look like Gregory Peck as far as he or she is concerned" (1982:16-17). Rewritings are of crucial social and cultural relevance because they determine the 'image' of a literary work when direct access to that work is limited or nonexistent. Maria Tymoczko (1995) has stressed the relevance of this idea in an essay about translations from smaller languages especially, arguing that the selection of texts and the particular mode of representation create an image which readers across the world take metonymically to stand for that culture as a whole.

All rewriting, then, takes place under the constraints of patronage, ideology and poetics. Heine could not be anthologized in Nazi Germany because he was Jewish. The Arabic *qasida* has no equivalent in Western poetic forms. To these constraints Lefevere adds another, 'universe of discourse', a concept which is not well integrated into the rest of the theory and defined vaguely as "the knowledge, the learning, but also the objects and the customs of a certain time, to which writers are free to allude in their work" (1985:232-33). Later Lefevere would speak of a 'cultural script', being "the accepted pattern of behavior expected of people who fill certain roles in a certain culture" (1992: 89). In an essay written jointly with Susan Bassnett and published after his death the reference is to a 'textual grid', "the collection of acceptable ways in which things can be said" (Bassnett & Lefevere 1998:5). The concept appears to straddle ideology and poetics; it is perhaps best thought of in terms of the modalities of normative force governing enunciations (prescriptions, proscriptions, preferences and permissions), as discussed in Chapter 6.

Translation, like other forms of rewriting, has to reckon with these constraints. It involves one extra constraint, language, which Lefevere demonstratively puts at the bottom of the list. Indeed most of his essays, and nearly all of his case studies and examples, are designed to illustrate the importance of patronage, ideology, poetics, "textual grids" and "conceptual and generic grids" (Bassnett & Lefevere 1998:49) at the expense of the language factor. Translation offers a privileged object of study, he contends, because it shows the workings of all these constraints more clearly than most other forms of rewriting. But it needs to be studied in conjunction with them, for they all partake in the packaging, remodelling, manipulation, construction and transmission of cultural goods (1991:143). Given the volume and significance of these refractions, not least in the mass media, the social and cultural relevance of studying them will be obvious.

Lefevere emphasizes that constraints are conditioning factors, not absolutes. Individuals can choose to go with or against them. Translators, too, can decide to defer to the powers that be, or foment opposition, be it poetic or political. Because translation means importation of goods from beyond the system's boundaries, it is always potentially subversive, which is why it tends to be heavily regulated (1985:237). In his case studies, however, Lefevere focused mostly on translations as merely reflecting the impact of a dominant poetics or ideology and therefore as providing little more than "an unfailing barometer of literary fashions" (1991:129). This barely takes us beyond, say, Reuben Brower's 'Seven Agamemnons' essay of 1959, which sought to demonstrate that translations of poetry "show [us] in the baldest form the assumptions about poetry shared by readers and poets" (1959a:175). It rarely grants translation more than a passive role, instead of seeing it as simultaneously determined and determining. The one-sidedness may stem from Lefevere's tendency to flit from one case study to another without ever digging very deep, but perhaps also from an inconsistency in his own theory. As we saw above, he puts rewriters, including translators, with the 'experts' who form part of the control mechanism of the literary system. But we are simultaneously to imagine the system as accommodating both writing and rewriting. This leaves it unclear whether rewriting is part of the system or of the system's control mechanism.

A similar and more important question may be raised regarding the status of Lefevere's own rewriting of translation. Criticism, like translation, is described as rewriting, but scholarly study and analysis are apparently something different. This is because criticism goes in for "the rough and tumble of the development of a literary system" (1985:219); it seeks to influence and manipulate. One of the good things about Deconstructionist criticism, he remarks, is that it puts criticism "squarely where it belongs: with literature, not with any kind of analysis of literature as a social phenomenon" (ibid.). By contrast, scholarly study, analysis and theory "would try to explain how both the writing and the rewriting of literature are subject to certain constraints, and how the interaction of writing and rewriting is ultimately responsible [...] for the evolution of a given literature" (ibid.). The distinction is similar to the one he had made a year earlier between 'refractive' and 'descriptive' translations (1984:93-94). The former seek to influence literary development, the latter merely serve as heuristic tools enabling access to foreign works. But just as Lefevere immediately concedes that each translation is a bit of both, it seems hard to maintain a neat distinction between critical and 'translational' rewriting on the one hand, and the scholarly rewriting of literature and translation on the other. In the cultural studies and postcolonial context to which Lefevere's work points, this separation between object-level and meta-level seems especially problematic.

Most of Lefevere's case studies highlight the power of patronage exercised through ideological constraints. They leave underexposed the fact that these constraints must operate within and through specific social and institutional structures. Equally underexposed is another aspect of the power relations affecting translation: that of the translator's loyalty and reliability. This aspect makes us appreciate the strategic importance of translators having access to information unavailable, or not easily available, to their clients. Especially in situations where translators are in short supply, controlling their activities amounts to acquiring a monopoly on information and knowledge. It also helps us to understand why translators who have exclusive or near-exclusive access to information otherwise unavailable to those in power tend to be closely supervised and vetted for political loyalty. Let me illustrate the issue with a couple of examples not from literary translation but from the history of interpreting.

The crucial importance of the political reliability of interpreters during the European reconnaissance and conquest of America has been discussed before (e.g. Delisle & Woodsworth 1995). The case of La Malinche, the woman who interpreted for Cortés during the Spanish conquest of Mexico, is well known. But already Columbus's own diary (or rather its reconstruction, as the original is lost) affords tantalizing insight into the tension between the European need to gain information and the native interpreters' own agenda. Scarcely six weeks after first sighting the island of Guanahaní, as he set about exploring neighbouring islands with the help of half a dozen natives captured on Guanahaní, Columbus realized he could not trust his captive interpreters: some of them escaped, others appeared to tell lies in desperate efforts to return home. He concluded that some of his own people would need to learn the local languages if he was going to have reliable interpreters (see the diary entries for 27 November 1492: "I often misunderstand what these Indians I have on board tell me, and I do not trust them, for they have tried repeatedly to escape. But now, God willing [...] I shall have all the language taught to one of my people"; and on 6 December: "The Indians I have brought with me [...] now distrust me so much for not making for their homeland that I have no faith in what they tell me"; Cummins 1992:84, 89).

Similar events and episodes occurred elsewhere. Japan remained hermetically closed to foreigners for two hundred years (*ca.* 1640-1850), except for the tiny Dutch trading post on the artificial island of Deshima, off Nagasaki. All the interpreters were Japanese government officials, and their activities were strictly controlled. The arrangement gave the Japanese authorities a decisive advantage. Not only was all incoming information processed by interpreters whose loyalty to the Japanese side was ensured, but the Dutch, whose movements were severely restricted, were effectively prevented from learning Japanese and gathering data about the country (Engels 1998). This power balance, incidentally, contradicts Lambert's hypothesis that a society which imports only from a single source tends to be unstable and finds itself in a position of dependency vis-à-vis the donor.

One of the best illustrations of the importance of the loyalty of interpreters concerns the decree issued by the French Council of State on 18 November 1669, ordering the establishment of a training institute for interpreters between French and Turkish. The decree, signed by Louis XIV's minister Jean-Baptiste Colbert, stipulates that the interpreters, who are to be trained from a tender age, must be French nationals and will be in the care of French Capuchin monks in Constantinople and Smyrna, "so that in future we can be assured of the fidelity of the interpreters and dragomans" ("afin qu'à l'avenir on puisse être assuré de la fidélité des drogmans et interprètes"; *Enfants de langue* 1995:20). The use of the word 'fidélité' throws interesting light on the notion of fidelity in translation history. It gestures to the same sense of political reliability which William Jones presumably had in mind when, in the preface to his *Grammar of the Persian Language* of 1771, he stressed the need for British East India Company officials to learn the languages of Asia because "it was found highly dangerous to employ the natives as interpreters, upon whose fidelity they could not depend" (in Naranjana 1992:16).

## Translation as Field and Habitus

In one of his last, posthumously published essays (Bassnett & Lefevere 1998:41-56), Lefevere discussed a number of English translations of Virgil's *Aeneid*, from the seventeenth to the nineteenth century. He pointed out that many of these were ostensibly addressed to readers who had probably learnt some Latin in school but may not have made much use of it in later years. Since Latin represented high culture, translations of the *Aeneid* gave readers renewed access, or in some cases first-time access, to this benchmark text. The translations generally did not seek to replace the original but to supplement it. Lefevere also speculates that especially the ascendant middle classes were eager to use translations to gain cultural respectability on a par with the aristocracy.

The essay itself phrases its argument in terms of Pierre Bourdieu's notion of 'cultural capital', understood as the means to acquire and maintain cultural status among those who enjoy similar status. Lefevere's use of Bourdieu is interesting, not only because it represents the last stage in his development, but because other researchers, too, have increasingly turned to Bourdieu's sociology of culture in their search for models to discuss translation in its social context. As mentioned earlier, Bourdieu is not a system theorist. The degree to which his approach can be construed as agreeing with system theory remains a moot point. While his insistence on the relational nature of his thinking provides an obvious point of overlap (Bourdieu 1994:17), in his own estimation the empirical urge underlying his work separates him from system theory, which he regards as based on an organicist, totalizing philosophy. A prominent system theorist like Siegfried Schmidt, on the other hand, has pointed out the striking similarities between Bourdieu's concepts and those of system theory. He argued for their compatibility, and tried to correct Bourdieu's perception of system theory as organicist (see the discussion in

Bourdieu et al. 1991). For Alain Viala, who has extensively applied Bourdieu's concepts to literary studies, rephrasing Bourdieu in system-theoretical terms would also be unproblematic (1997:65). This debate continues. In the following paragraphs I will concentrate on two lines of approach which take their cue from Bourdieu. One concentrates on genre and history, the other on the translator.

In a couple of recent essays the Canadian researcher Jean-Marc Gouanvic (1997, 1997a) has employed Bourdieu's notions of 'fields' and of homologies between social and cultural fields to explain the migration of one particular genre, science fiction, by means of translation. Gouanvic's methodology is grounded in a critique of polysystem theory, which in his opinion pays insufficient attention to the social functions of cultural products. We can also see it as addressing a weakness in Lefevere's approach, which talks in general terms about ideology but underplays the role of institutions. According to Gouanvic, the sociology of culture as developed by Bourdieu can remedy these shortcomings because it consistently combines the semiotic with the social.

Bourdieu himself introduced the key notions of 'field' and 'habitus' in an attempt to overcome two dangers which, as he sees it, threaten research in the human sciences: naive teleological or 'finalist' thinking, which sees the end of a known process as illuminating the path towards that goal, and mechanistic determinism, which interprets processes as the inevitable unravelling of a set of initial conditions (1977:72ff.). Bourdieu's concept of 'field' bears some resemblance to the notion of system. It can be understood as a structured space with its own laws of functioning, its structure being determined by the relations between the positions which agents occupy in the field (1993:6). Gouanvic speaks of it as a "place or context where a certain set of orientations, dispositions and self-justifications are considered legitimate" (1997a:142). A field however is also a site of competition and struggle, with as its ultimate stake the authority to define the field itself, its values and its boundaries. The term 'habitus' stands for "a system of durable, transposable dispositions", of "internalized structures, common schemes of perception, conception and action"; the result of inculcation and habituation, the habitus is simultaneously structured and structuring, and directed towards practice (Bourdieu 1990:53-60).

Gouanvic has studied the emergence and evolution of science fiction as a genre in French culture in the postwar period. Following Bourdieu he regards the texts in question as cultural products entering into the logic of a cultural marketplace, where they possess material but also symbolic value. Cultural goods, that is, are at once commodities with an economic price tag, and symbolic goods. In the field of cultural production it is primarily status and prestige, or 'symbolic capital', which is to be accumulated and traded. French science fiction feeds on translations of American originals, and Gouanvic will read this translated status as constituting a particular form of cultural capital.

Gouanvic's object of study, then, consists of the science fiction genre viewed as a 'field' in Bourdieu's sense, a space where agents occupy certain positions and, through their actions, take up further positions as they struggle for dominance. His analysis traces the way in which, in the early 1950s, a small group of non-conformist writers including Boris Vian and Raymond Queneau successfully launched science fiction as a 'translated' genre in France, in the teeth of denunciations by establishment figures like Michel Butor, Arthur Koestler and François Truffaud. Crucial to the genre's success were two sociocultural 'homologies', or structural similarities. Firstly, there existed in both France and the United States groups of readers receptive to the genre. The homology here concerns the composition of these groups: both were lower middle class, and technophile. Secondly, in the course of the 1950s French publishers and aficionados put in place a production and distribution system for the genre homologous to the one created in the US in the 1920s and '30s. This material infrastructure comprised specialized outlets, book series and magazines, in the margins of more canonical literary forms.

At the time, Vian and Queneau already enjoyed a literary reputation, and hence 'legitimacy', which placed them in a stronger position when they deployed a combination of translations and critical essays to introduce American science fiction texts as 'a new genre' in 1951. The decisive factor however was the genre's aura of 'Americanness'. The cultural prestige, or 'cultural capital', of postwar America as perceived in France meant that the translations could be emphatically marketed as based on American originals. In the postwar years American cultural dominance became evident in other sectors too, from popular culture to translations and re-translations of older canonical writers such as Nathaniel Hawthorne and Henry James. In science fiction this hegemony has continued to the present day. Whereas Vian and Queneau were originally attracted to science fiction in part because it offered possibilities for social criticism, the subsequent wholesale 'americanization' of the genre represents a displacement of those stakes which we can understand by considering the genre's social function.

In his conclusion Gouanvic stresses that in studying translation we need to look not only at translators but at all the agents involved and at the entire field, including production, distribution, consumption and critical meta-discourses, taking account of both translated and non-translated texts, and of the social function of a given genre. Linking social groups with genres is crucial, he argues, because the struggle for symbolic power is concerned less with individual texts than with classes and types of text which relate to the interests of certain groups occupying certain positions in the field.

The principal gain in this type of study consists in its marrying of the genre-specific and the social via the idea of homologies. It may be worth inquiring, though, just how much Gouanvic's homologies actually explain, and which ones are required for an explanation. Pointing to the middle-class and technophile nature of a section of the French reading public, for example, does not account for their preference for specifically American products, and the postwar French admiration for things American does not possess a homologous counterpart on the American side of the Atlantic. Other explanations may be possible (what were the technophile French middle classes reading before science fiction was served up?). Clearly, more work will need to be done to demonstrate the superior power of this line of reasoning over existing ones. But the potential is undoubtedly there, and as a complement to Lefevere's rather unwieldy notion of patronage the emphasis on fields and institutions opens up promising directions.

Daniel Simeoni (1998) has explored the usefulness of Bourdieu's notion of habitus for translation studies, linking the idea of a specific 'translating habitus' with the concept of norms. His contribution modifies the norms concept, and suggests specific topics for further empirical research.

Simeoni picks his starting point some way off, in the generalized, social habitus which Norbert Elias characterized back in 1939 as 'embodied social learning' and which Bourdieu described in the 1970s as a set of 'dispositions'. Like social conventions and norms, this generalized habitus constitutes for Simeoni the "pivot around which systems of social order revolve" (1998: 24). In addition to this, translators develop a more specific, professional habitus geared to the practical requirements of the task. Learning to translate means refining a social habitus into a specialized habitus. In this respect Simeoni is intrigued by the self-image of 'voluntary servitude' which translators appear to develop. Are translators born subservient, do they acquire subservience, or do they have subservience thrust upon them? Simeoni looks for answers in two directions.

Firstly, translation is a heteronomous activity in that it always caters for other fields and is therefore oriented towards these client fields, be they agriculture, cookery books, banks, literature or the medical profession. Whereas Bourdieu could analyze how, for example, literature emerged in the nineteenth century as an autonomous field with its own rules and values, in Simeoni's view translation displays no such internal organization and at best constitutes a pseudo- or would-be field. Translators obey the discursive and other rules pertaining to the client field, hence their submissiveness.

Secondly, the habitus concept stresses not only the structured but equally the structuring character of the 'habitual' practice of translating. Just as following a norm reinforces that norm, submissive translators play into the hands of custom and order. The reverse side of this coin is that translators can govern norms as much as they are governed by them. Although Simeoni stops well short of endorsing it, there would seem to be an opening here for self-conscious, resistant translation of the type Lawrence Venuti (1995) advocates.

Simeoni discerns several possibilities for empirical translation research using the habitus concept. We could gain insight into the 'sociogenesis' of translating practices by focusing on the cultural group in which a translator received his or her training, and tracing the inculcation of a specialized habitus. The psychological study of translators at work could make good use of the concept as well. The important point here, Simeoni notes, is not to reduce the translator's habitus to a collection of purely intellectual skills or a mindset. It is an embodied, somatic disposition comprising an affective as well as a cognitive dimension. This makes it an eminently suitable tool to investigate, for instance, how translators tackle texts they regard as 'difficult', what they experience as 'difficult' or what creates tension in a translator's daily routine. Being a 'subject-grounded category' (Simeoni 1998:29), the habitus idea should prove useful to researchers interested in the translation process as such and to those in favour of paying more attention to real-life translators and their working environments than to impersonal norm systems. For all that, habitus need not be in competition with norms concepts. Since the latter encompass also the patterns of expectation alive in a community or a field, they may be better suited to explain how translations fare once they leave the translator's desk and, more broadly, to explicitate historical concepts of translation.

Two other points are worth making. Simeoni's emphasis on the 'bodily inscription' of the translator's routines offers a pertinent corrective to the somewhat skeletal notion of norms. It also happens to be entirely in line with what the philosopher Charles Taylor said in 1992 about what it means 'to follow a rule'. Taylor welcomed Bourdieu's habitus concept precisely because it incorporated – and this is the right word here – lived experience and bodily comportment, including the degree of suspense and uncertainty which goes with the enactment of rules. In this connection Taylor (1992:183) underlined the relevance of Aristotle's notion of *phronèsis*, a situated, practical understanding of the particulars of a given situation. The notion would seem to identify an essential aspect of the way in which the translator's habitus works on a specific context. Taylor's cautionary observation that there is a crucial 'phronetic gap' between the concrete enactment of a disposition, or norm, or rule, and its formulation or representation, deserves to be taken to heart as well.

I wonder if, or to what extent, Simeoni's scepticism as regards the existence of a 'field of translation' is justified. Translation, Simeoni argues, is heteronomous, obedient to client systems, therefore lacking in the kind of autonomy manifested, for instance, by the literary field as constructed by Bourdieu for nineteenth-century France. It can be objected to this that such a comparison is not very helpful. The autonomy of the literary field is a construction like any other, and remains relative. No one produces or consumes 'literature' *per se*, but texts which involve themes, ideas, situations and motifs which are of relevance also outside literature. When literary works are suppressed or censored, it is usually not for purely literary reasons. Since 'literariness' cannot readily be isolated, and individuals as well as institutions in the literary field as elsewhere act according to interlocking logics, autonomy and heteronomy must go together. It is not immediately obvious why this would not hold for translation as well. On the contrary, it provides a good reason to investigate how translation could be thought of as a 'field' or a 'system' in its own right. If translation was wholly heteronomous and translators naturally subservient, would there be any need to exercise the tight controls over the interpreters we met at the end of the previous section?

Grounds for suggesting a field of translation may be found to the extent that, inadvertently or not, concepts of translation are often formulated in general terms; that we can witness discussions about the 'constitutive' norms of translation, and about the need to distinguish between translation and other operations felt to be similar but different and therefore differently labelled; that we encounter rivalling translations in which the rivalry is focused on modes of representation rather than on genre-bound categories; that translators' associations issue codes of conduct purporting to apply to any and all forms of translation; that translator training institutes claim to foster general as well as subject-specific translation skills. After all, when Timothy Buck denies Helen Lowe-Porter's versions of Thomas Mann the status of translations, the disagreement is not only about Thomas Mann but also about translation, and about who decides what translation is. In the following chapter I will sketch one possible way of conceptualizing translation in terms of a social system. The theoretical model will derive, not from Bourdieu, but from Niklas Luhmann.

# 10. Translation as System

As I remarked at the beginning of the previous chapter, there are obvious similarities between Bourdieu and Luhmann. Both have proved prolific, innovative, controversial, and influential well beyond their sociological specialism. Both are primarily concerned with the functioning of modern industrialized society and its subdivisions, including culture. They are relational thinkers, acutely aware of theoretical and methodological issues. Neither has written about translation, but both, Bourdieu more than Luhmann, have in recent years seen their ideas taken up by translation researchers.

The differences between them are no less obvious. If Bourdieu is a sociologist with an anthropological strain, Luhmann is tarred with a system-theoretical brush. Some of Luhmann's writing remains forbiddingly abstract. Luhmann's ideas have also evolved considerably over the years, as he shifted from thinking of systems as means of reducing complexity to an emphasis on self-reproducing and self-referential systems. On the whole Luhmann's outlook, more so than Bourdieu's, is decidedly anti-foundational and constructivist: he sees knowledge and observation as the application of distinctions which are properties of the observing system rather than of the world as such (Laermans 1997:107). This has brought him close to postmodern and post-structuralist modes of thought (De Berg & Prangel 1995; *New German Critique* 1994).

Much of Luhmann's work over the last fifteen years or so has been concerned with large-scale functional systems like the economy, the legal system, politics, education, religion, science and art. The theoretical groundwork for these studies was laid in his *Soziale Systeme* of 1984 (English: Luhmann 1995a). He has also applied system-theoretical insights to social phenomena such as ecological communication (1989) and protest movements (1996). Attempts to apply Luhmann's concepts in literary and art-historical studies have been made by David Roberts (1992), Dietrich Schwanitz (1990), Niels Werber (1992), Kitty Zijlmans (1990) and others. Siegfried Schmidt's analyses of the literary system in eighteenth-century Germany (Schmidt 1989, 1991, 1992, 1997) are indebted to Luhmann but add different touches.

In the following pages I will explore some of the ways in which Luhmann's work might be utilized for the study of translation. Some of these reflect my own current interests. Throughout, it will be good to remember J. Herwig-Lempp's remark that the point of working with system concepts is not necessarily to grasp the system as a whole, but to consider an entity in system terms in order to elicit answers to certain questions (in Fokkema 1991:164). Among such questions could be: How can we conceptualize translation despite its heteronomy? How to account for continuity, diversity and change in concepts and practices of translation? Viewing translation as a social system

– or for that matter as a field in Bourdieu's sense – may open up interesting perspectives. Formidable problems are bound to remain, if only because Luhmann's theory of functionally differentiated systems is historically tied to modern industrialized societies; he has had little to say about pre-modern societies. What we may gain from the attempt, however, is a way of conceptualizing translation as simultaneously autonomous and heteronomous, a means of studying disputes over what is or what is not translation, a tool to think about the internal organization and evolution of the social and intellectual space we call translation.

Let me begin by introducing some of the key terms and concepts. Luhmann does not think of social systems as consisting of individuals or collectives. Individuals are made up of physical bodies, which have cells as their constituent parts, and states of consciousness, i.e. psychic systems. The interaction of the biological with the psychic system makes our lives possible. The domain of the social and the interpersonal however requires communication. For Luhmann, social systems consist of communications, in the sense that communications are the elements social systems are made of. All social systems are 'sense systems', or 'meaning systems' (Luhmann's German term is *Sinnsysteme*): communicative signals, interpretive acts and connecting responses constitute the system and keep it going. Communications are events, acts, fleeting things which need to be connected over time. The boundaries between social systems are those watersheds where meaning is processed differently on one side as compared with the other.

This can apply to smaller units like families or holiday camps or university departments, or to the large functional systems of society. Luhmann envisages modern industrial society as made up of a number of such 'functionally differentiated' social systems, primarily politics, economics, religion, the law, science, the arts, and education. System differentiation consists in the re-introduction of a 'system versus environment' boundary within a system. Functional differentiation results in some systems processing certain aspects of reality, thereby leaving other systems free to focus on other aspects. Each can be described as a social system in itself, differentiated from its environment, i.e. the collection of other systems, by the fact that within each system, communications are of a different intensity and quality as compared with the environment. Although the various systems obviously interact and need each other, each system looks at the rest of the world from its own point of view. The legal system, for instance, reads the world in terms of what is lawful and what is not, whereas in the political system power is the measure of things. The main advantage of this decentralized and 'decentred' organization of society, in Luhman's view, is that it makes it easier for society to cope with the world's complexity. Historically this form of societal organization emerged in the West in roughly the seventeenth and eighteenth centuries.

If this is, grossly simplified, the basis on which Luhmann has built his imposing analyses of social systems, the theoretical apparatus has seen various additions and modifications in recent years. In what follows I will take up only some of these, in particular the emphasis on social systems as being self-reproducing (or 'autopoietic') and self-referential, and Luhmann's comments on second-order observation.

If we want to see how Luhman's theory of social systems might be of use to translation studies, there are two fairly obvious, and overlapping, points of entry. One is the work done by the German researcher Andreas Poltermann, the first to apply Luhmann's system-theoretical ideas to literary translation and translation norms. The other is to link the notion of norms with what Luhmann says about expectations. I will explain these two approaches first, and then go on to other questions. These will bear on the possibility of viewing translation in terms of self-reproducing and self-reflexive systems. This latter aspect will lead us back, via a somewhat vertiginous route, to the problematics of description in translation studies.

## Expectations Structure

Poltermann's essay on 'Norms of Literary Translation' (1992) is concerned with norm changes, primarily in Germany, in the context of literature as a differentiated social system in Luhmann's sense. Literature as a 'differentiated social system' means that it possesses a degree of autonomy with regard to other systems such as religion, politics, or education. The emergence of literature as a differentiated system with its own function and rules is usually dated to the eighteenth century. The historical process of differentiation is obviously a complex matter (Schmidt 1989 has described it for literature in Germany). As literature abandons, for example, its primary role as an instrument of moral instruction, it no longer wants to be judged by moral criteria but instead lays claim to its own literary or aesthetic rules. Literature begins to concentrate on selective functions like social critique and the production of alternative models of reality. Self-descriptions, in the form of literary criticism and handbooks on poetics, emphasize the unity and difference of the system. The participants in literary communication adopt various social roles, which take account of such things as the overwhelmingly written nature of modern literature, the anonymity of the reading public, and the need for expert critics to mediate between writers and readers.

Among the consequences of these changes for literary translation Poltermann singles out the role of philological renderings, which in the case of theatre translation, for instance, lead to a marked difference between versions destined for the stage and those, like Wilhelm von Humboldt's *Agamemnon* of 1816, intended to be read. The latter thus align themselves with the increasingly written character of literary communication. In passing Poltermann offers an interesting system-theoretical explanation for the fact

that the first translations of foreign works tend to stick more closely to domestic genre expectations than subsequent renderings. Meeting genre expectations
can be seen as a way of reducing complexity, making 'alien' elements easier
to handle within the system. The alternative solutions that were not selected,
however, continue to lead a virtual existence as 'temporalized complexity'. In
translation criticism and in subsequent translations, which need to legitimize
themselves with regard both to existing versions and to the original, the contingency of the first translation is shown up and the temporarily stored
complexity of alternative solutions gradually unfolds over time (Poltermann
1992:19).

Poltermann's account treats literary and translation norms in terms of
genre expectations, allowing him to comment on the relevance both of meeting expectations and of confounding them. This way of looking at norms ties
in with what was said in the final section of Chapter 6 about focusing on
selectivity and exclusion in studying norms. It also accords with Luhmann's
view of communication, which itself has phenomenological roots, and possesses elements in common with speech act theory (Luhmann 1984:191ff.;
Blom 1997:70ff.).

Luhmann does not conceive of communication in terms of the transmission of a pre-given message. Rather, meaning is construed by the recipient as
a result of recognizing selectivity. What is offered acquires meaning against
the backdrop of the possibilities that were more or less readily available but
were excluded in the event. The element of selection concerns both the enunciation, i.e. the intentional act of utterance, and the information, i.e. the 'theme'
or the 'data' which are highlighted. Because communication takes place at a
certain moment in a temporal sequence, in a given context, 'understanding' or
'making sense' of a communication means being alive not only to its 'theme'
and 'mode of utterance', but also to the selective aspects of both, to their
negative foils, the difference between what is included and what is excluded
(Luhmann 1986a:85ff; 1990:12ff.).

It follows that texts and other utterances have no fixed meaning, recover-
able from the semantics of the words. They are invested with meaning in
selective, differential contexts. When we look at texts in this way, through
their "temporalized semantics" (De Berg 1990:50), we can probe their significance by asking questions like: How likely, or how new, was this
communication in the circumstances? Why this theme, and this mode of transmission, against which set of likely alternatives? What issue or problem is
being addressed, and what is occluded? And how does this communication
contribute to the establishment of a new context, a new range of possibilities
for subsequent communications? Applied to translation: it is part of the meaning of a translation that a particular original was selected from among a range
of candidates, that it was selected for translation and not for some other form
of importation, recycling or rewriting, and that a particular translating style

was selected, one mode of representing the original against other more or less likely, more or less permissible modes.

The reference to 'likely' and 'permissible' modes reminds us that we are talking about cognitive and normative expectations within a limited range of options. It also allows us to formulate norm concepts in a system-theoretical context. The domain of translation, or the social institution which is termed 'translation', has limits, a socially acknowledged boundary differentiating it, sometimes sharply, sometimes only diffusely, from other modes of dealing with anterior discourses. The expectations which police the boundaries of translation are called the 'constitutive norms' of translation (see Chapter 6). Breaching them means that the product will not be called 'translation', at least not by the group that lays claim to the definition of translation. Within the field of translation we speak of 'regulatory norms', expectations concerning what is appropriate with regard to certain types or areas of discourse. These expectations form the structure of the social system of translation, in a sense compatible with Luhmann's terminology. Luhmann holds that whereas communications are the building blocks of social systems, expectations about communications constitute their cement, their structure. Social structures are structures of expectation in an otherwise contingent world (Luhman 1984:139, 377ff.). Structure here means that some occurrences, and some processes and combinations, are more likely than others.

Luhmann's comments on style are of interest in this respect. Referring to the arts in general, he suggests that style 'organizes' the contribution of an individual work to the ongoing production and consumption of art. In this way "[t]he style of a work allows us to recognize what it owes to other works of art and what it means for other, new works of art" (1990:196-97; 1986: 632). By recognizing style, including styles of translating, we establish filiations branching into the past and adjust future expectations. The process, which works by means of contrast as well as parallelism, has multiple orientations. It links the translation we are reading with other texts belonging to the same type or sharing stylistic features, regardless of whether those texts are translations or originals; and it links this particular translation with other translations, whether of the same genre or not. To the extent that in the former case we can speak of translation's external reference and in the latter of its self-reference, we can thus bring into view the idea of translation itself as a social system.

## Translation as a Social System

We can look upon translation as a recognized social phenomenon, both an intellectual category and a cultural practice. The meaning of the term is codified in dictionaries, fixed by informal as well as professional activities called translation, constantly affirmed by translators' associations and by educational, scholarly, journalistic and other public and private discourses. As was suggested above, it is reasonable also to assume that we bring both cognitive and normative expectations to translation. Both sets of expectations are continually being negotiated, confirmed, adjusted and modified by practising translators and by all who speak about translation.

In this sense we can envisage the world of translation itself as a system, an adaptive, self-regulating, self-reflexive and self-reproducing system in Luhmann's terms. This implies that we account for the simultaneous autonomy and heteronomy of translation, and explore how Luhmann's descriptions of social systems apply to translation. Naturally, the interest of such an exercise lies partly in the excitement of the exploration itself, and partly in the kind of issues it brings to the surface.

If social systems consist of communications, then the elements which build the translation system must be actual translations and statements about translation. The system's temporal dimension, its internal memory, so to speak, reflects the fact that communication generates communication, under the right conditions. A system can only continue to exist if communications connect. We can translate because there are translations which we recognize as translations *and* because, when we translate or speak about translation, we routinely take account of the conditioning factors governing the concepts and practices which count as 'translation' in our world. This creates the necessary connectivity and a sufficient 'horizon of expectations' to produce further translations and statements about translation. The expectations constitute what Luhmann called the 'structure' of the system. These structures, which are themselves the products of communication, in turn fix the conditions for the connectivity of further communications. This, in a nutshell, is the idea of a self-reproducing or 'autopoietic' system: structure and process support each other.

If we regard translation as constituting a functional system, its primary function can be said to consist in producing representations of anterior discourses across semiotic boundaries, and typically that representations can be taken as re-enacting anterior discourses. The system's identity as a separate functional system, its 'guiding difference' (Luhmann's term is *Leitdifferenz*), is based on this specific representational role. Some of the practical consequences of this role are profoundly paradoxical. One consequence, for example, is that interlingual translation may need to create an impression of equivalence – an illusion of equivalence, Anthony Pym (1995a) would say – if it is to produce target texts that can serve as replacements of their source texts (see Chapter 7). Another is the fact that the translator, in re-enacting another utterance, does not speak in his or her own name only, which results in translations possessing a hybrid discursive subject, somewhat like direct or indirect quotation (Folkart 1991; Pym 1992b; Hermans 1996b). No doubt an approach employing Bakhtin's notions of dialogism and heteroglossia could take these issues further.

A social system's primary means of differentiation and self-organization is a binary 'code', an operational distinction furnishing the ultimate point of orientation for discourse. Science, for Luhmann, uses the 'true/false' distinction as its basic code; politics is centred on power; the legal system on legal versus illegal. My suggestion as regards translation would be for the distinction between 'valid' or 'not valid' as representation. Because the distinction bearing on the validity of the representation marks the system's constitutive difference, it also creates the boundary between the system itself and its environment. In the course of history the terms of this basic 'code' can be, and have been, fleshed out in very different ways, in the form of what Luhmann calls 'programmes'. They take the form of different criteria and preferences, or different poetics of translation, in the way different sets of concrete laws, for example, embody different 'programmes' of the legal system. All the normative expectations and codifications of translation can be expressed in these terms. Neoclassical translation as practised by Houdar de la Motte is programmed differently from Hölderlin's literalism. Ezra Pound and Vladimir Nabokov both acknowledge word-for-word and sense-for-sense as divergent but coexisting programmes.

While social systems are open in that they require input from their environment, this input is processed in the system's own terms. Luhmann speaks of 'operational closure' in this connection. Churches, for example, interpret the world from a religious point of view. In the case of translation this means that texts and other semiotic constructs are processed with an eye to their 'translational' aspects. At the same time, however, translation does not operate in and for itself, but caters for other interests, other systems – hence its heteronomy. Translations enter, and interact with, existing discursive forms and practices. On the whole, we expect translations to defer to the client system's prevailing discourse, although, depending on circumstances, more complex forms of interaction, pliancy and recalcitrance can and will occur. A theoretical account of this form of entanglement or complicity may be found in the notions of 'structural coupling' or 'resonance' between systems, whereby the norms, criteria and resources of one system are put at the disposal of or forced upon another system, there to be respected or resisted, as the case may be.

Since translation is on the whole less clearly differentiated, less autonomous, than, say, modern art or religion, it is particularly prone to interference. Here we encounter the engine that drives translation and induces change in the social system of translation. Only systems which constantly adapt to their environment can continue to exist – and adaptation can take the form of influencing neighbouring systems. The nature of translation's programmes alters as translational communications respond to all manner of internal and external interference. Connectivity cannot be taken for granted.

In the combination of autonomy and heteronomy, of self-reference and external reference, we can recognize translation's formative role in history. Translation actively contributes to the shaping of cultural and other discourses because, whatever its actual complexion, it possesses a momentum of its own,

an internal memory resulting from operational closure. This is what makes
translation irreducible, even when it defers to prevailing discourses. The self-
reference of translation sees to it that the translative operation never wholly
extinguishes a source text's otherness. It is also one of the means to irritate
client systems.

    To the extent that the translation system has its own momentum, its iden-
tity and relative stability as a system, it continually reproduces itself. The way
in which translation is maintained and continually modified as a social system
governed by particular sets of expectations, determines the way in which we
produce and process translations and communicate about them, whether in
everyday or in academic conversation, at a translator training institute, in a
newspaper review or a translator's preface. Adopting this perspective implies,
though, that the term 'translation' has no fixed, inherent, immanent meaning.
The category 'translation', including what I called its representational function, is constantly being reproduced by means of communication. Its semantics
changes in this process of reproduction, just as historically its basic code ('valid/
not valid as representation') is occupied by different terms, oppositions and
values, i.e. by different 'programmes'. Its durability or stability, as a concept
and a practice, stems from its autopoiesis as a system, i.e. from recursive
operations of self-production and self-reflexiveness. Our contemporary discourses, including those of translation studies, including the words on this
page, are part of that process.

## Self-reference and Description

In his English translation (published in 1921) of Louis Hemon's classic French-
Canadian novel *Maria Chapdelaine*, the Canadian translator William Hume
Blake had one character advise another to "regard well"; on another page,
something is said to be "sacredly amusing". These deliberate literalisms allow Sherry Simon to glimpse what she calls "the translator's signature" (1997:
195, 197) and to gauge their cultural and political significance. We could also
say that the translator was implicitly commenting on the nature of translation,
and on the choice of a particular style of translating. He was signalling his
awareness of engaging with an existing tradition of translation and its treatment of linguistic and cultural otherness.

    Something similar occurs when Vladimir Nabokov rails against earlier
translators of Pushkin's *Eugene Onegin* and takes a demonstratively different
tack in his own version, sporting "copious footnotes, footnotes reaching up
like skyscrapers to the top of this or that page" (1992:143). The Zukofskys'
near-phonetic renderings of Catullus quoted in an earlier chapter, David Luke's
retranslation of Mann's *Death in Venice*, and the translators of Heidegger or
Derrida who feel obliged to keep putting the original German and French
words between brackets in their translations because the originals exploit the

economy of their respective idioms in ways that refuse to be parallelled in other languages – in all these cases we have translators implicitly or explicitly commenting on their own activity as translators. In doing so, they are observing themselves translating.

One way of dealing with such self-reflexive moments in translation is to read them as marking the difference between self-reference and external reference; another is to relate them to Luhmann's idea of second-order observation. This latter path will lead us towards some fundamental problems of translation description.

Contrasting self-reference and external reference in translations shows up the system's simultaneous autonomy and heteronomy. A translation's external reference can be understood as its assimilation to other signifying practices. A translated car maintenance manual is used to maintain cars in much the same way as a non-translated manual. A translation is recognized as a well-formed text among other texts in the receptor culture. It refers back to its original in ways bearing similarities to the ways in which other rewritings refer to pre-existing texts. In each case translation interacts with other discourses and the social systems of which they form a part.

Self-reference contributes to the autopoiesis of translation. It draws attention to prevailing programmes as legitimate modes of representation, and may question these programmes or even the boundaries of what constitutes translation. In harking back to existing renderings, and, in so doing, claiming the right to speak about translation, self-reference is grounded in similarities and contrasts with existing translations and discourses about translation. It thus helps to structure, to maintain and to modify the system.

Approaching the matter in terms of second-order observation opens up perspectives of a different kind. If we envisage the process of translation as a matter of observing a source text and making decisions about how to render it, then self-reflexive comments and activities constitute observations of those observations. Luhmann calls this second-order observation (1990a:23ff; 1993; 1995:92ff.). Second-order observation involves an altered vantage point. As someone looks at an object, they cannot simultaneously look at themselves looking at the object. The eye cannot watch itself watching – just as Tristram Shandy, in Laurence Sterne's eponymous novel, cannot include in his description of himself the description of himself describing himself. But when translators like those mentioned above mark the distance between their own work and that of a predecessor, or flag instances of untranslatability, they are observing their own operations. These observations constitute second-order observations in relation to the first-order observation involved in translating.

Of course, when these translators are observing their own operations, they cannot simultaneously observe that second-order observation. But we can observe translators observing themselves. Our comments on translation and translators are a matter of second-order observation with regard to the

translators' own second-order observations. In turn, we cannot observe ourselves observing translators. There always remains a blind spot.

The relevance of this line of reasoning is that it takes us into two epistemological paradoxes, both of which bear on questions of description, more
particularly on the problematic relation between the describer and the object
of description.

The first paradox concerns the fact that there is no fundamental difference between translators acting as second-order observers of their own work,
and translation researchers acting a second-order observers of the translators'
second-order observations. Both belong to the social system of translation in
that they produce and respond to communications within the sphere of translation. This is a point similar to the one we saw Lieven D'hulst making in the
section on 'Historicizing Theory' in Chapter 7: there is no clear dividing line
between scholarly and other statements about translation. In other words, a
systems theory of Luhmann's constructivist ilk leads to a questioning of any
neat separation between object-level and meta-level. Since that separation is
one of the cornerstones of the empirical approach to translation, we have a
problem.

Perhaps the problem looks worse than it is. Literary studies, too, have
witnessed debates between scientists and culturalists, those who think of their
activities as primarily scientific and divorced from literature, and those who
stress that interpretation and criticism are not immune from literature itself.
Some empiricists refrain from making interpretive statements about literary
texts altogether, and concentrate instead on the mechanics of the market. By
contrast, schools of thought such as Deconstruction, gender-based, postcolonial
and cultural studies have insisted on the untenability of a detached, Archi-
medean and value-free point of view, arguing that the human sciences take
part in the production of culture and ideology.

In translation studies, remarkably, this discussion has hardly begun.
Luhmann's juggling with first and second-order observation, his awareness
that one cannot simultaneously observe an object and one's observation of it,
could contribute to such a discussion by suggesting that neither one stance
nor the other provides a firm foundation (and this observation, too, is made
from a particular vantage point in systems theory). The early descriptivists
were undoubtedly right in criticizing the limitations inherent in prescriptive
approaches to translation. However, their own primary orientation towards
the academic discourses of literary theory, historiography and semiotics cannot immunize them from the concepts of translation they work on, just as their
own position cannot be wholly neutral, detached, objective or external. The
ambivalence always remains. In pointing up this ambivalence, the anti-
foundationalist aspect of constructivist theories can guard against a form of
description which forgets that describers are always positioned somewhere,
and have blind spots.

The paradox, and the ensuing ambivalence, need not paralyze research. If translation studies want to create a self-reflexive and self-critical space while avoiding the pitfalls of prescriptivism, they have to operate at the level of theory, analysis and history. Their task then consists in theorizing the historical contingency of different modes and uses of translation together with the concepts and discourses – historical and contemporary – which legitimize them. The relative strength of this position lies in the awareness of its own ambivalence and contingency.

The second paradox, too, is a matter of the snake biting its own tail. The intellectual historian Quentin Skinner identifies the problem in his essay 'Conventions and the Understanding of Speech Acts' (1970). Skinner here asks how we can assess what, borrowing a term from speech act theory, he calls the 'illocutionary force' of a statement made by someone who is speaking, in a different context, to someone else rather than to us. The issue, Skinner reminds us, is relevant to historians and anthropologists, who 'overhear' utterances produced by others for others. We can represent it as involving a person $A$, at a time and/or place $t2$, who is trying to understand an utterance by a speaker $S$ who was speaking at $t1$. As Skinner points out, the problem "is neither philosophically trivial in itself, nor in the practice of these disciplines can it be readily overcome" (1970:136). Of course, $A$ has to know enough about the concepts and conventions available to $S$ at $t1$ so that $A$ can grasp the semantics of $S$'s utterance and what force $S$'s enunciation of that utterance must have registered when it was uttered. In addition,

> it also seems indispensable that $A$ should be capable of performing some act of translation of the concepts and conventions employed by $S$ at $t1$ into terms which are familiar at $t2$ to $A$ himself, not to mention others to whom $A$ at $t2$ may wish to communicate his understanding. (ibid.)

If we want to gauge the meaning of Plutarch's *Lives*, we have to know something about the conventions of Plutarch's time and place to grasp both the semantics of his words and the force registered by his uttering those words then and there. What if the object of our attention is not Plutarch but, say, a sixteenth-century translation of Plutarch? If we want to understand and communicate about Jacques Amyot's version, or Thomas North's, we not only need to have a sense of their concepts and practices of translation, we also need to be able to translate these into our metalanguage of translation. To understand and speak about someone else's translation, we must translate that translation.

In terms of Roman Jakobson's 1959 essay 'On Linguistic Aspects of Translation', even intralingual translation is translation, if perhaps improperly. As is well known, Jakobson's essay holds that intralingual translation or rewording, interlingual translation or "translation proper", and intersemiotic translation or transmutation, all constitute forms of translation. The very fact that Jakobson spoke of interlingual translation as "translation proper" indicates that the semiotics-based statements in the essay were being made in the context of concepts of translation which regarded only interlingual translation as 'proper' translation. But since translation studies align themselves with semiotics, they are not in a position to quarrel with Jakobson's recuperation of rewording as a form of translation (Hermans 1997:16ff.). It follows that our accounts of translation, whether intralingual or interlingual, constitute themselves a form of translation.

In a way, this only re-states what was said above. The study of translation is implicated, oddly and improperly, in the practice of translation. If translation descriptions perform the operations they are simultaneously trying to describe, the distinction between object-level and meta-level is rendered problematic. Descriptive translation studies have been keen to keep object-level and meta-level well apart, but it turns out that the object constantly contaminates its description – a point first made, from a Deconstructionist position, by Matthijs Bakker (1995). Even the scholarly study of translation is implicated in the self-description of translation as a cultural construct. There is a worm in the bud of descriptive translation studies and their claim to disciplinary rigour.

But if describing is also translating, then the norms aspect re-enters the picture too. In translating other people's concepts of translation (or what looks to us like our 'translation'), our accounts are inevitably based on concepts of translation. They will also be inscribed with the values and the manipulations which accompany translation, and hence tell us something about the individuals and communities performing the translative operation, i.e. about ourselves. The study of translation rebounds on our own categories and assumptions, our own modes of conceptualizing and translating translation.

Here again things are less new than they may appear. Other branches of the human sciences struggle with their entanglement in the objects they describe. In the study of translation the issue only becomes acute when we move beyond our immediate horizon, whenever we wish to speak about 'translation' generally, as a transhistorical or transcultural phenomenon, or when we attempt to comprehend and convey what another, especially a distant culture means by whatever terms they use to denote an activity or product that appears to translate as our 'translation'.

Since we cannot step outside ourselves or do without interpretation, there are no ready solutions to this epistemological aporia. But there may be ways of coming to terms with it. Recent practices in ethnography offer one example. Luhmann's system theory may supply another. Let me conclude this chapter with a brief look at each.

Edmund Leach observed in 1973 that for ethnography and anthropology "the essential problem is one of translation", adding optimistically that "social anthropologists are engaged in establishing a methodology for the translation of cultural language" (1973:772). The anthropologists in the field found the problem rather more intractable than Leach had anticipated.

Its complexity can be illustrated with a couple of examples. Jesuit missionaries proselytizing in China in the sixteenth and seventeenth centuries needed to express Christian concepts like 'God' and 'heaven', 'soul' and 'sin', in Chinese. When Matteo Ricci wrote his Chinese treatise on *The True Meaning of the Master of Heaven* (1604), the only terms available to him were those which echoed Confucian and Buddhist vocabulary. As a result, the Christian concepts he was trying to convey were inevitably locked in what Lefevere would call a 'universe of discourse' wholly incommensurable with the Christian message; these texts were read, moreover, by people who did not think in terms of transcendent or eternal truths (Gernet 1985:48-49, 146-47). Because the missionaries in China could only hope to reach the Chinese in Chinese, they had no option but to preach Christian ideas drenched in Chinese concepts. The debate over the Chinese name of the Western, Christian God has raged ever since.

When, in the 1940s and '50s, the Oxford ethnographer Edward Evans-Pritchard studied the beliefs of the Nuer in the southern Sudan, he faced a similar problem, but the other way round. He emphasized the utter otherness and incompatibility of Nuer words and concepts with Western, Christian terms. His *Nuer Religion* (1956) highlights the Westerner's formidable problem of understanding something which is alien, at best approachable through painstaking 'contextual interpretation', of rendering *that* in a language like English, and therefore in terms that are tainted by our concepts, our history, our values. It was Evans-Pritchard who, in a lecture of 1951, described the central task of ethnography as "the translation of culture" (Needham 1978:8).

In his *Belief, Language, and Experience* (1972), which patiently traces Evans-Pritchard's account of Nuer beliefs, Rodney Needham offered an extended reflection on the perplexing problems of this 'translation of culture'. Needham points out, for example, that, if we want to compare different Western interpretations of Nuer concepts, we need to assess what 'adjustments' would be required of the various languages involved to make them accommodate the Nuer terms. But we lack a metalanguage to carry out such a comparison. It could only be constructed on the basis of the comparability of cultural concepts, and the concepts can only be compared on the basis of a suitable metalanguage. That lands us in a vicious circle (Needham 1972:222). We cannot escape from perspectival observation, value-ridden interpretation, compromised and compromising translation.

In recent decades postmodern, postcolonial ethnographers have become aware of their discipline's roots in colonial history and of its entanglement in structures of power and domination. As a result, ethnography has become markedly more self-reflexive and self-critical, aware of its own historicity and institutional position, of its presuppositions and blind spots, of the pitfalls of representation by means of language and translation (Sturge 1997; Wolf 1997). If translation studies are to come to terms with the paradoxes and entanglements of description, they might do well to look closely at practices like those in contemporary ethnography, and at theories of self-reflexive systems.

The anti-foundationalism of Luhmann's system theory could be of use here. Luhmann realizes that every description remains partial. Self-description can only be partial because describers cannot include their own descriptions in their descriptions. This is because they cannot observe themselves observing, but also because the self-description alters the thing described (it now includes the self-description). External description does not fare any better. To be external the description must belong to another system. Legal translation or community-based interpreting, for example, can be described from the position of education and academic scholarship. But the educational and academic worlds can only look at what happens in their environments through their own codes and programmes, their own distinctions. This knocks the supports from under any attempt at immanent objectivity.

The theory of self-reflexive systems, as Luhmann has pointed out (e.g. Luhmann 1993), posits a de-centred and polycontextual world in which there is no single privileged way of attributing or processing meaning. System theory does not exclude itself from this unresolvable relativism. But at least this postmodern flaunting of epistemological doubt offers the advantage of taking little for granted and of leaving room for paradox, hesitation and experiment. It is one way of dealing with what has become known as the crisis of representation in the human sciences (Marcus & Fischer 1986:7-16). Once we know that our knowledge is constructed, we can learn to live with the limitations of perspective.

In this way system theory can fulfil several functions in translation studies. It can make us rethink the way in which translation exists in society and open up avenues for research on translation as a social system. It can also ask awkward questions of the discipline of translation studies itself, and help to find solutions to fundamental problems.

# 11. Criticisms

Most internal criticism has already been dealt with in the preceding chapters. This chapter is therefore concerned only with criticism levelled from outside the empirical/systemic paradigm. An exhaustive catalogue is obviously out of the question. What follows is a brief and highly selective account, which is concerned with types of criticism rather than with individual critics.

Several categories can be distinguished. At one end of the spectrum we encounter criticism voiced from a position fundamentally at odds with the entire orientation and purpose of the descriptive approach. This is the case, for example, with Peter Newmark's criticism. At the other end we find comments which take issue with certain theoretical or methodological aspects of the paradigm while being largely sympathetic to it. The critical line taken by members of the Göttingen research centre on literary translation fits this category. In between these two poles various types of criticism can be heard which are prepared to acknowledge the achievements of the Manipulation group but perceive weaknesses and shortcomings on the basis of a different agenda. This is the case, for example, with criticism stemming from hermeneutics, cultural materialism, gender-based and postcolonial studies. Let us review some of these comments and differences.

Peter Newmark's dissatisfaction with descriptivism cuts deeper than the carping at turgid style and a paucity of examples mentioned in Chapter 1. It boils down to two issues. The first can be seen in Newmark's essay 'What Translation Theory is About' (1980). The key statement of this position paper runs as follows:

> Translation theory's main concern is to determine appropriate translation methods for the widest possible range of texts or text categories. Further, it provides a framework of principles, restricted rules, and hints for translating texts and criticizing translations, a background for problem solving. [...] Lastly, translation theory attempts to give some insight into the relation between thought, meaning, and language; the universal cultural and individual aspects of language and behaviour, the understanding of cultures [...]. (1980:1-2)

For Newmark, the study and theory of translation has its rationale in the benefit that can accrue from it for the practice of translating and of translator training. This is exactly what the descriptive paradigm contested from the start. The Manipulation group claims a place for a kind of translation studies that is not immediately 'of use', in James Holmes' words. They put first what for Newmark comes last.

The major point of actual conflict follows from this basic difference. It concerns the descriptivists' unwillingness to work towards explicit value judgements regarding translation quality or to formulate criteria for accuracy in translation, both crucial to Newmark's vision (1991:54). In his assessment the functionalist principle of descriptive analysis is to blame, because its relativism will not recognize an immanent or universal essence in what translation is or should be:

> All studies are relativised to a consideration of the functions of a translation at a given period. Any idea that functions might be universal and not entirely bound to a literary coterie or social class at a particular period, that translation may have an essence if not necessarily a prototype, is seen as beside the point. In the language of these writers, function becomes its own self-justification. (ibid.)

Newmark himself takes the view that "[t]ranslators cannot be neutral, where matters of fact or morality are concerned. They have to intervene, inside or outside their texts" (Newmark 1993:79). The Manipulation group's more relativistic and historicizing stance, with its interest in figuring out how and why certain translations came into being rather than in any absolute rights and wrongs of a case, indeed refuses to dictate to translators, or even to try and render itself directly useful to them. At the same time, the question of value in descriptive work is rather more complex than descriptivists often make it out to be, as I tried to show in the previous chapter and in Chapter 7. Still, as far as the primary orientation of research into translation is concerned, the differences with a stance like Newmark's appear to be unbridgeable.

This is not the case with the 'special research centre' ('Sonderforschungsbereich') on literary translation which flourished at the University of Göttingen from 1986 to 1997. The Göttingen centre, the largest in the world except for teams working on machine translation, brought together some fifty researchers overall and produced over fifty books (for a sampling, see the Bibliography under Czennia, Essmann & Schöning, Frank, Kittel, Lönker, Poltermann, Ranke, Schultze, Turk). Its thematic focus was on the history of literary translation in Germany from the eighteenth century to the present day, with specific projects on such things as the translation of theatre and narrative fiction, translation anthologies, etc. Despite its size and astounding productivity the centre has had only limited impact outside the German-speaking area. Its publications have been mostly in German, and the centre as a whole did not develop a coherent theoretical or methodological framework, preferring instead to devote their energy to extensive and detailed case studies. Nonetheless several sophisticated lower-level methodologies were elaborated, such as the set of parameters for studying the translation of cultural references in literary texts, mentioned in Chapter 5.

Although from its earliest publications the Göttingen centre acknowledged its affinity with the descriptive and systemic paradigm in translation studies, they stressed their own priorities under the banner of 'historical-descriptive' fieldwork (Frank 1987). They resisted the extension of the field beyond conventional forms of translation, keeping their distance from Lefevere's inclusive notion of rewriting. They also remained keen to combine philological, text-based 'internal' analyses with the investigation of 'external' aspects such as the institutional embedding of translation. Their actual criticism of the Manipulation school's approach homes in on two points: the exclusive orientation on the target pole, and the systems concept.

For the Göttingen researchers, the stridency with which the Manipulation group advocated a target-oriented approach betrayed an overreaction against earlier and equally blinkered source-based approaches. The resulting near-exclusive attention for the target pole, they argued, was too restrictive as a basis for sustained historical research (Frank 1987:xiii). Instead the centre opted for a 'transfer-oriented' model, "squarely based on the literary, linguistic, and cultural differences between source and target sides that need to be mediated by an act of translation" (Frank & Bödeker 1991:61). Harald Kittel claimed a transfer-oriented stance as inherently more comprehensive than either source-oriented or target-oriented approaches (1992:v-vi). The Göttingen critics had a point insofar as the Manipulation school tended to neglect detailed comparative study of specific texts; on the other hand, nothing in the target-oriented model actually prevented a broader view. The fact that Newmark roundly dismissed the whole Göttingen-based 'transfer' approach along with all other non-applied descriptive work as "an overblown platitude" (1993: 149) only underscores the similarities between the two, when seen from a distance.

The systems idea provided another flashpoint. One whole volume in the Göttingen series of books was devoted to it (Kittel 1992), and concluded with a highly critical examination of the concept. Armin Paul Frank distrusted its scientistic overtones and pointed to the ever present danger of mistaking one's binary classifications – such as the polysystem dualism of 'primary' versus 'secondary' – for real states of affairs, with the attendant risk of a grossly reductive understanding (Frank 1989a:91-93; 1992:377). Again, the criticism may not be unjustified as far as polysystem theory is concerned (see Chapter 8), and the ontological objection was raised elsewhere too (Korpel 1992:11-12). However, Frank's rudimentary notion of system, which he saw entirely in parallel with the Saussurean idea of *langue* (1992:378) or in the context of the exact sciences (1989a:93-94), failed to address the diversity and flexibility of system concepts in the humanities and social sciences, including those being explored by some of his own colleagues, among them Andreas Poltermann (see Chapter 10). This was a discussion that was conducted fitfully and never concluded.

Frank's own vision of a research programme focused on the 'internal' history of translation. It comprises four stages, each one broader than the one before it (1992:383-86). The project begins with the investigation of what Franks calls the 'echo chamber' (1989:195-99; 1989a:95) of individual translations, the intricate pattern of textual relations which includes not only those between translation and original, but also various other textual traces: those of the actual transfer process (e.g. the use made of certain dictionaries), of linguistic and literary usage at the receptor pole, of earlier translations (plundered, echoed or purposely avoided), of translation norms and concepts, of actual working conditions (e.g. signs of haste) and of other control factors (e.g. commissions, instructions, editorial comments). Then comes the extension to larger corpora of translations, like those which the Göttingen group called 'comet's tails', or filiations of interrelated versions springing from a single original (Frank 1989:266). A third stage would involve an exploration of the set of foreign works made available by means of translation in certain epochs and places, and stage four would document the ascertainable use made of translations (reprints, incorporation into anthologies, critical, scholarly and creative responses).

None of this is incompatible with either a descriptive or a systemic perspective. Indeed a programme like this could have fitted into Chapter 5 above. What the Göttingen research teams have made clear, however, is the complex intertextuality of translation in its historical unfolding and the virtues of open-minded philological acumen. If the Manipulation group stressed contextualization, the impressively detailed analyses carried out in Göttingen foregrounded intertextualization. Both are needed.

Speaking from the vantage point of literary hermeneutics, Antoine Berman's last book launched a critique of descriptivism which sought to revalue the translator's subjectivity (1995:50-61). Some of Berman's comments appear to be based on misunderstandings, though. Berman read the concept of norms, for example, as deterministic, arguing that since norms tended to prescribe translations of the naturalizing kind, and translators were supposed to obey norms, a norms-based approach denied all creativity to translation and translators. It does nothing of the sort. In the same way he assumed, erroneously, that the 'target-oriented' research option, more particularly Toury's suggestion that it is generally a good idea for the researcher to begin by looking at the context in which the translation was probably meant to serve some purpose, automatically favoured target-accommodating translations.

Berman was however correct in criticizing Even-Zohar's assumption about the 'secondary' role played by the large majority of translations, which indeed underplays their creative and formative aspect. André Lefevere, as we saw (Chapter 9), also rejected the 'primary' versus 'secondary' opposition in Even-Zohar's theory. Berman further stressed that the often problematic status awarded to translations in many cultures need not imply they are therefore also peripheral or negligible. Translations, for Berman, are not normally integrated in the receiving culture but remain there as 'foreign bodies', constituting a series of their own. However, Berman went off on a more dubious tack when he contended that there exists an immanent Idea of translation which manifests itself through different terms and forms in History (1995:61; Berman's capitals). A descriptivist response would undoubtedly assert a less idealized, more relativistic position: if we begin by viewing translation as a label attached to a number of practices, it is important, despite the problems highlighted in the previous chapter, to attempt to map out what the term covers and what other terms are conceptually near.

Although he is not a hermeneuticist, Anthony Pym, like Antoine Berman, has been keen to raise the profile of the individual translator's agency, which a mechanistic application of the norms concept is bound to downgrade. Pym has summed up his criticism of the way descriptive studies have operated with norms as follows (1998:110-15): it is not clear what exactly norms constrain; too much emphasis is placed on stability rather than change; insufficient attention is paid to the gap separating translation practice from what is said about it; there is no reason to assume norms are culture-specific; and – a more puzzling point – the study of norms "tends to make the object exterior to us, allowing the past to be used for ideologically relativist ends" (1998:115). The discussion of norms concepts and their applications in Chapters 6, 7 and 10 above should have answered most of these objections.

The main thrust of Pym's critique of the notion of systems has been that systemic approaches remain "fundamentally unable to model social causation" (1998:ix,124). While this may be true of the Formalist streak running through polysystem theory, it hardly applies to approaches based on Luhmann or Bourdieu, which are explicitly social in nature. It is also worth bearing in mind that if descriptive – and most other – approaches are not prepared to point to direct causation, this is because social and cultural causation is likely to be a complicated and anything but clear-cut affair, involving multilayered correlation and filtering. It is enough to glance, for example, at the awesome complexity of the 'structural-functional' models designed to map the social history of German nineteenth-century literature (Heydebrand *et al.* 1988) to realize that Pym is asking for the holy grail. Pym's own proposals to think in terms of intercultural regimes are fascinating in themselves but offer little obvious advantage over field or systems concepts, especially as he presents them as "[his] own particular brand of system" (1998:118).

Postcolonial, cultural-materialist and gender-based approaches to translation possess a broader conceptual hinterland and have generated a large amount of interest, discussion and research in recent years. They have vigorously foregrounded the social, political and ideological contexts and effects of translation, the kind of contextualization which the 'cultural turn' in translation studies also favoured, but which these researchers now elaborate from a committed, oppositional and critical angle. Viewed from that angle, the formalism and literary insulation of some descriptive work leaves too many large and important questions unaddressed. In Tejaswini Niranjana's assessment, for example, most studies of translation elide both the political force of translation and its complicity in processes of subjugation and domination. Speaking of Toury's work in particular she contends that "the 'empirical science' of translation comes into being through the repression of the asymmetrical relations of power that inform the relations between languages" (1992: 60). The call here is not just to focus on certain aspects of translation, but to do so from an explicit ideological standpoint.

This postcolonial position would probably meet with Lawrence Venuti's approval. His cultural materialism also entails a politically committed stance, as is borne out by the 'Call to Action' which concludes his study of *The Translator's Invisibility* (1995). For Venuti, "[r]esearch into translation can never be simply descriptive" (1995:312), since even the decision to occupy oneself with the study of so marginalized a cultural practice like translation constitutes an act of opposition. Venuti's eloquent appeal to translators to stand up and be counted with resistant translations implies a charge of timidity and complacency directed at a descriptivism apparently reluctant to mount the barricades.

To the extent that both translation and its scholarly study are intertwined as cultural practices, Venuti's critique of descriptivism has some justification. But as I suggested in the previous chapter, this need not be the last word on the matter. Every vantage point contains its blind spot. While Venuti's position has the virtue of consistency, it stands or falls with the righteousness of his cause and the moral high ground of his indignation. If we want to create sufficient and sustainable room for self-reflexive criticism of that or any other position, we cannot very well do it from a practising translator's point of view. We must do it from a theoretical angle, one that aligns itself with the theoretical and scholarly discourses to which Venuti's language and style of argument also appeal. This is why, to my mind at least, the critical task of translation theory does not consist in advocating this or that resistant or oppositional or compliant or fluent or any other mode of translating. Rather, as indicated in the previous chapter, it consists in theorizing the historical contingency of these modes together with the concepts and discourses underpinning them. A non-prescriptive study of translation should not seek to impose on the practice of translation, but to account for its deployment and conceptualization in history, including contemporary history. It should also seek to theorize its own contingency, and the precariousness of its own dependence on and distance from prevailing practices of translation.

An argument along these lines can also be developed in connection with gender-based approaches (Von Flotow 1997; Simon 1996). Here, as Rosemary Arrojo (1994) has pointed out, a double standard is often at work: translations deliberately gendered from a feminist viewpoint are applauded, other interventions are branded as distortions. From a gender studies perspective the partisanship is justified by arguing that, as objective positions or value-free descriptions do not exist, it is better to take an overt stance in defence of a noble cause than to connive with the status quo by remaining silent. By way of response a descriptive paradigm which does not want to paint itself into the corner of a discredited objectivism or an untenable detachment could still point out that exclusive commitment leaves little room for self-relativization and critical distance towards one's own presuppositions, and that in most historical cases there are reasons and relations to be discovered which we run the risk of overlooking if moral outrage leads us to focus on just one glaring aspect.

The more committed approaches to translation are currently making most of the running in translation studies. The Manipulation school will need to see where its descriptive models, its contextualization of translation and its re-thinking of its own position may eventually lead. I will attempt to provide a few pointers in the concluding chapter.

# 12. Perspectives

In her book *Excitable Speech* (1997) Judith Butler points out that, when a new baby comes into the world and the doctor who receives the child observes 'It's a girl', that speech act effects a performative. The utterance 'It's a girl' is more than a mere statement of fact. It begins, in Butler's words, "that long string of interpellations by which the girl is transitively girled: gender is ritualistically repeated, whereby the repetition occasions both the risk of failure and the congealed effect of sedimentation" (1997:49).

Butler's inquiry concerns the authority that lends speech acts their force. The one who speaks the performative does so by citing it, for it always predates the particular utterance. Speakers establish themselves as the authors of the performatives they pronounce, but they simultaneously invoke the derivative status of that authorship. If a performative succeeds, Butler argues,

> ... then it is not because an intention successfully governs the action of speech, but only because that action echoes prior actions, and *accumulates the force of authority through the repetition or citation of a prior and authoritative set of practices*. It is not simply that the speech act takes place *within* a practice, but that the act is itself a ritualized practice (1997:51; emphasis in the original).

As with babies, or insults, or death sentences, so with translations. When the label 'translation' attaches itself to certain texts, it amounts to more than a statement of fact or a description of status. It constitutes a performative, implying the suggestion, the request or demand that the text be classified and treated in certain ways. But because the ritualized labelling action rehearses prior actions, we cannot know from a single, isolated occurrence exactly what the gesture means. The citational nature of the term 'translation' obliges us to probe its social, cultural and historical dimension if we are to ascertain its force. Translation takes place within an existing practice, reiterating and extending it. Whether we call this the social system of translation, or a translation tradition, or the sociocultural embedding of translation, we can only make provisional, time-bound statements about it.

Perhaps the core of the descriptive project in translation studies can be characterized by its willingness to take 'translation' not merely as a descriptive term but rather as a performative, an active bid to belong to a certain category. Texts are made into translations by being called translations, in particular contexts. The investigation of these contexts, and hence of the local validity of 'translation', keeps descriptivists occupied. In that sense John McFarlane's insight in the 1950s that "translation is as translation does" and that its study should be "diagnostic rather than hortatory" stands undiminished.

The most central and powerful tenet of descriptive translation studies has been that translation cannot be defined a priori, once and for all. What 'translation' means has to be established, however provisionally, by means of tentative theories, paradoxical methodologies and patient study.

The other major contribution of descriptivism, the contextualization of translation, follows from this. It involved a reorientation which brought first culture and then politics and power into the picture. It reminded the discipline of its social relevance. It would also take descriptivism beyond its initial parameters, as increasingly the descriptivists' own claims to be immune to evaluation and to stand outside the object they described came under critical fire from various more overtly ideological positions.

While the present book has given an overview of some of the key ideas of descriptive and systemic approaches to translation, it has also suggested that we are dealing with a still unfinished project. The basic ideas have proved fruitful and resilient, but some are in need of revision and overhaul. The behaviourist and objectivist reflexes, the rush to immanent laws, and the old structuralist taxonomic and binary fury have come to look dated and discredited. Questions of value and evaluation, of the translator's agency, and of the problematic position from which statements about translation are made, need closer consideration.

Where is the descriptive and systemic paradigm likely to go? A number of directions suggest themselves.

The history of translation is bound to remain a key area of research. It will need an eye for theoretical aspects of historiography, for the long-term impact of translations, for the relations between discourses about and practices of translation, for the simultaneously overdetermined and formative role of translation in the context of prevailing power hierarchies, for both the autonomy and heteronomy of translation as a cultural practice, and for the translator's actual working environment. Historical research will need to be not only more concrete, alive to the intricacies of specific circumstances and the material and symbolic stakes of the situation, but also more circumspect, aware of the interpretive and evaluative determinants of its conduct.

Appropriate tools need to be devised to study translation in our contemporary social and technological world, tools which can cope with the mobility and interpenetration of communities, with multiple identities and mixed languages, and with the multilevel processing of visual and verbal, spoken and written texts in the mass media. But the methodologies required to study text-based translation and various forms of interpreting also merit further attention, especially as translating and interpreting in the non-Western world are becoming better known in the West.

If there is an obvious lack in translation studies generally today, it is located at the level of theory. The discipline generally, but the descriptive school in particular, urgently needs to take account of developments in some of the more vigorous intellectual and social movements of our time, including gender

studies, poststructuralism, postcolonial and cultural studies, and the new interdisciplinarity invading the human sciences. This renewed theorical reflection
should not necessarily serve only to back up case studies. It should linger on
the modes and conditions of knowledge with which the study of translation
itself operates. It needs to be a self-reflexive, provisional theorizing which is
prepared to be awkward and experimental, and is more alert than translation
studies have traditionally been to the wealth of ideas in neighbouring disciplines.

The structuralist-inspired model of empirical-descriptive translation studies as it was elaborated in the 1970s and '80s, new and exciting as it once was,
is now a thing of the past. The relative absence of innovation within the paradigm itself, and the rise of other, more committed approaches, point in that
direction. Just as a designation like 'the Manipulation group' is tied to a particular historical moment and bound to disappear, so the distinctive identity of
the paradigm that formed the subject of this book is unravelling. Several of
the paradigm's key achievements have become absorbed into the discipline
of translation studies itself. However, that does not mean descriptive and systemic studies no longer have a role to play.

'Whatever Happened to Descriptive Poetics?', Brian McHale recently
asked in a short but pertinent essay (McHale 1994). He pointed out that what
used to be known as 'descriptive poetics' in literary studies had been squeezed
between close textual interpretation on the one hand, and grand theory on the
other. McHale expressed concern at the resulting flattening of critical practice.
Instead of different levels of metalanguage, each with its own range, contemporary analyses tended to move straight from some highly abstract theoretical
frame to the primary texts themselves. As theory was collapsed into interpretation, the texts became mere source material for high-level theorizing.

What has gone missing, McHale suggests, is the middle range, the awkward in-between level where descriptive studies can inform interpretive practice
and yet resist the voraciousness of abstract theory. As McHale sees it, this
middle range is worth reclaiming:

> Instead of theory being brought to bear directly on the text, so as to
> yield an interpretation that is, in effect, merely a mirror or double of the
> theory that underwrites it, the introduction of a descriptive level com-
> pels our discourse to *hesitate*, to linger over or circulate among a range
> of possibilities. Instead of rushing to specify a text's meaning in the
> light of a theory, the descriptive project encourages us to map out a
> range of possible meanings, or to seek to grasp the *conditions* of mean-
> ing in specific texts. (1994:65)

Descriptive translation studies, too, operate to their greatest advantage in the
middle range, where they can query theoretical assumptions without losing
touch with the varied historical and sociocultural practices of translation, and

can delay the attribution of meaning to individual texts by reflecting on the methodological and theoretical implications of such a move.

This is where descriptive and systemic approaches to translation, with their contextualizing historical and sociological reflexes, can find their place. They can challenge and replenish both theoretical speculation and text-based research. They can be the critical conscience of translation studies, urging historical awareness as well as theoretical reflection, attention to words as well as to the conditioning of our ways of making sense of them.

# Glossary

*Acceptability*. Assimilation to the norms and values of the receiving (or 'target') culture. For Even-Zohar and Toury it represents one of two theoretical extremes (the opposite pole is 'adequacy') to which translations tend. The notion is similar to what other researchers have called naturalizing, endogenizing, target-accommodating or domesticating translation. See p. 76.

*Adequacy*. Retention of the features and textual relations of the original in a translation. For Even-Zohar and Toury it represents one of two theoretical extremes (the opposite pole is 'acceptability') to which translations tend. The notion is similar to what other researchers have called exoticizing, exogenizing, source-oriented or foreignizing translation. See pp. 56, 76.

*Adequate Translation (AT)*. Toury's term for a theoretical construct that would contain an explicitation of all the pertinent textual relations and functions of a source text and could serve as the invariant in the comparison between translations and originals. The concept proved unworkable and was subsequently dropped. See p. 56.

*Architranseme*. Van Leuven-Zwart's term for the common denominator between two transemes, used as the invariant of the comparison between them. See p. 59.

*Autopoiesis*. Self-reproduction. In Luhmann's theory of social systems the system reproduces the elements of which it consists; these elements are communications, which, under the right conditions, give rise to further communications. See p. 142.

*Communication*. As Luhmann uses the term, it means the co-occurrence of three elements: enunciation (or utterance), information, and interpretation. For Luhmann, communication begins not with the sender of a message, but with a receiver interpreting something as a message by processing it as meaningful. See p. 140.

*Constructivism*. The philosophical view that all our knowledge is constructed, i.e. dependent on certain presuppositions rather than being reducible to ultimate, firm essences. See p. 137.

*Convention*. A regularity in behaviour, together with the common knowledge about and the mutual expectations regarding the preferred behaviour of all members of a group or community (Lewis). See pp. 80-81.

*Equivalence*. The name sometimes given to the relation between a translation and its source text. See pp. 47ff., 96ff.

*Field*. In Bourdieu's theory, a structured space of social activity with its own laws of functioning and its own relations of force, its structure determined by the relations between the positions agents occupy in the field. Each field is assumed to be relatively autonomous, but structurally homologous with other fields. See p. 132.

*Functional differentiation*. Luhmann's term for a feature of modern societies; it consists in the development of social systems oriented towards specific functions as a way of coping with the complexity of the world. See p. 138.

*Habitus*. A set of 'durable, transposable dispositions' (Bourdieu), both structured and structuring, and, as principles which generate and organize practices and representations, geared towards practical decision-making. See pp. 132, 134.

*Metatext*. A text which speaks about another text. Holmes and Popovič call translations metatexts because they refer back to the original texts from which they derive and which they claim to represent. See p. 25.

*Norm*. A regularity in behaviour, together with the common knowledge about and the mutual expectations concerning the way in which members of a group or community ought to behave in certain types of situation. The content of a norm is a value, a notion of what is correct. The directive force of a norm guides the behaviour of individuals so as to secure the content of the norm. See p. 73ff.

*Patronage*. Lefevere's term for persons or institutions that can further, hinder or otherwise interfere with the production and distribution of cultural goods, such as literary texts or translations. See p. 126.

*Polysystem*. A term invented by Even-Zohar to indicate a complex system or a system consisting of (sub-)systems. He defines such a system as 'the network of relations that can be hypothesized for a certain set of assumed observables'. A literary system would then be defined as 'the network of relations that is hypothesized to obtain between a number of activities called 'literary', and consequently these activities themselves observed via that network', or alternatively 'the complex network of activities, or any section thereof, for which systemic relations can be hypothesized to support the option of considering them "literary".' See p. 106ff.

*Pseudotranslation*. An original work which purports to be a translation. See pp. 25, 50.

*Repertoire*. In Even-Zohar's polysystem theory, 'the aggregate of laws and elements (...) that govern the production of texts'. See p. 107.

*Repertoreme*. A term used by Even-Zohar and Toury to denote an item of an institutionalized or stereotyped repertoire. See p. 93.

*Rewriting*. Lefevere's term for various forms of text processing such as adapting or summarizing texts, reviewing, compiling anthologies, writing critical commentaries or literary histories, and also translating. See p. 127.

*Second-order observation*. The observation of observation (Luhmann). An observer can observe something but not everything, if only because he cannot observe himself observing. Only a second-order observer can see both the first observer and what that observer perceives. However, the second-order observer cannot observe himself observing the first-order observer, etc. The relevance of the notion becomes clear when we read 'description' for 'observation'. See p. 145.

*Self-reproduction*. See *autopoiesis*.

*Social System*. A functionally differentiated, self-reproducing system consisting of communications which process meaning, and separated from its environment by a boundary (Luhmann). See p. 138.

*System*. Often defined simply as a complex of interacting elements, separated from its environment by a boundary. Other definitions characterize a system as a structured whole with internal connections between the elements being more intensive and qualitatively different from those with elements outside the system. See also 'polysystem' and 'social system'. See pp. 42, 102ff.

*Target-oriented Approach*. An approach in the study of translation which tends to start from, and generally puts the emphasis on, the translating or receiving pole, rather than on the source text or culture. See p. 37.

*Texteme*. A term used by Even-Zohar and Toury to denote a linguistic item which forms part of a text and therefore carries textual functions in it. See also 'repertoreme'. See p. 93

*Transeme*. Van Leuven-Zwart's term for a textual unit which is chosen as the unit of analysis in the comparison between originals and translations. See p. 58.

# Bibliography

*The titles most directly relevant to descriptive and systemic translation studies are marked with an asterisk.*

Aaltonen, Sirkku (1997) 'Translating Plays or Baking Apple Pies. A Functional Approach to the Study of Drama Translation', in Snell-Hornby et al. 1997, 89-98.

Aaltonen, Sirkku (1996) *Acculturation of the Other. Irish Milieux in Finnish Drama Translation*. Joensuu: Joensuu University Press.

Álvarez, Román & Vidal, Carmen-África (1996) eds. *Translation, Power, Subversion*. Clevedon etc.: Multilingual Matters.

Arntz, Reiner & Thome, Gisela (1990) eds. *Übersetzungswissenschaft. Ergebnisse und Perspektiven. Festschrift Wolfram Wilss*. Tübingen: Gunter Narr.

Arrojo, Rosemary (1994) 'Fidelity and the Gendered Translation', *TTR* 7, 2, 142-63.

Asad, Talal (1986) 'The Concept of Cultural Translation in British Social Anthropology', in *Writing Culture. The Poetics and Politics of Ethnography* (ed. James Clifford & George Marcus), Berkeley etc.: University of California Press, 141-64.

Baker, Mona (1998) ed. *Routledge Encyclopedia of Translation Studies*. London & New York: Routledge.

Baker, Mona (1996) 'Linguistics & Cultural Studies. Complementary or Competing Paradigms in Translation Studies?', in *Übersetzungswissenschaft im Umbruch. Festschrift Wolfram Wilss* (ed. Angelika Lauer et al.), Tübingen: Gunter Narr, 9-19.

Baker, Mona (1995) 'Corpora in Translation Studies. An Overview and Suggestions for Future Research', *Target* 7, 2, 223-44.

Bakker, Matthijs (1995) 'Metasprong en wetenschap: een kwestie van discipline', in Delabastita & Hermans 1995, 141-62.

Bakker, Matthijs & Naaijkens, Ton (1991) 'A Postscript: Fans of Holmes', in Van Leuven-Zwart & Naaijkens 1991, 193-208.

Ballard, Michel & D'hulst, Lieven (1996) eds. *La traduction en France à l'âge classique*. Lille: Presses universitaires du septentrion..

Barthes, Roland (1970) *S/Z*. Paris: Seuil.

Bartsch, Renate (1987) *Norms of Language. Theoretical and Practical Aspects*. London: Longman.

Bassnett, Susan (1997) ed. *Translating Literature*. Cambridge: D.S. Brewer.

Bassnett, Susan (1993) *Comparative Literature. A Critical Introduction*. Oxford: Blackwell.

Bassnett, Susan (1992) 'Writing in No Man's Land. Questions of Gender and Translation', *Ilha Do Desterro. Studies in Translation* 28: 63-73.

Bassnett, Susan (1991a) 'Translating for the Theatre. The Case Against Performability', *TTR* 4, 1, 99-113.

Bassnett, Susan (1991) *Translation Studies*. London: Methuen (revised ed.; first published 1980).

Bassnett, Susan (1990) 'Translating for the Theatre: Textual Complexities', *Essays in Poetics* 15, 1, 71-84.

Bassnett, Susan (1985) 'Ways Through the Labyrinth. Strategies and Methods for Translating Theatre Texts', in Hermans 1985, 87-103.

Bassnett, Susan (1978) 'Translating Spatial Poetry: An Examination of Theatre Texts in Performance', in Holmes et al. 1978, 161-76.

Bassnett, Susan & Lefevere, André (1998) *Constructing Cultures. Essays on Literary Translation*. Clevedon etc.: Multilingual Matters.

*Bassnett, Susan & Lefevere, André (1990) eds. *Translation, History and Culture*. London & New York: Pinter.

Beil, Ulrich (1996) 'Zwischen Fremdbestimmung und Universalitätsanspruch. Deutsche Weltliteraturanthologien als Ausdruck kultureller Selbstinterpretation', in Eßmann & Schöning 1996, 261-310.

Ben-Ari, Nitsa (1992) 'Didactic and Pedagogic Tendencies in the Norms Dictating the Translations of Children's Literature: the Case of Postwar German-Hebrew Translations', *Poetics Today* 13, 221-30.

Ben-Porat, Ziva & Hrushovski, Benjamin (1974) *Structuralist Poetics in Israel*. Tel Aviv: Tel Aviv University.

Berg, Henk de (1997) 'Communication as Challenge to Systems Theory', *Canadian Review of Comparative Literature* 24, 1, 141-51.

Berg, Henk de (1995) 'A Systems Perspective on Communication', *Poetics Today* 16, 4, 709-36.

Berg, Henk de (1993) 'Die Ereignishaftigkeit des Textes', in De Berg & Prangel 1993, 32-52.

Berg, Henk de & Prangel, Matthias (1995) eds. *Differenzen. Systemtheorie zwischen Dekonstruktion und Konstruktivismus*. Tübingen: Francke.

Berg, Henk de & Prangel, Matthias (1993) eds. *Kommunikation und Differenz. Systemtheoretische Ansätze in der Literatur- und Kunstwissenschaft*. Opladen: Westdeutscher Verlag.

Berman, Antoine (1995) *Pour une critique des traductions: John Donne*. Paris: Gallimard.

Bernheimer, Charles (1995) ed. *Comparative Literature in the Age of Multiculturalism*. Baltimore & London: Johns Hopkins University Press.

Bertalanffy, Ludwig von (1971) *General System Theory. Foundations, Development, Application*. Harmondsworth: Penguin..

Bex, Tony (1994) 'The Relevance of Genre', in *Literature and the New Interdisciplinarity. Poetics, Linguistics, History* (ed. Roger Sell & Peter Verdonk), Amsterdam & Atlanta: Rodopi, 107-29.

Blodgett, E.D. (1989) 'Translated Literature and the Literary Polysystem. The Example of May's *Evangeline*', *Meta* 33, 157-68.

Blom, Tannelie (1997) *Complexiteit en contingentie. Een kritische inleiding tot de sociologie van Niklas Luhmann*. Kampen: Kok Agora.

Borges, Jorge Luis (1981) 'Pierre Menard, Author of the *Quixote*' (transl. James

Irby), in his *Labyrinths*, Harmondsworth: Penguin, 62-71.

Bourdieu, Pierre (1996) *The Rules of Art*. Transl. Susan Emanuel. London: Polity Press.

Bourdieu, Pierre (1994) *Raisons pratiques. Sur la théorie de l'action*. Paris: Seuil.

Bourdieu, Pierre (1993) *The Field of Cultural Production. Essays on Art and Literature*. Transl. Randal Johnson. Cambridge: Polity Press.

Bourdieu, Pierre (1991a) 'Questions of Method', in Ibsch et al. 1991, 19-36.

Bourdieu, Pierre (1991) *Language and Symbolic Power*. Transl. G. Raymond & M. Adamson. Cambridge: Polity Press.

Bourdieu, Pierre (1990) *The Logic of Practice*. Transl. Richard Nice. London: Polity.

Bourdieu, Pierre (1984) *Questions de sociologie*. Paris: Minuit.

Bourdieu, Pierre (1977) *Outline of a Theory of Practice*. Transl. Richard Nice. Cambridge: Cambridge University Press.

Bourdieu, Pierre; Van Rees, Kees, Schmidt, Siegfried & Verdaasdonk, Hugo (1991) 'Panel Discussion: The Structure of the Literary Field and the Homogeneity of Cultural Choices', in Ibsch et al. 1991, 427-43.

Bragt, Katrin van (1995) *Bibliographie des traductions françaises (1810-1840). Répertoires par disciplines*. Leuven: Presses universitaires de Louvain.

Bragt, Katrin van (1982) 'The Tradition of a Translation and Its Implications: 'The Vicar of Wakefield' in French Translation', *Dispositio* 7, 63-76.

Broeck, Raymond van den (1992) *Over de grenzen van het vertaalbare*. Antwerpen & Harmelen: Fantom.

Broeck, Raymond van den (1991) 'The Generative Model of the Translation Process', in Van Leuven-Zwart & Naaijkens 1991, 105-14.

Broeck, Raymond van den (1989) 'Literary Conventions and Translated Literature', in D'haen et al. 1989, 57-75.

Broeck, Raymond van den (1988a) 'Translation Theory after Deconstruction', *Linguistica Antverpiensia* 22, 266-88 (also in *Translation Theory in Scandinavia*, ed. Patrick Chaffey et al., Oslo, 24-57).

Broeck, Raymond van den (1988) ed. *Literatuur van elders*. Leuven: Acco.

Broeck, Raymond van den (1987) 'Jacques Derrida en de toren van Babel: deconstructie en vertaling', *Linguistica Antverpiensia* 21, 127-48.

Broeck, Raymond van den (1986) 'Translating for the Theatre', *Linguistica Antverpiensia* 20, 96-110.

Broeck, Raymond van den (1984-85) 'Verschuivingen in de stilistiek van vertaalde literaire teksten: een semiotische benadering', *Linguistica Antverpiensia* 18-19, 111-46.

Broeck, Raymond van den (1981) 'The Limits of Translatability Exemplified by Metaphor Translation', *Poetics Today* 2, 4, 73-87.

Broeck, Raymond van den (1978) 'The Concept of Equivalence in Translation Theory: Some Critical Reflections', in Holmes et al. 1978, 29-47.

Broeck, Raymond van den (1974) 'Deskriptief en theoretisch onderzoek van de vertaling. Perikelen van een discipline in wording', *Leuvense Bijdragen* 68, 261-78.

Broeck, Raymond van den (1966-67) 'De paradoxen van het vertalen', *Spiegel der letteren* 10, 180-99.

Broeck, Raymond van den & Lefevere, André (1979) *Uitnodiging tot de vertaalwetenschap*. Muiderberg: Coutinho.

Brower, Reuben (1959a) 'Seven Agamemnons', in Brower 1959, 173-95.

Brower, Reuben (1959) ed. *On Translation*. Cambridge: Harvard University Press.

Buck, Timothy (1997) 'Retranslating Mann: A Fresh Attempt on *The Magic Mountain*', *The Modern Language Review* 92, 656-9.

Buck, Timothy (1996) 'Loyalty and Licence: Thomas Man's Fiction in English Translation', *The Modern Language Review* 91, 898-921.

Buck, Timothy (1995) 'Neither the letter nor the spirit. Why most English translations of Thomas Mann are so inadequate', *The Times Literary Supplement*, 13 October 1995, 17.

Burnett, Leon (1985) 'Mandel'shtam's "Word" and Translation', in Hermans 1985, 164-97.

Butler, Judith (1997) *Excitable Speech. A Politics of the Performative*. London & New York: Routledge.

Carbonell i Cortés, Ovidi (1997) *Traducir al Otro. Traducción, exotismo, poscolonialismo*. Cuenca: Universidad de Castilla-La Mancha.

Carbonell i Cortés, Ovidi (1996) 'The Exotic Space of Cultural Translation', in Álvarez & Vidal 1996, 79-98.

Cattrysse, Patrick (1997) 'Audiovisual Translation and New Media', in *From One Medium to Another. Basic Issues for Communicating the Scriptures in New Media* (ed. P.A. Soukup & R. Hodgson), Kansas City & New York: Sheed and Ward & American Bible Society, 67-89.

Cattrysse, Patrick (1994) 'The Study of Film Adaptation: a State of the Art and Some 'New' Functional Proposals', in Eguíluz et al. 1994, 37-55.

*Cattrysse, Patrick (1992a) 'Film (Adaptation) as Translation: Some Methodogical Proposals', *Target* 4, 1, 53-70.

Cattrysse, Patrick (1992) *Pour une théorie de l'adaptation filmique. Le film noir américain*. Bern etc: Peter Lang.

Chamberlain, Lori (1992) 'Gender and the Metaphorics of Translation', in *Rethinking Translation* (ed. Lawrence Venuti), London: Routledge, 57-74. Originally printed 1988 in *Signs* 13, 454-72.

Chesterman, Andrew (1997a) 'Ethics of Translation', in Snell-Hornby et al. 1997, 147-57.

Chesterman, Andrew (1997) *Memes of Translation. The Spread of Ideas in Translation Theory*. Amsterdam & Philadelphia: John Benjamins.

Chesterman, Andrew (1996) 'On Similarity', *Target* 8, 159-64.

Chesterman, Andrew (1993) 'From "Is" to "Ought": Laws, Norms and Strategies in Translation Studies', *Target*, 5, 1-20.

Chesterman, Andrew (1989) ed. *Readings in Translation Theory*. Helsinki: Oy Finn Lectura.

Chevrel, Yves (1988) 'Les traductions et leur rôle dans le système littéraire français', in Kittel 1988, 30-55.

Cheyfitz, Eric (1991) *The Poetics of Imperialism. Translation and Colonization from 'The Tempest' to 'Tarzan'*, New York & Oxford: Oxford University Press.

Copeland, Rita (1991) *Rhetoric, Hermeneutics, and Translation in the Middle Ages*. Cambridge: Cambridge University Press.

Crane, Diana (1972) *Invisible Colleges. Diffusion of Knowledge in Scientific Communities*. Chicago & London: University of Chicago Press.

Crick, Joyce (1985) 'Coleridge's *Wallenstein*: Available Dictions', in Hermans 1985d, 128-60

Culler, Jonathan (1997) *Literary Theory. A Very Short Introduction*. Oxford & New York: Oxford University Press.

Cummins, John (1992) *The Voyage of Christopher Columbus. Columbus' Own Journal of Discovery Newly Restored and Translated*. London: Weidenfeld & Nicolson.

Czennia, Bärbel (1992) 'Zum Aussagewert motivgeschichtlicher Übersetzungsstudien', *Target* 4, 71-96.

Danan, Martine (1996) 'A la recherche d'une stratégie internationale: Hollywood et le marché français des années trente', in *Les transferts linguistiques dans les médias audiovisuels* (ed. Yves Gambier), Villeneuve d'Ascq: Presses universitaires du Septentrion, 1996, 109-30.

Danan, Martine (1991) 'Dubbing as an Expression of Nationalism', *Meta* 36, 606-14.

Davis, Kathleen (1997) 'Signature in Translation', in Delabastita 1997, 23-44.

Dawkins, Richard (1995) *River Out of Eden. A Darwinian View of Life*. London: Phoenix.

Delabastita, Dirk (1997) ed. *Traductio. Essays on Punning and Translation*. Manchester & Namur: St Jerome & Presses Universitaires de Namur.

Delabastita, Dirk (1994) 'Focus on the Pun. Wordplay as a Special Problem in Translation Studies', *Target* 6, 223-43.

Delabastita, Dirk (1993a) '*Hamlet* in the Netherlands in the Late Eighteenth and Early Nineteenth Centuries. The Complexities of the History of Shakespeare's Reception,' in Delabastita & D'hulst 1993, 219-33.

*Delabastita, Dirk (1993) *There's a Double Tongue. An Investigation into the Translation of Shakespeare's Wordplay*. Amsterdam & Atlanta: Rodopi.

Delabastita, Dirk (1991) 'A False Opposition in Translation Studies: Theoretical versus/and Historical Approaches', *Target* 3, 137-52.

*Delabastita, Dirk (1990) 'Translation and the Mass Media', in Bassnett & Lefevere 1990, 97-109.

Delabastita, Dirk (1989) 'Translation and Mass Communication: film and TV translation as evidence of cultural dynamics', *Babel* 35, 4, 193-218.

Delabastita, Dirk (1987) 'Translating Puns. Possibilities and Restraints', *New Comparison* 3, 143-59.

Delabastita, Dirk (1985) 'Shakespeare's Sonnets in Translation: A TT-Oriented Approach', in Hermans 1985c, 106-27.

*Delabastita, Dirk & D'hulst, Lieven (1993) eds. *European Shakespeares. Translating Shakespeare in the Romantic Age*. Amsterdam & Philadelphia: John Benjamins.

Delabastita, Dirk & Hermans Theo (1995) eds. *Vertalen historisch bezien. Tekst, metatekst, theorie*. The Hague: Bibliographia Neerlandica.

Delisle, Jean & Woodsworth, Judith (1995) eds. *Translators through History*. Amsterdam & Philadelphia: John Benjamins.

Derrida, Jacques (1985) 'Des Tours de Babel', in *Difference in Translation* (ed. Joseph Graham), Ithaca & London: Cornell University Press, 165-248.

Derrida, Jacques (1982) *The Ear of the Other. Otobiography, Transference, Translation*. Transl. Peggy Kamuf. Lincoln & London: University of Nebraska Press.

D'haen, Theo, Grübel, Rainer & Lethen, Helmut (1989) eds. *Convention and Innovation in Literature*. Amsterdam & Philadelphia: John Benjamins.

D'hulst, Lieven (1997a) 'Les premiers doctorats français sur la traduction', *Linguistica Antverpiensia* 30, 49-66.

D'hulst, Lieven (1997) 'La traduction: un genre littéraire à l'époque romantique?', *Revue d'histoire littéraire de la France* 97, 391-400.

D'hulst, Lieven (1996) 'Unité et diversité de la réflexion traductologique en France (1722-1789)', in Ballard & D'hulst 1996, 83-100.

*D'hulst, Lieven (1995a) 'Pour une historiographie des théories de la traduction: questions de méthode', *TTR* 8, 1, 13-33.

D'hulst, Lieven (1995) 'Enkele stellingen over de historiografie van de vertaalwetenschap', in Delabastita & Hermans 1995, 7-22.

D'hulst, Lieven (1993a) 'La traduction en France à l'époque romantique et l'évolution de la culture française', in Lambert & Lefevere 1993, 159-64.

D'hulst, Lieven (1993) 'Observations sur l'expression figurée en traductologie française (XVIIIe-XIXe siècles)', *TTR* 6, 1, 83-111.

D'hulst, Lieven (1992) 'Sur le rôle des métaphores en traductologie contemporaine', *Target* 4, 33-52.

D'hulst, Lieven (1991) 'Pourquoi et comment écrire l'histoire des théories de la traduction', in *Actes du XIIe congrès mondial de la FIT*, Belgrade: Prevodilac, 57-62.

*D'hulst, Lieven (1990) ed. *Cent ans de théorie française de la traduction (1748-1847)*. Lille: Presses Universitaires de Lille.

D'hulst, Lieven (1989a) 'Le discours sur la traduction en France (1800-1850)', *Revue de littérature comparée* 63, 2, 179-87

D'hulst, Lieven (1989) 'Sur la poésie traduite en ses enjeux au XIXe siècle: le dossier des traductions françaises de la 'Lénore' de Bürger', *Linguistica antverpiensia* 23, 51-81.

D'hulst, Lieven (1987a) 'La traduction des poètes classiques à l'époque romantique', *Les études classiques* 55, 65-74.

D'hulst, Lieven (1987) *L'évolution de la poésie en France (1780-1830). Introduction à une analyse des interférences systémiques*. Leuven: Leuven University Press.

D'hulst, Lieven (1986) 'Quelques notes sur le "champ" des études de traduction', *Linguistica Antverpiensia* 20, 59-62.

D'hulst, Lieven (1982) 'The Conflict of Translational Models in France (end of 18th-beginning of 19th century), *Dispositio* 7, 41-52.

D'hulst, Lieven (1981) 'Les variantes textuelles des traductions littéraires', *Poetics Today* 2, 4, 133-41.

D'hulst, Lieven (1979) 'Recente ontwikkelingen in literair vertaalonderzoek', *Spiegel der letteren* 21, 1, 26-37.

Dimič, Milan & Garstin, Marguerite (1988) 'The Polysystem Theory: A Brief Introduction with Bibliography', in *Problems of Literary Reception* (ed. E.D. Blodgett & A.G.Purdy), Edmonton: University of Alberta, 177-96.

*Doorslaer, Luc van (1995) 'Quantitative and Qualititative Aspects of Corpus Selection in Translation Studies', *Target* 7, 245-60.

Dubois, Jacques & Durand, Pascal (1989)'Literary Field and Classes of Texts' (transl. Priscilla Parkurst Ferguson), in *Literature and Social Practice* (ed. Philippe Desan, Priscilla Parkhurst Ferguson & Wendy Griswold), Chicago & London: University of Chicago Press, 137-53.

Du-Nour, Myriam (1995) 'Retranslation of Children's Books as Evidence of Changes of Norms', *Target* 7, 327-46.

Ďurišin, Dionýz (1972) *Vergleichende Literaturforschung*. Berlin: Akademieverlag.

Eguíluz, F., Merino, R., Olsen, V., Pajares, E. & Santamaría, J.-M. (1994) eds. *Transvases culturales: literatura, cine, traducción*. Vitoria-Gasteiz: Universidad del País Vasco/Euskal Herriko Unibertsitatea.

Eikhenbaum, Boris (1978) 'Literary Environment' [1929], in Matejka & Pomorska 1978, 56-65.

*Enfants de langue* (1995) *Enfants de langue et Drogmans. Dil O ğlanlari ve Tercümanlar*. Istanbul: Yapi Kredi.

Engels, Yukino (1998) *A Study of 'Oranda Tsûji': in preparation for an extended study of translation history in Japan through 'Oranda Tsûji'*. MSc. dissertation, Department of Language Engineering, University of Manchester Institute of Science and Technology.

Essmann, Helga & Schöning, Udo (1996) eds. *Weltliteratur in deutschen Versanthologien des 19. Jahrhunderts*. Berlin: Erich Schmidt.

Evans-Pritchard, Edward (1956) *Nuer Religion*. Oxford: Oxford University Press.

Even-Zohar, Basmat (1992) 'Translation Policy in Hebrew Children's Literature: the Case of Astrid Lindgren', *Poetics Today* 13, 231-45.

Even-Zohar, Itamar (Forthcoming) *Studies in Polysystems of Cultures*.

Even-Zohar, Itamar (1997a) 'The Making of Culture Repertoire and the Role of Transfer', *Target* 9, 355-63.

Even-Zohar, Itamar (1997) 'Factors and Dependencies in Culture: A Revised Outline for Polysystem Culture Research', *Canadian Review of Comparative Literature* 24, 1, 15-34.

Even-Zohar, Itamar (1996) 'The Role of Literature in the Making of the Nations of Europe: a Socio-Semiotic Examination', *Applied Semiotics / Sémiotique appliquée* 1, 20-30 (http://www.epas.utoronto.ca:8080/french/as-sa/index.html).

*Even-Zohar, Itamar (1990) 'Polysystem Studies', *Poetics Today*, 11, 1 (special issue).

Even-Zohar, Itamar (1981a) 'The Emergence of a Native Hebrew Culture in

Palestine: 1882-1948, *Studies in Zionism* 4, 167-84.

Even-Zohar, Itamar (1981) 'Translation Theory Today. A Call for Transfer Theory', *Poetics Today* 2, 4, 1-7.

Even-Zohar, Itamar (1978a) 'The Position of Translated Literature within the Literary Polysystem', in Holmes et al. 1978, 117-27 (also in Even-Zohar 1978).

*Even-Zohar, Itamar (1978) *Papers in Historical Poetics*. Tel Aviv: Porter Institute for Poetics and Semiotics.

Even-Zohar, Itamar (1971) *Introduction to a Theory of Literary Translation*. PhD Thesis, University of Tel Aviv.

Flotow, Luise von (1997) *Translation and Gender. Translating in the 'Era of Feminism'*. Manchester & Ottawa: St Jerome & University of Ottawa Press.

Fokkema, Douwe (1991) 'Changing the Canon: A Systems-Theoretical Approach', in Ibsch et al. 1991, 363-70.

Fokkema, Douwe (1989) 'The Concept of Convention in Literary Theory and Empirical Research', in D'haen et al. 1989, 1-16.

Fokkema, Douwe (1985) 'The Concept of Code in the Study of Literature', *Poetics Today* 6, 643-56.

Fokkema, Douwe & Ibsch, Elrud (1987) *Modernist Conjectures. A Mainstream in European Literature 1910-1940*. London: Hurst.

Folkart, Barbara (1991) *Le conflit des énonciations. Traduction et discours rapporté*. Candiac: Editions Balzac.

Frank, Armin Paul (1992a) 'Zu einer 'konkreten Theorie' des übersetzerischen Umgangs mit Fremdheitspotential: *Waste Land*-Übersetzungen französisch und deutsch', in Lönker 1992, 63-8.

Frank, Armin Paul (1992) 'Towards a Cultural History of Literary Translation. 'Histories', 'Systems' and Other Forms of Synthesizing Research', in Kittel 1992, 369-87.

Frank, Armin Paul (1991) 'Translating and Translated Poetry: the Producer's and the Historian's Perspectives', in Van Leuven-Zwart & Naaijkens 1991, 115-40.

Frank, Armin Paul (1990) 'Forty Years of Studying the American-German Translation Transfer. A Retrospect and Some Perspectives', *American Studies / Amerika Studien*, 35, 1, 7-20.

Frank, Armin Paul (1989a) '"Translation as System" and *Übersetzungskultur*: On Histories and Systems in the Study of Literary Translation', *New Comparison* 8, 85-98.

Frank, Armin Paul (1989) ed. *Der lange Schatten kurzer Geschichten. Amerikanische Kurzprosa in deutschen Übersetzungen*. Berlin: Erich Schmidt.

Frank, Armin Paul (1988) 'Rückblick und Ausblick', in Kittel 1988, 180-206.

Frank, Armin Paul (1987) 'Einleitung', in Schultze 1987, ix-xvii.

Frank, Armin Paul & Bödeker, Birgit (1991) 'Trans-culturality and Inter-culturality in French and German Translations of T.S. Eliot's *The Waste Land*', in Kittel & Frank 1991, 41-61.

Frank, Armin Paul & Schultze, Brigitte (1988) 'Normen in historisch-deskriptiven Übersetzungsstudien', in Kittel 1988, 96-121.

Gaddis Rose, Marilyn (1996) ed. *Translation Horizons. Beyond the Boundaries of 'Translation Spectrum'. Translation Perspectives IX*. Binghamton: State University of New York.

Gallego Roca, Miguel (1994) *Traducción y literatura: los estudios literarios ante las obras traducidas*. Madrid: Jucar.

Geest, Dirk de (1997) 'Systems Theory and Discursivity', *Canadian Review of Comparative Literature* 24, 1, 161-75.

Geest, Dirk de (1996) *Literatuur als systeem, literatuur als vertoog. Bouwstenen voor een functionalistische benadering van literaire verschijnselen*. Leuven: Peeters.

*Geest, Dirk de (1992) 'The Notion of 'System': Its Theoretical Importance and Its Methodological Implications for a Functionalist Translation Theory,' in Kittel 1992, 32-45.

Gentzler, Edwin (1993) *Contemporary Translation Theories*. London & New York: Routledge.

Gernet, Jacques (1985) *China and the Christian Impact. A Conflict of Cultures*. Transl. Janet Lloyd. Cambridge & Paris: Cambridge University Press & Editions de la Maison des Sciences de l'Homme.

Gile, Daniel (1991) 'Methodological Aspects of Interpretation (and Translation) Research', *Target* 3, 153-74.

Goris, Olivier (1993) 'The Question of French Dubbing: Towards a Frame for Systematic Investigation', *Target* 5, 169-90.

Gorlée, Dinda (1997-98) 'Translation: Between Imaging, Modeling and Manipulation', in *Semiosis*, 85/90, 74-83.

Gorlée, Dinda (1993) *Semiotics and the Problem of Translation. With Special Reference to the Semiotics of Charles S. Peirce*. Thesis, Amsterdam (UvA).

Gorlée, Dinda (1986) 'Translation Theory and the Semiotics of Games and Decisions', in *Translation Studies in Scandinavia. SSOTT II* (ed. Lars Wollin & Hans Lindquist), Malmö: Liber, 37-50.

Gorp, Hendrik van (1996) 'Traductions, versions et extraits dans la Nouvelle Bibliothèque des Romans et la Bibliothèque Britannique (1796-1802)', in Ballard & D'hulst 1996, 291-304.

Gorp, Hendrik van (1985) 'Translation and Literary Genre. The European Picaresque Novel in the 17th and 18th Centuries', in Hermans 1985, 136-48.

Gorp, Hendrik van (1981) 'Traductions et évolution d'un genre littéraire. Le roman picaresque en Europe au 17e et 18e siècle', *Poetics Today* 2, 4, 209-19.

Gorp, Hendrik van (1978) 'La traduction littéraire parmi les autres métatextes', in Holmes et al. 1978, 101-16.

Gouanvic, Jean-Marc (1997a) 'Translation and the Shape of Things to Come. The Emergence of American Science Fiction in Post-War France'. *The Translator* 3, 125-52 [An earlier French version in *TTR* 7, 1994, 1, 117-52].

Gouanvic, Jean-Marc (1997) 'Pour une sociologie de la traduction: le cas de la littérature américaine traduite en France après la Seconde Guerre mondiale (1945-1960)', in Snell-Hornby et al. 1997, 33-44.

Graeber, Wilhelm (1996) 'Le charme des fruits défendus: les traductions de l'anglais et la dissolution de l'idéal classique', in Ballard & D'hulst 1996, 305-19.

Graeber, Wilhelm (1993) 'Das Ende deutscher Romanübersetzungen aus zweiter Hand', *Target* 5, 215-28.

Graeber, Wilhelm (1990) ed. *Französische Übersetzervorreden des 18. Jahrhunderts*. Frankfurt: Peter Lang.

Graeber, Wilhelm & Roche, Geneviève (1988) eds. *Englische Literatur des 17. und 18. Jahrhunders in französischer Übersetzung und deutscher Weiterübersetzung. Eine kommentierte Bibliographie*. Tübingen: Niemeyer.

Grähs, Lillebill, Korlén, Gustav & Malmberg, Bertil (1978) eds. *Theory and Practice of Translation*. Bern: Peter Lang.

Gutt, Ernst-August (1996) 'Implicit Information in Literary Translation: A Relevance-Theoretic Perspective', *Target* 8, 239-56.

Gutt, Ernst-August (1991) *Translation and Relevance. Cognition and Context*. Oxford: Blackwell.

Halverson, Sandra (1997) 'The Concept of Equivalence in Translation Studies: Much Ado about Something', *Target* 9, 207-34.

Harris, Brian (1990) 'Norms in Interpretation', *Target* 2, 115-19.

Hejl, Peter (1993) 'Culture as a Network of Socially Constructed Realities', in *Cultural Participation. Trends since the Middle Ages* (ed. Ann Rigley & Douwe Fokkema), Amsterdam & Philadelphia: John Benjamins, 227-50.

Hellmann, Kai-Uwe (1996) 'Einleitung', in Luhmann 1996, 7-45.

Hermans, Theo (1997a) 'The Task of the Translator in the European Renaissance', in Bassnett 1997, 14-40.

Hermans, Theo (1997) 'Translation as Institution', in Snell-Hornby et al. 1997, 3-20.

Hermans, Theo (1996c) *Translation's Other*. Inaugural lecture. London: University College London.

Hermans, Theo (1996b) 'The Translator's Voice in Translated Narrative', *Target* 8, 23-48.

Hermans, Theo (1996a) 'Norms and the Determination of Translation', in Álvarez & Vidal 1996, 24-51.

Hermans, Theo (1996) *Door eenen engen hals. Nederlandse beschouwingen over vertalen 1550-1670*. The Hague: Bibliographia Neerlandica.

Hermans, Theo (1995) 'Disciplinary Objectives: The Shifting Grounds of Translation Studies', in *Perspectivas de la traducción inglés-español* (eds. P. Fernández Nistal & J.M. Bravo Gonzalo), Valladolid: Universidad de Valladolid, 9-26.

Hermans, Theo (1994a) 'Translation between Poetics and Ideology', *Translation and Literature* 3, 138-145.

Hermans, Theo (1994) 'Vertaalwetenschap in de Lage Landen', *Neerlandica extra muros* 32, 3, 1-13.

Hermans, Theo (1993) 'On Modelling Translation. Models, Norms and the Field of Translation', *Livius* 4, 69-88.

Hermans, Theo (1992) 'Renaissance Translation between Literalism and Imitation', in *Geschichte, System, Literarische Übersetzung / Histories, Systems, Literary Translations* (ed. Harald Kittel), Berlin: Erich Schmidt, 95-116.

Hermans, Theo (1991b) *Studies over Nederlandse vertalingen. Een bibliografische lijst*. The Hague: Bibliographia Neerlandica.

Hermans, Theo (1991a) 'Translating 'Rhetorijckelijck' or 'Ghetrouwelijck'. Dutch Renaissance Approaches to Translation', in *Standing Clear* (ed. J. Fenoulhet & T. Hermans), London: Centre for Low Countries Studies, 151-72.

Hermans, Theo (1991) 'Translational Norms and Correct Translations', in Van Leuven-Zwart & Naaijkens 1991, 155-70.

Hermans, Theo (1988a) 'Van 'Hebban olla vogala' tot Ernst van Altena: literaire vertaling en Nederlandse literatuurgeschiedenis', in Van den Broeck 1988, 11-26.

Hermans, Theo (1988) 'On Translating Proper Names, with reference to *De Witte* and *Max Havelaar*', in *Modern Dutch Studies* (ed. M. Wintle), London: Athlone, 11-24.

Hermans, Theo (1987) 'Huygens on Translation', *Dutch Crossing* 33, 3-27.

Hermans, Theo (1986) 'Literary Translation: the Birth of a Concept', *New Comparison* 1, 28-42 . Reprinted in Lambert & Lefevere 1993, 93-104.

Hermans, Theo (1985d) 'Vondel on Translation', *Dutch Crossing* 26, 38-72.

Hermans, Theo (1985c) ed. *Second Hand. Papers on the Theory and Historical Study of Literary Translation* . Antwerp: ALW.

Hermans, Theo (1985b) 'Images of Translation: Metaphor and Imagery in the Renaissance Discourse on Translation', in Hermans 1985, 103-35 .

Hermans, Theo (1985a) 'Introduction. Translation Studies and a New Paradigm', in Hermans 1985, 7-15.

*Hermans, Theo (1985) ed. *The Manipulation of Literature. Studies in Literary Translation*. London & Sydney: Croom Helm.

Hermans, Theo (1982) *The Structure of Modernist Poetry*. London & Canberra: Croom Helm.

Hermans, Theo (1980) 'P.C. Hooft: the Sonnets and the Tragedy', *Dutch Crossing* 12, 10-26. Reprinted in *Dispositio* 19-21, 1982, 95-110.

Hermans, Theo (1979) 'Translation, Comparison, Diachrony', *Comparison* 9, 58-91.

Heydebrand, Renate von, Pfau, Dieter & Schönert, Jörg (1988) eds. *Zur theoretischen Grundlegung einer Sozialgeschichte der Literatur. Ein struktural-funktionaler Entwurf*. Tübingen: Max Niemeyer.

Heylen, Romy (1993) *Translation, Poetics, and the Stage. Six French Hamlets*. London & New York: Routledge.

Hjort, Anne Mette (1992) ed. *Rules and Conventions. Literature, Philosophy, Social Theory*. Baltimore & London: Johns Hopkins University Press.

Hjort, Anne Mette (1990) 'Translation and the Consequences of Scepticism', in Bassnett & Lefevere 1990, 38-45.

Holmes, James S (1988a) 'The Name and Nature of Translation Studies' [1972], in *Translated!*, ed. R. van den Broeck, Amsterdam: Rodopi, 67-80.

*Holmes, James S (1988) *Translated! Papers on Literary Translation and*

*Translation Studies*, ed. R. van den Broeck. Amsterdam: Rodopi.

Holmes, James S (1978) 'Describing Literary Translations: Models and Methods', in Holmes et al. 1978, 69-82 (reprinted in Holmes 1988).

Holmes, James S (1970) ed. *The Nature of Translation. Essays on the Theory and Practice of Literary Translation*. The Hague & Paris / Bratislava: Mouton / Slovak Academy of Sciences.

*Holmes, James S; Lambert, José & Van den Broeck, Raymond (1978) eds. *Literature and Translation. New Perspectives in Literary Studies*. Leuven: Acco.

Horguelin, Paul (1977) ed. *Translating, a Profession. La traduction, une profession*. Montréal: Conseil des traducteurs et interprètes du Canada.

Huntemann, Willi (1990) 'Überlegungen zum Begriff der Sozialen Konvention', in Schultze et al. 1990, 15-33.

Hyun, Theresa (1997) 'Byron Lands in Korea. Translation and Literacy/Cultural Changes in Early Twentieth-Century Korea', *TTR* 10, 1, 283-99.

Hyun, Theresa (1995) 'Translation Norms and the Importation of Symbolist Poetry in Early Modern Korea', in Hyun & Lambert 1995, 54-61.

Hyun, Theresa (1992a) 'Translation Policy and Literary/Cultural Changes in Early Modern Korea (1895-1921)', *Target* 4, 191-208.

Hyun, Theresa (1992) *Translation and Early Modern Korean Literature*. Seoul: Siwa Sihaksa.

Hyun, Theresa & Lambert, José (1995) eds. *Translation and Modernization*. Tokyo: Tokyo University Press.

Ibsch, Elrud, Schram, Dick & Steen, Gerard (1991) eds. *Empirical Studies of Literature. Proceedings of the Second IGEL conference, Amsterdam 1989*. Amsterdam & Atlanta: Rodopi.

Jakobson, Roman (1959) 'On Linguistic Aspects of Translation', in Brower 1959, 232-39.

Jansen, Peter (1995) ed. *Translation and the Manipulation of Discourse. Selected Papers of the CERA Research Seminars in Translation Studies 1992-93*. Leuven: CETRA Chair.

Kelly, Louis (1979) *The True Interpreter. Theory and Practice of Translation in the West*. Oxford: Blackwell.

Kelsen, Hans (1991) *General Theory of Norms*. Transl. Michael Hartney. Oxford: Clarendon [German original 1979].

King, Graham (1978) *Garden of Zola (Emile Zola and His Novels for English Readers)*. New York: Barnes & Noble.

Kittel, Harald (1995) ed. *International Anthologies of Literature in Translation*. Berlin: Erich Schmidt.

*Kittel, Harald (1992) ed. *Geschichte, System, Literarische Übersetzung. Histories, Systems, Literary Translations*. Berlin: Erich Schmidt.

Kittel, Harald (1988a) 'Kontinuität und Diskrepanzen', in Kittel 1988, 158-79.

Kittel, Harald (1988) ed. *Die literarische Übersetzung. Stand und Perspektiven ihrer Erforschung*. Berlin: Erich Schmidt.

Kittel, Harald & Frank, Armin Paul (1991) eds. *Interculturality and the Historical Study of Literary Translations*. Berlin: Erich Schmidt.

Koller, Werner (1995) 'The Concept of Equivalence and the Object of Translation Studies', *Target* 7, 2, 191-222.

Koller, Werner (1992) *Einführung in die Übersetzungswissenschaft*. 4th rev. ed.
Heidelberg & Wiesbaden: Quelle & Meyer.

Koller, Werner (1990) 'Zum Gegenstand der Übersetzungswissenschaft' in Arntz
& Thome 1990, 19-30.

Koller, Werner (1978) 'Äquivalenz in kontrastiver Linguistik und Übersetzungswissenschaft', in Grähs et al. 1978, 69-92.

Koller, Werner (1972) *Grundprobleme der Übersetzungstheorie. Unter besonderer
Berücksichtigung schwedisch-deutscher Übersetzungsfälle*. Bern & München:
Francke.

Korpel, Luc (1993a) 'Rhetoric and Dutch Translation Theory (1750-1820)', *Target* 5, 55-69.

Korpel, Luc (1992) *Over het nut en de wijze der vertalingen. Nederlandse vertaal-
reflectie (1750-1820) in een Westeuropees kader*. Amsterdam & Atlanta:
Rodopi.

Korpel, Luc (1986) 'The Discourse on Translation in the Netherlands (1750-1800)',
*New Comparison* 1, 43-56.

Kratochwil, Friedrich (1989) *Rules, Norms and Decisions. On the Conditions of
Practical and Legal Reasoning in International Relations and Domestic Affairs*. Cambridge etc.: Cambridge University Press.

Krawietz, Werner & Welker, Michael (1992) *Kritik der Theorie sozialer Systeme.
Auseinandersetzungen mit Luhmanns Hauptwerk*. Frankfurt: Suhrkamp.

Kuhn, Thomas (1970) *The Structure of Scientific Revolutions*. 2nd, enlarged ed.
Chicago & London: University of Chicago Press.

Laermans, Rudi (1997) 'Communication on Art, or the Work of Art as Communication? Bourdieu's Field Analysis Compared with Luhmann's Systems
Theory', *Canadian Review of Comparative Literature* 24, 1, 103-13.

Lambert, José (1997) 'Itamar Even-Zohar's Polysystem Studies: An Interdisciplinary Perspective on Culture Research', *Canadian Review of Comparative
Literature* 24, 1, 7-14.

Lambert, José (1996a) 'Le discours implicite sur la traduction dans l'*Encyclopédie*',
in Ballard & D'hulst 1996, 101-19.

Lambert, José (1996) 'Translation and/as Research for Societies' in *Translation
Studies in Hungary*, ed. Kinga Klaudy, José Lambert & Anikó Sohár, Buda-
pest: Scholastica, 11-25.

Lambert, José (1995c) 'Literary Translation. Research Updated', in *La traducción
literaria* (ed. Josep Borillo), Castelló: Universitat Jaume I, 19-42.

Lambert, José (1995b) 'Translation, or the Canonization of Otherness', in
Poltermann 1995, 160-78.

Lambert, José (1995a) 'Literatures, Translation and (De)Colonization', in Hyun
& Lambert 1995, 98-117.

Lambert, José (1995) 'Translation, Systems and Research: The Contribution of
Polysystem Studies to Translation Studies', *TTR* 8, 1, 105-52.

Lambert, José (1994) 'Ethnolinguistic Democracy, Translation Policy and

Contemporary World (Dis)order', in Eguíluz et al. 1994, 23-36.

*Lambert, José (1993a) 'Auf der Suche nach literarischen und übersetzerischen Weltkarten', in *Übersetzen, verstehen, Brücken bauen*, vol. 1 (ed. Armin Paul Frank et al.), Berlin: Erich Schmidt, 85-105.

Lambert, José (1993) 'Shakespeare en France au tournant du XVIIIe siècle. Un dosier européen', in Delabastita & D'hulst 1993, 25-44.

Lambert, José (1992) 'Shakespeare and French Nineteenth-Century Theatre. A Methodological Discussion', in Kittel 1992, 66-90.

Lambert, José (1991a) 'In Quest of Literary World Maps', in Kittel & Frank 1991, 133-44 [first published in French, 1989].

*Lambert, José (1991) 'Shifts, Oppositions and Goals in Translation Studies: Towards a Genealogy of Concepts', in Van Leuven-Zwart & Naaijkens 1991, 25-37.

Lambert, José (1990) 'Le sous-titrage et la question des traductions. Rapport sur une enquête', in Arntz & Thome 1990, 228-38.

Lambert, José (1989a) 'L'époque romantique en France: les genres, la traduction et l'évolution littéraire', *Revue de littérature comparée* 2, 25-30.

Lambert, José (1989) 'La traduction, les langues et la communication de masse. Les ambiguïtés du discours international', *Target* 1, 215-37.

*Lambert, José (1988) 'Twenty Years of Research on Literary Translation at the Katholieke Universiteit Leuven', in Kittel 1988, 122-38.

Lambert, José (1986) 'Les relations littéraires internationales comme problème de réception', *Œuvres et Critiques* 11, 2, 173-89.

Lambert, José (1985) 'Literature in South Africa. Suggestions for Systemic Research', *South African Journal of Literary Studies* 1, 2, 34-42.

Lambert, José (1984/5) 'De l'histoire des traductions à la pratique de la traduction', *Linguistica Antverpiensia* 18/19, 74-83.

Lambert, José (1984) 'Théorie littéraire, histoire littéraire, étude des traductions', in *Renouvellements dans la théorie de l'histoire littéraire* (ed. Eva Kushner), Montréal: Société Royale du Canada, 119-30.

Lambert, José (1983) 'L'éternelle question des frontièrers: littératures nationales et systèmes littéraires', in *Langue, dialecte, littérature* (ed. C. Angelet et al.), Leuven: Leuven University Press, 355-70.

Lambert, José (1982) 'How Emile Deschamps Translated Shakespeare's *Macbeth*, or Theatre System and Translation System in French', *Dispositio* 7, 53-62.

Lambert, José (1981) 'Théorie de la littérature et théorie de la traduction en France (1800-1850), interprétées à partir du polysystème', *Poetics Today*, 2, 4, 161-70.

Lambert, José (1978a) 'Echanges littéraires et traduction, ou: études théoriques vs. études descriptives', in Grähs et al. 1978, 237-48.

Lambert, José (1978) 'Echanges littéraires et traduction: discussion d'un projet', Holmes et al. 1978, 128-41.

Lambert, José (1976) *Ludwig Tieck dans les lettres françaises. Aspects d'une résistance au romantisme allemand*. Paris & Leuven: Didier & Presses universitaires de Louvain.

Lambert, José & Delabastita, Dirk (1996) 'La traduction des textes audiovisuels: modes et enjeux culturels', in *Les transferts linguistiques dans les médias audiovisuels* (ed. Yves Gambier), Villeneuve d'Ascq: Presses universitaires du Septentrion, 1996, 33-58.

Lambert, José; D'hulst, Lieven & Van Bragt, Katrin (1985) 'Translated Literature in France, 1800-1850', in Hermans 1985, 149-63.

Lambert, José & Van Gorp, Hendrik (1985a) 'Towards Research Programmes: the Function of Translated Literature within European Literatures', in Hermans 1985c, 183-97.

Lambert, José & Van Gorp, Hendrik (1985) 'On Describing Translations', in Hermans 1985, 42-53.

Lambert, José & Lefevere, André (1993) eds. *Translation in the Development of Literatures / La traduction dans le développement des littératures*. Bern/Leuven: Peter Lang/Leuven University Press.

Lambert, José & Lefevere, André (1977) 'Translation, Literary Translation and Comparative Literature. Traduction, traduction littéraire et littérature comparée', in Horguelin 1977, 329-42.

Lambert, José & Toury, Gideon (1989) 'On *Target*'s Targets', *Target* 1, 1-7.

Leach, Edmund (1973) 'Ourselves and Others', *The Times Literary Supplement*, 6 July, 772.

Lefevere, André (1998) 'Translation Practice(s) and the Circulation of Cultural Capital. Some Aeneids in English', in Bassnett & Lefevere 1998, 25-40.

Lefevere, André (1997) 'Translation and the Creation of Images, or 'Excuse me, is this the same poem?'', in Bassnett 1997, 64-79.

Lefevere, André (1996b) 'Translation: Who is Doing What For/Against Whom and Why?', in Gaddis Rose 1996, 45-55.

Lefevere, André (1996) 'The Extract: Literary Guerilla as Literary Interchange', in Ballard & D'hulst 1996, 275-90.

Lefevere, André (1995) 'German Literature for Americans 1840-1940', in Kittel 1995, 40-55.

Lefevere, André (1992b) ed. *Translation/History/Culture. A Sourcebook*. London & New York: Routledge.

Lefevere, André (1992a) *Translating Literature: Practice and Theory in a Comparative Literature Context*. New York: Modern Language Association of America.

*Lefevere, André (1992) *Translation, Rewriting and the Manipulation of Literary Fame*. London & New York: Routledge.

Lefevere, André (1991) 'Translation and Comparative Literature: the Search for the Center', *TTR* 4, 1, 129-44.

Lefevere, André (1990) 'Translation: Its Genealogy in the West', in Bassnett & Lefevere 1990, 14-28.

Lefevere, André (1989) 'The Dynamics of the System: Convention and Innovation in Literary History', in D'haen et al. 1989, 37-55.

Lefevere, André (1986) 'Why the Real Heine Can't Stand up in/to Translation: Rewriting as the Way to Literary Influence', *New Comparison* 1, 83-92;

reprinted in Lambert & Lefevere 1993, 173-80.

Lefevere, André (1985b) 'Systems in Evolution: Historical Relativism and the Study of Genre', *Poetics Today* 6, 665-67.

Lefevere, André (1985a) 'What is Written Must be Rewritten. *Julius Caesar*: Shakespeare, Voltaire, Wieland, Buckingham', in Hermans 1985c, 88-105.

Lefevere, André (1985) 'Why Waste Our Time on Rewrites? The Trouble with Interpretation and the Role of Rewriting in an Alternative Paradigm', in Hermans 1985, 215-43.

Lefevere, André (1984a) 'Translations and Other Ways in which One Literature Refracts Another', *Symposium* 38, 127-42.

Lefevere, André (1984) 'That Structure in the Dialect of Men Interpreted', *Comparative Criticism* 6, 87-100.

Lefevere, André (1983) 'Poetics (Today) and Translation (Studies)', *Modern Poetry in Translation* 42/42, 190-95.

Lefevere, André (1982a) 'Literary Theory and Translated Literature', *Dispositio* 7, 3-23.

Lefevere, André (1982) 'Mother Courage's Cucumbers: Text, System and Refraction in a Theory of Literature', *Modern Language Studies* 12, 4, 3-20.

Lefevere, André (1981) 'Programmatic Second Thoughts on 'Literary' and 'Translation' or: Where Do We Go From Here', *Poetics Today* 2, 4, 39-50.

Lefevere, André (1978a) 'Translation Studies: the Goal of the Discipline', in Holmes et al. 1978, 234-35.

Lefevere, André (1978) 'Translation: The Focus of the Growth of Literary Knowledge', in Holmes et al. 1978, 7-28.

Lefevere, André (1977a) *Literary Knowledge. A Polemical and Programmatic Essay on Its Nature, Growth, Relevance and Transmission*. Assen & Amsterdam: Van Gorcum.

Lefevere, André (1977) ed. *Translating Literature: the German Tradition*. Assen: Van Gorcum.

Lefevere, André (1975) *Translating Poetry. Seven Strategies and a Blueprint*. Assen & Amsterdam: Van Gorcum.

Lefevere, André (1972) 'The Translation of Literature: An Approach', *The Bible Translator* 23, 1, 110-5 [first published in *Babel* 1970].

Lefevere, André & Vanderauwera, Ria (1979) eds. *Vertaalwetenschap. Literatuur, wetenschap, vertaling en vertalen*. Leuven: Acco.

Leuven-Zwart, Kitty van (1992) *Vertaalwetenschap. Ontwikkelingen en perspectieven*. Muiderberg: Coutinho.

Leuven-Zwart, Kitty van (1990) 'Translation and Original. Similarities and Dissimilarities, II', *Target* 2, 69-96.

Leuven-Zwart, Kitty van (1989) 'Translation and Original. Similarities and Dissimilarities, I', *Target* 1, 151-82.

Leuven-Zwart, Kitty van (1986) 'Vertellers in vertalingen: de verteller vertaald - de vertaler verteld', *Forum der Letteren* 27: 188-204.

Leuven-Zwart, Kitty van (1984) *Vertaling en origineel. Een vergelijkende beschrijvingsmethode voor integrale vertalingen, ontwikkeld aan de hand van*

*Nederlandse vertalingen van Spaanse narrative teksten.* Dissertation, University of Amsterdam.

Leuven-Zwart, Kitty van & Naaijkens, Ton (1991) eds. *Translation Studies. The State of the Art.* Amsterdam: Rodopi..

Levý, Jiří (1976)'The Translation of Verbal Art', in *Semiotics of Art. Prague School Contributions*, ed. L. Matejka & I. Titunik, Cambridge (Mass.) & London: MIT Press, 218-26.

Levý, Jiří (1969) *Die literarische Übersetzung. Theorie einer Kunstgattung.* Transl. Walter Schamschula. Frankfurt & Bonn: Athenäum (first published in Czech, 1963).

Levý, Jiří (1968) 'Die Übersetzung von Theaterstücken', *Babel* 14, 77-82.

Levý, Jiří (1967) 'Translation as a Decision Process', in: *To Honor Roman Jakobson*, vol. 2, The Hague & Paris: Mouton, 1171-82.

Levý, Jiří (1965) 'Will Translation Theory be of Use to Translators?', in *Übersetzen. Vorträge und Beiträge vom internationalen Kongreß literarischer Übersetzer,* Frankfurt & Bonn: Athenäum, 77-82.

Lewis, David (1969) *Convention. A Philosophical Study.* Cambridge (Mass.): Harvard University Press.

Linn, Stella (1993) 'Een opzet voor een vertaaldescriptief onderzoek', *Linguistica Antverpiensia* 27, 161-91.

Littau, Karin (1996) 'Translation in the Age of Postmodern Production: from Text to Intertext to Hypertext', *Forum for Modern Language Studies* 33, 1, 81-96.

Littau, Karin (1993) 'Intertextuality and Translation. *The Waste Land* in French and German', in *Translation the Vital Link* (ed. C. Picken), London: Chameleon, 63-69.

Lönker, Fred (1992) ed. *Die literarische Übersetzung als Medium der Fremderfahrung.* Berlin: Erich Schmidt.

Lotman, Yury (1990) *Universe of the Mind. A Semiotic Theory of Culture.* Transl. Ann Shukman. London & New York: Tauris.

Lotman, Yury (1977) 'The Dynamic Model of a Semiotic System' [1974], transl. Ann Shukman, *Semiotica* 21, 193-210.

Luhmann, Niklas (1997) *Die Gesellschaft der Gesellschaft.* Frankfurt: Suhrkamp.

Luhmann, Niklas (1996) *Protest. Systemtheorie und soziale Bewegungen.* Ed. Kai-Uwe Hellmann. Frankfurt: Suhrkamp.

Luhmann, Niklas (1995a) *Social Systems.* Transl. John Bednarz. Stanford: Stanford University Press (German original 1984).

Luhmann, Niklas (1995) *Die Kunst der Gesellschaft.* Frankfurt: Suhrkamp.

Luhmann, Niklas (1994) 'How Can the Mind Participate in Communication?', in *Materialities of Communication*, ed. H.U. Gumbrecht & K.L. Pfeiffer, transl. William Whobrey, Stanford: Stanford University Press, 371-88.

Luhmann, Niklas (1993) 'Deconstruction as Second-Order Observing', *New Literary History* 24, 763-82.

Luhmann, Niklas (1992) 'Die operative Geschlossenheit psychischer und sozialer Systeme' in *Das Ende der grossen Entwürfe*, ed. H.R. Fischer, A. Retzer & J. Scheweitzer, Frankfurt: Suhrkamp, 117-31.

Luhmann, Niklas (1990a) 'Welkunst', in N. Luhmann, F. Bunsen & D. Baecker, *Unbeochbachtbare Welt. Über Kunst und Architektur*, Bielefeld: Cordula Haux, 7-45.

Luhmann, Niklas (1990) *Essays on Self-Reference*. New York: Columbia University Press.

Luhmann, Niklas (1989) *Ecological Communication*. Transl. John Bednarz. London: Polity Press.

Luhmann, Niklas (1986a) 'Systeme verstehen Systeme', in *Zwischen Intransparanz und Verstehen. Fragen an die Pädagogik*, ed. N. Luhmann & K.E. Schorr, Frankfurt: Suhrkamp, 72-117.

Luhmann, Niklas (1986) 'Das Kunstwerk und die Selbtsreproduktion der Kunst', in *Stil. Geschichte und Funktionen eines kulturwissenschaflichen Diskurselements*, ed. H.U. Gumpert & K.L. Pfeiffer, Frankfurt: Suhrkamp, 620-72.

Luhmann, Niklas (1984) *Soziale Systeme. Grundriss einer allgemeinen Theorie*. Frankfurt: Suhrkamp.

Luhmann, Niklas (1982a) 'Territorial Borders as System Boundaries', in *Cooperation and Conflict in Border Areas*, ed. R. Strassoldo & G. Delli Zotti, Milan: Franco Angeli, 235-71.

Luhmann, Niklas (1982) *The Differentiation of Society*. Transl. Stephen Holmes & Charles Larmore. New York: Columbia University Press.

Luhmann, Niklas (1981) 'Ist Kunst codierbar?', in his *Soziologische Aufklärung 3*, Opladen: Westdeutscher Verlag, 245-66.

Luhmann, Niklas (1979) *Trust and Power*. Intro. G. Poggi. Chichester etc.: John Wiley & Sons.

Mann, Thomas (1996) *Death in Venice and Other Stories*. Transl. David Luke. London: Minerva.

Marcus, George & Fischer, Michael (1986) *Anthropology as Cultural Critique. An Experimental Moment in the Human Sciences*. Chicago & London: University of Chicago Press.

Matejka, Ladislav & Pomorska, Krystyna (1978) eds. *Readings in Russian Poetics. Formalist and Structuralist Views*. Ann Arbor: University of Michigan.

McFarlane, John (1953) 'Modes of Translation', *The Durham University Journal* 45, 3, 77-93.

McHale, Brian (1994) 'Whatever Happened to Descriptive Poetics?', in *The Point of Theory. Practices of Cultural Analysis* (ed. Mieke Bal & Inge Boer), Amsterdam: Amsterdam University Press, 56-65.

Merino Álvarez, Raquel (1997) 'Complejidad y diversidad en los Estudios Descriptivos de Traducción: *La Alhambra* de Washington Irving en España' in *Aproximaciones a los estudios de traducción*, ed. P. Fernández Nistal & J.M. Bravo Gonzalo, Valladolid: Universidad de Valldolid, 51-70.

Merino Álvarez, Raquel (1994a) 'A Framework for the Description of Drama Translations', in Robyns 1994, 139-50.

Merino Álvarez, Raquel (1994) *Traducción, tradición y manipulación. Teatro inglés en España 1950-1990*. León/Vitoria: Universidad de León/Universidad del País Vasco.

Merkle, Denise (1994) 'Emile Zola devant la censure victorienne', *TTR* 7, 1, 77-91.

Merton, Thomas (1973) 'The Normative Structure of Science' [1942], in his *The Sociology of Science. Theoretical and Empirical Investigations* (ed. Norman W. Storer), Chicago: Chicago University Press, 267-78.

Miko, František (1970) 'La théorie de l'expression et la traduction', in Holmes 1970, 61-77.

Mounin, Georges (1963) *Les problèmes théoriques de la traduction*. Paris: Gallimard.

Mukařovský, Jan (1978) *Structure, Sign and Function. Selected Essays*. Transl. and ed. John Burbank & Peter Steiner. New Haven & London: Yale University Press.

Mukařovský, Jan (1970) *Aesthetic Function, Norm and Value as Social Facts* [1936]. Transl. Mark Suino. Ann Arbor: University of Michigan.

Müller, Harro (1994) 'Luhmann's Systems Theory as a Theory of Modernity' (transl. Larson Powell), *New German Critique* 61, 39-54.

Naaijkens, Ton (1992) 'Transitional Literature and Translation. Apollinaire's *Zone* in the Dutch Polysystem', in Kittel 1992, 228-49.

Nabokov, Vladimir (1992) 'Problems of Translation: *Onegin* in English' [1955], in *Theories of Translation* (ed. Rainer Schulte & John Biguenet), Chicago & London: University of Chicago Press, 127-43.

Needham, Rodney (1978) *Essential Perplexities*. Oxford: Oxford University Press.

Needham, Rodney (1972) *Belief, Language and Experience*. Oxford: Oxford University Press.

Neubert, Albrecht, & Shreve, Gregory (1992) *Translation as Text*. Kent, Ohio: Kent State University Press.

*New German Critique* (1994) Special issue on Niklas Luhmann.

Newmark, Peter (1993) *Paragraphs on Translation*. Clevedon: Multilingual Matters.

Newmark, Peter (1991a) 'The Curse of Dogma in Translation Studies', *Lebende Sprachen* 36, 3, 105-108.

Newmark, Peter (1991) *About Translation*. Clevedon: Multilingual Matters.

Newmark, Peter (1988) *Approaches to Translation*. New York etc.: Prentice-Hall.

Newmark, Peter (1986) 'Translation Studies: Eight Tentative Directions for Research and Some Dead Ducks', in *Translation Studies in Scandinavia* (ed. Lars Wollin & Hans Lindquist), Malmö: CWK Gleerup, 37-50.

Newmark, Peter (1980) 'What Translation Theory is About', *Quinquereme* 3, 1, 1-21.

Nida, Eugene (1976) 'A Framework for the Analysis and Evaluation of Theories of Translation', in *Translation. Applications and Research* (ed. R.W. Brislin), New York: Gardner Press, 47-91.

Nida, Eugene (1969) 'Science of Translation' [1969] in Chesterman 1989, 80-98.

Nida, Eugene (1964) *Toward a Science of Translating*. Leiden: Brill.

Nida, Eugene (1959) 'Principles of Translation as Exemplified by Bible Translating', in Brower 1959, 11-31.

Niranjana, Tejaswini (1992) *Siting Translation. History, Post-Structuralism and the Colonial Context*. Berkeley: University of California Press.

Nooy, W. de (1991) 'Social Networks and Classification in Literature', *Poetics* 20, 507-37.

Nord, Christiane (1997) *Translating as a Purposeful Activity. Functionalist Approaches Explained*. Manchester: St Jerome.

Nord, Christiane (1991a) 'Scopos, Loyalty, and Translational Conventions', *Target* 3, 1, 91-110.

Nord, Christiane (1991) *Text Analysis in Translation. Theory, Methodology, and Didactic Application of a Model for Translation-Oriented Text Analysis*. Transl. Christiane Nord & Penelope Sparrow. Amsterdam & Atlanta: Rodopi.

Norton, Glyn (1984) *The Ideology and Language of Translation in Renaissance France and Their Humanist Antecedents*. Genève: Droz.

Paker, Saliha (1991) 'The Age of Translation and Adaptation, 1850-1914. Turkey', in *Modern Literature in the Near and Middle East 1850-1970* (ed. Robin Ostle), London & New York: Routledge, 17-32.

Paker, Saliha (1986b) 'Hamlet in Turkey', *New Comparison* 2, 89-105.

Paker, Saliha (1986) 'Translated European Literature in the Late Ottoman Literary Polysystem', *New Comparison* 1, 67-82; reprinted in Lambert & Lefevere 1993, 181-92.

Paker, Saliha & Toska, Zehra (1997) 'A Call for Descriptive Translation Studies in the Turkish Tradition of Rewrites', in Snell-Hornby et al. 1997, 79-88.

Pegenaute Rodríguez, Luis (1994) 'The Unfortunate Journey of Laurence Sterne through Spain. The Translations of His Works into Spanish', *The Shandean* 6, 25-53.

Pegenaute Rodríguez, Luis (1992) 'Traducción literaria de mensajes (des)cifrados: limitaciones metalingüisticas a la equivalencia', *Estudios humanísticos Filología* 14, 11-23.

Perrot d'Ablancourt, Nicolas (1972) *Lettres et préfaces critiques*. Ed. H. Zuber. Paris Didier.

Poltermann, Andreas (1995a) 'Literaturkanon – Medienereignis – Kultureller Text. Formen interkultureller Kommunikation und Übersetzung', in Poltermann 1995, 1-58.

Poltermann, Andreas (1995) ed. *Literaturkanon – Medienereignis – Kultureller Text. Formen interkultureller Kommunikation und Übersetzung*. Berlin: Erich Schmidt.

*Poltermann, Andreas (1992) 'Normen des literarischen Übersetzens im System der Literatur', in Kittel 1992, 5-31.

Poltermann, Andreas (1990) [Review of Toury 1980], *Jahrbuch für internationale Germanistik* 21, 2, 115-23.

Poltermann, Andreas (1987) 'Die Erfindung des Originals. Zur Geschichte der Übersetzungskonzeptionen in Deutschland im 18. Jahrhundert', in Schultze 1987, 14-52.

Popovič, Anton (1979) 'De afbakening van het begrip vertaling: stellingen', in Lefevere & Vanderauwera 1979, 24-31.

Popovič, Anton (1976a) 'Aspects of Metatext', *Canadian Review of Comparative Literature* 1976, 225-35.

Popovič, Anton (1976) *Dictionary for the Analysis of Literary Translation*. Edmonton: University of Alberta.

Popovič, Anton (1970) 'The Concept 'Shift of Expression' in Translation Analysis', in Holmes 1970, 78-87.

Popovič, Anton (1967) 'Die theoretischen Probleme der Übersetzung', *Literatur und Kritik* 2, 611-7.

Puurtinen, Tiina (1989) 'Assessing Acceptability in Translated Children's Books', *Target* 1, 201-14.

Pym, Anthony (1998) *Method in Translation History*. Manchester: St Jerome.

Pym, Anthony (1995a) 'European Translation Studies, 'une science qui dérange' and Why Equivalence Needn't be a Dirty Word', *TTR* 8, 1, 153-76.

Pym, Anthony (1995) 'Translational and Non-Translational Regimes informing Poetry Anthologies. Lessons on Authorship from Fernando Maristany and Enrique Díez-Canedo', in Kittel 1995, 251-70.

Pym, Anthony (1994) 'Twelfth-Century Toledo and Strategies of the Literalist Trojan Horse', *Target* 6, 43-66.

Pym, Anthony (1993) 'The Problem of Sovereignty in Regimes of European Literature Transfer', *New Comparison* 15, 137-46.

Pym, Anthony (1992b) 'Discursive Persons and the Limits of Translation', in *Translation and Meaning, Part 2* (ed. B. Lewandowska-Tomasczyk & M. Thelen), Maastricht: Rijkshogeschool Maastricht, 159-68.

Pym, Anthony (1992a) 'The Relations between Translation and Material Text Transfer', *Target* 4, 171-90.

Pym, Anthony (1992) *Translation and Text Transfer*. Frankfurt: Peter Lang.

Ranke, Wolfgang (1995) 'Integration und Ausgrenzung. Ausländische Klassiker in deutschen Literaturgeschichten des 19. Jahrhunderts', in Poltermann 1995, 92-118.

Ranke, Wolfgang (1993) 'Shakespeare Translations for Eighteenth-Century Stage Productions in Germany: Different Versions of *Macbeth*', in Delabastita & D'hulst 1993, 163-82.

Ranke, Wolfgang (1992) 'Historisches Theatersystem und bearbeitende Übersetzung für die Bühne. Überlegungen am Beispiel von Bürgers und Schillers *Macbeth*-Versionen,' in Kittel 1992, 117-41.

Reiss, Katharina (1989) 'Was heisst und warum betreibt man Übersetzungswissenschaft?', *Lebende Sprachen* 34, 3, 97-100.

Reiss, Katharina (1976) *Texttyp und Übersetzungsmethode. Der operative Text*. Kronberg: Scriptor.

Reiss, Katharina (1971) *Möglichkeiten und Grenzen der Übersetzungskritik*. München: Max Hueber .

Reiss, Katharina & Vermeer, Hans (1984) *Grundlegung einer allgemeinen Translationstheorie*. Tübingen: Max Niemeyer.

Ridley, Matt (1996) *The Origins of Virtue*. London etc.: Viking.

Roberts, David (1992) 'The Paradox of Form: Literature and Self-Reference', *Poetics* 21, 75-91.

Robinson, Douglas (1997c) *Translation and Empire. Postcolonial Theories Explained*. Manchester: St Jerome.

Robinson, Douglas (1997a) *Becoming a Translator. An Accelerated Course*. London & New York: Routledge.

Robinson, Douglas (1997) *What Is Translation? Centrifugal Theories, Critical Interventions*. Kent & London: Kent State University Press.

Robyns, Clem (1995) 'Defending the National Identity: Franglais and Francophony', in Poltermann 1995, 179-210.

Robyns, Clem (1994a) 'Translation and Discursive Identity', in Robyns 1994, 57-81; also in *Poetics Today* 15, 405-28.

Robyns, Clem (1994) ed. *Translation and the (Re)production of Culture. Selected Papers of the CERA Research Seminars in Translation Studies 1989-1991*. Leuven: CERA Chair.

Robyns, Clem (1992) 'Towards a Sociosemiotics of Translation', *Romanische Zeitschrift für Literaturgeschichte* 16, 211-26.

Robyns, Clem (1990) 'The Normative Model of Twentieth-Century Belles Infidèles: Detective Novels in French Translation', *Target* 2, 23-42.

Schäffner, Christina (1997) 'Where is the Source Text?', in Wotjak & Schmidt 1997, 193-211.

Schiavi, Giuliana (1996) 'There is always a Teller in a Tale', *Target* 8, 1-22.

Schjoldager, Anne (1994) 'Interpreting Research and the 'Manipulation School' of Translation Studies'. *Hermes* 12, 65-89 (abbreviated version in *Target* 7, 29-46).

Schmidt, Siegfried (1997) 'A Systems-Oriented Approach to Literary Studies', *Canadian Review of Comparative Literature* 24, 1, 119-36.

Schmidt, Siegfried (1992) 'Conventions and Literary Systems', in Hjort 1992: 215-249.

Schmidt, Siegfried (1991) 'Literary Systems as Self-Organizing Systems', in Ibsch et al. 1991, 413-24.

Schmidt, Siegfried (1989) *Die Selbstorganisation des Sozialsystems Literatur im 18. Jahrhundert*. Frankfurt: Suhrkamp.

Schultze, Brigitte (1987) ed. *Die literarische Übersetzung. Fallstudien zu ihrer Kulturgeschichte*. Berlin: Erich Schmidt.

Schultze, Brigitte; Fischer-Lichte, Erika; Paul, Fritz & Turk, Horst (1990) eds. *Literatur und Theater. Traditionen und Konventionen als Problem der Dramenübersetzung*. Tübingen: Gunter Narr.

Schwanitz, Dietrich (1990) *Systemtheorie und Literatur*. Opladen: Westdeutscher Verlag.

Schwartz, Werner (1985) *Schriften zur Bibelübersetzung und zur mittelalterlichen Übersetzungstheorie*. London: Institute of Germanic Studies.

Shavit, Zohar (1997) 'Cultural Agents and Cultural Interference: the Function of J.H. Campe in an Emerging Jewish Culture', *Target* 9, 111-30.

Shavit, Zohar (1992) 'Literary Interference between German and Jewish-Hebrew Children's Literature during the Enlightenment: the Case of Campe', *Poetics Today* 13, 41-61.

Shavit, Zohar (1991) 'Canonicity and Literary Institutions', in Ibsch et al. 1991, 231-8.

Shavit, Zohar (1986) *Poetics of Children's Literature*. Athens & London: University of Georgia Press.

Shavit, Zohar (1981) 'Translation of Children's Literature as a Function of its Position in the Literary Polysystem', *Poetics Today* 2, 4, 171-9.

Sheffy, Rakefet (1997) 'Models and Habituses. Problems in the Idea of Cultural Repertoires', *Canadian Review of Comparative Literature* 24, 1, 35-47.

Sheffy, Rakefet (1990) 'The Concept of Canonicity in Polysystem Theory', *Poetics Today* 11, 511-22.

Shreve, Gregory (1997) 'Prolegomena to an Empirical Translation Studies', in Wotjak & Schmidt 1997, 41-58.

Shreve, Gregory (1996) 'On the Nature of Scientific and Empirical Translation Studies', in Gaddis Rose 1996, 69-86.

Shuttleworth, Mark & Cowie, Moira (1997) *Dictionary of Translation Studies*. Manchester: St Jerome.

Simeoni, Daniel (1998) 'The Pivotal Status of the Translator's Habitus', *Target* 10, 1-39.

Simon, Sherry (1997) 'Translation and Cultural Politics in Canada' in *Translation and Multilingualism. Post-Colonial Contexts* (ed. Shantha Ramakrishna), Delhi: Pencraft International, 192-204.

Simon, Sherry (1996) *Gender in Translation. Cultural Identity and the Politics of Transmission*. London & New York: Routledge.

Simon, Sherry (1992) 'The Language of Cultural Difference: Figures of Alterity in Canadian Translation', in Venuti 1992, 159-76.

Simon, Sherry (1990) 'Translating the Will to Knowledge: Prefaces and Canadian Literary Politics', in Bassnett & Lefevere 1990, 110-17.

Simon, Sherry (1989) *L'inscription sociale de la traduction au Québec*. Québec: Office de la langue française.

Skinner, Quentin (1970) 'Conventions and the Understanding of Speech Acts', *The Philosophical Quarterly* 20, 118-38.

Skinner, Quentin (1969) 'Meaning and Understanding in the History of Ideas', *History and Theory* 8, 3-53.

Snell-Hornby, Mary (1995a) 'The Integrated Linguist: On Combining Models of Translation Critique', in *La traducción literaria* (ed. Josep Borillo), Castelló: Universitat Jaume I, 43-58. Also in Wotjak & Schmidt 1997, 73-88.

Snell-Hornby, Mary (1995) *Translation Studies. An Integrated Approach*. Revised ed. Amsterdam: John Benjamins.

Snell-Hornby, Mary (1991) 'Translation Studies – Art, Science, or Utopia?' in Van Leuven-Zwart & Naaijkens 1991, 13-23.

Snell-Hornby, Mary (1988) *Translation Studies. An Integrated Approach*. Amsterdam: John Benjamins.

Snell-Hornby, Mary (1986) ed. *Übersetzungswissenschaft. Eine Neuorientierung*. Tübingen: Francke.

Snell-Hornby, Mary, Jettmarová, Zuzanna & Kaindl, Klaus (1997) eds. *Translation as Intercultural Communication. Selected Papers from the EST Congress,*

*Prague 1995*. Amsterdam & Philadelphia: John Benjamins.

Somekh, Sasson (1981) 'The Emergence of Two Sets of Stylistic Norms in Early Literary Translation into Arabic Prose', *Poetics Today* 2, 4, 193-200.

Sorvali, Irma (1996) *Translation Studies in a New Perspective*. Frankfurt etc.: Peter Lang.

Stegeman, Jelle (1991) *Übersetzung und Leser. Untersuchungen zur Übersetzungs-äquivalenz dargestellt an der Rezeption von Multatulis 'Max Havelaar' und seinen deutschen Übersetzungen*. Berlin/New York: De Gruyter.

Steiner, George (1975) *After Babel. Aspects of Language and Translation*. Oxford: Oxford University Press.

Steiner, T.R. (1975) *English Translation Theory 1650-1800*. Assen/Amsterdam: Van Gorcum.

Stendhal (1970) *Vies de Haydn, de Mozart et de Métastase* [1815] in his *Œuvres complètes* vol. 41 (ed. Victor del Litto & Ernest Abravanel), Geneva: Edito-Service.

Steyaert, Chris & Janssens, Maddy (1997) 'Language and Translation in an International Business Context: Beyond an Instrumental Approach', *Target* 9, 1, 131-54.

Sturge, Kate (1997) 'Translation Strategies in Ethnography', *The Translator* 3, 1, 21-38.

Taivalkoski, Kristiina (1998) *Fielding travesti. Etude comparée descriptive de la traduction faite par l'Abbé Desfontaines de 'Joseph Andrews' de Henry Fielding*. Thèse de troisième cycle, Université de Helsinki.

Taylor, Charles (1992) 'To Follow a Rule...', in Hjort 1992, 167-85. Reprinted in *Bourdieu: Critical Perspectives* (ed. Craig Calhoun et al.), London: Polity Press, 1993, 45-60.

Thirlwall, J.C. (1966) *In Another Language. A Record of the Thirty-Year Relationship between Thomas Mann and his English Translator Helen Lowe-Porter*. New York: Alfred Knopf.

Tötösy de Zepetnek, Steven (1992) 'Systemic Approaches to Literature. An Introduction with Selected Bibliographies', *Canadian Review of Comparative Literature* 19, 1/2, 21-93. Internet: http://www.ualberta.ca/ARTS/ricl.html

Toury, Gideon (1997) 'What is It that Renders a Spoonerism (Un)translatable?', in Delabastita 1997, 271-91.

*Toury, Gideon (1995) *Descriptive Translation Studies and Beyond*. Amsterdam & Philadelphia: John Benjamins.

Toury, Gideon (1993) 'Translation of Literary Texts vs. Literary Translation', in *Recent Trends in Empirical Translation Research* (ed. S. Tirkkonen & J. Laffling), Joensuu: University of Joensuu, 10-24 .

Toury, Gideon (1991a) 'Experimentation in Translation Studies: Achievements, Prospects and Some Pitfalls', in *Empirical Research in Translation and Intercultural Sudies* (ed. Sonja Tirkkonen-Condit), Tübingen: Narr, 45-66.

Toury, Gideon (1991) 'What are Descriptive Studies into Translation Likely to Yield apart from Isolated Descriptions?', in Van Leuven-Zwart & Naaijkens 1991, 179-192.

Toury, Gideon (1990a) 'The Coupled Pair 'Problem + Solution' in Translation Studies', in *Translation Theory in Scandinavia* (ed. P.N. Chaffy et al.), Oslo, 1-23.

Toury, Gideon (1990) 'From One Signifier to Another. Modified Phonetic Transpositon in Word-Formation and Translation', in Arntz & Thome 1990, 191-8.

Toury, Gideon (1988) 'Translating English Literature via German – and Vice Versa. A Symptomatic Reversal in the History of Modern Hebrew Literature', in Kittel 1988, 139-57.

Toury, Gideon (1986a) 'Monitoring Discourse Transfer. A Test-Case for a Developmental Model of Translation', in *Interlingual and Intercultural Communication* (ed. J. House & S. Blum-Kulka), Tübingen: Gunter Narr, 79-94.

Toury, Gideon (1986) '[Translation:] A Cultural-Semiotic Perspective', in *Encyclopaedic Dictionary of Semiotics* (ed. Thomas Sebeok), vol. 2, Berlin: De Gruyter, 1111-24.

Toury, Gideon (1985) 'A Rationale for Descriptive Translation Studies', in Hermans 1985, 16-41.

Toury, Gideon (1984) 'Translation, Literary Translation and Pseudotranslation', *Comparative Criticism* 6, 73-85.

Toury, Gideon (1982) 'A Rationale for Descriptive Translation Studies', *Dispositio* 7, 23-40.

Toury, Gideon (1981) 'Translated Literature: System, Norm, Performance', *Poetics Today* 2, 4, 9-27.

*Toury, Gideon (1980) *In Search of a Theory of Translation*. Tel Aviv: Porter Institute for Poetics and Semiotics.

Toury, Gideon (1979) 'Interlanguage and its Manifestations in Translation', *Meta* 24, 223-31.

Toury, Gideon (1978) 'The Nature and Role of Norms in Literary Translation', in Holmes et al. 1978, 83-100 (reprinted in Toury 1980).

Toury, Gideon (1974) 'Literature as a Polysystem', *Ha-Sifrut / Literature*, 18-19, 1-19 (Hebrew, with English summary).

Toury, Gideon & Lambert, José (1989) 'On *Target*'s Targets', *Target* 1, 1-7.

Trivedi, Harish (1995) *Colonial Transactions. English Literature and India*. Manchester & New York: Manchester University Press.

Turk, Horst (1990) 'Konventionen und Traditionen. Zum Bedingungsrahmen der Übersetzung für das Theater oder für die Literatur', in Schultze et al. 1990, 63-93.

*Tymoczko, Maria (1999) *Translation in a Postcolonial Context. Early Irish Literature in English Translation*. Manchester: St Jerome.

Tymoczko, Maria (1995) 'The Metonymics of Translating Marginalized Texts', *Comparative Literature* 47, 1, 11-24.

Tymoczko, Maria (1991) 'Two Traditions of Translating Early Irish Literature', *Target* 3, 207-24.

Tymoczko, Maria (1990) 'Translation in Oral Tradition as a Touchstone for Translation Theory and Practice', in Bassnett & Lefevere 1990, 46-55.

Tymoczko, Maria (1987) 'Translating the Humour in Early Irish Hero Tales. A Polysystems Approach', *New Comparison* 3, 83-103.

Tymoczko, Maria (1986) 'Translation as a Force for Literary Revolution in the Twelfth-Century Shift from Epic to Romance', *New Comparison* 1, 7-27; reprinted in Lambert & Lefevere 1993, 75-92.

Tymoczko, Maria (1985) 'How Distinct are Formal and Dynamic Equivalence?', in Hermans 1985, 63-86.

Tymoczko, Maria (1984) 'Translating Old Irish: A Perspective on Translation Theory', *Babel* 30, 3, 144-47.

Tymoczko, Maria (1983) 'Translating the Old Irish Epic *Táin Bó Cúailnge*: Political Aspects', *Pacific Quarterly Moana* 8, 2, 6-21.

Tymoczko, Maria (1982) 'Strategies for Integrating Irish Epics into European Literature', *Dispositio* 7, 123-40.

Tynjanov, Yury (1982) 'Das literarische Faktum' [1924], transl. Brigitta Schröder, in his *Poetik. Ausgewählte Essays*, Leipzig & Weimar: Kiepenheuer, 7-30.

Tynjanov, Yury (1978) 'On Literary Evolution' [1927], in Matejka & Pomorska 1978, 66-78.

Tynjanov, Yury & Jakobson, Roman (1978) 'Problems in the Study of Literature and Language' [1928], in Matejka & Pomorska 1978, 79-81.

Vanderauwera, Ria (1985a) 'The Response to Translated Literature. A Sad Example', in Hermans 1985, 198-214.

Vanderauwera, Ria (1985) *Dutch Novels Translated into English. The Transformation of a 'Minority' Literature*. Amsterdam: Rodopi.

Vanderauwera, Ria (1982) 'Texts and Contexts of Translation: A Dutch Classic in English', *Dispositio* 7, 111-22.

Venuti, Lawrence (1995) *The Translator's Invisibility. A History of Translation*. London & New York: Routledge.

Venuti, Lawrence (1992) ed. *Rethinking Translation. Discourse, Subjectivity, Ideology*. London & New York: Routledge.

Vermeer, Hans (1990a) 'Texttheorie und translatorisches Handeln', *Target* 2, 219-42.

Vermeer, Hans (1990) *Skopos und Translationsauftrag. Aufsätze*. Heidelberg: Institut für Übersetzen und Dolmetschen, Universität Heidelberg.

Viala, Alain (1997) 'Logique du champ littéraire', *Canadian Review of Comparative Literature / Revue Canadienne de littérature comparée* 24, 1, 63-75.

Vidal Claramonte, Carmen África (1995) *Traducción, manipulación, desconstrucción*. Salamanca: Colegio de España.

Voltaire (1879) 'Appel à toutes les nations de l'Europe des jugements d'un écrivain anglais ou Manifeste au sujet des honneurs du pavillon entre les théatres de Londres et de Paris' [1761], in *Œuvres complètes de Voltaire*, vol. 24 (Mélanges III), Paris: Garnier, 190-224.

Vuorinen, Erkka (1997) 'News Translation as Gatekeeping', in Snell-Hornby et al. 1997, 161-71.

Weissbrod, Rachel (1991) 'Translation of Prose Fiction from English to Hebrew: A Function of Norms (1960s and 1970s)', in *Translation: Theory and Prac-*

*tice. Tension and Interdependence* (ed. Mildred Larson), Binghamton: SUNY, 206-23.

Werber, Niels (1992) *Literatur als System. Zur Ausdifferenzierung literarischer Kommunikation.* Opladen: Westdeutscher Verlag.

Wolf, Michaela (1997) 'Translation as a Process of Power. Aspects of Cultural Anthropology in Translation', in Snell-Hornby et al. 1997, 123-34.

Wotjak, Gerd & Schmidt, Heide (1997) ed. *Modelle der Translation / Models of Translation. Festschrift Albrecht Neubert.* Frankfurt: Vervuert.

*Yahalom, Shelly (1981) 'Le système littéraire en état de crise. Contacts inter-systémiques et comportement traductionnel', *Poetics Today* 2, 4, 143-60.

Yahalom, Shelly (1980) 'Du non-littéraire au littéraire. Sur l'élaboration d'un modèle romanesque au XVIIIe siècle', *Poétique* 11, 406-21.

Zijlmans, Kitty (1993) 'Kunstgeschiedenis als systeemtheorie', in *Gezichtspunten. Een inleiding in de methoden van de kunstgeschiedenis* (ed. M. Halbertsma & K. Zijlmans), Nijmegen: SUN, 311-44.

Zijlmans, Kitty (1990) *Kunst, geschiedenis, kunstgeschiedenis. Methode en prak-tijk van een kunsthistorische aanpak op systeemtheoretische basis.* Leiden: Alpha.

Zlateva, Palma (1990) 'Translation: Text and Pre-Text. 'Adequacy' and 'Accept-ability' in Crosscultural Communication', in Bassnett & Lefevere 1990, 29-37.

# Index